# THERE ARE WORSE THINGS I COULD DO

*Adrienne Barbeau*

CARROLL & GRAF PUBLISHERS
NEW YORK

THERE ARE WORSE THINGS I COULD DO

Carroll & Graf Publishers
An Imprint of Avalon Publishing Group, Inc.
245 West 17th Street
11th Floor
New York, NY 10011

AVALON
publishing group incorporated

Library of Congress Cataloging-in-Publication Data is available.

ISBN-13: 978-0-78671-637-1
ISBN-10: 0-78671-637-1

9 8 7 6 5 4 3 2 1

Printed in the United States of America
Interior design by Maria Torres
Distributed by Publishers Group West

*For Billy, who makes everything possible,*
*and Armen, who would have given a copy to everyone she met*

# Contents

# The Journals

I STARTED KEEPING A JOURNAL WHEN I WAS IN FIFTH grade. It was a gift from my best "boy" friend and if *he* gave it to me, I was going to write in it every day. I loved the pale green imitation leather with the words FIVE YEAR DIARY embossed on it in gold. The best part about it was the lock and key, so my mother couldn't see what I'd written: "I read *Nancy Drew* today. We weeded in the garden. We made brownies. I threw up." By seventh grade I was writing down all the compliments I got from the boys in my class: "Terry McDonnell said he liked my saddle shoes." When you've got short kinky hair, glasses, and no breasts, you're not allowed to wear makeup, and your parents are the only divorced parents you know, you need all the encouragement you can get. By ninth grade I was writing in code so my mother wouldn't figure out the guy I was dating was an eleventh-grader with grease in his hair—God forbid.

Today I have thousands of pages of daily entries with barely a mention of my career (which made it a little more difficult to write this book). I can read about every man I ever dated, every witty or wise or sexy or unpleasant word we exchanged, every meal I cooked during every romance, and just how passionate the lovemaking was, but there's nothing there about opening nights on Broadway or meeting Nancy Reagan and Jimmy Carter or starring in my own pilot for CBS. That was my job; what I did for a living. That wasn't what I was interested in writing about.

Auditioning for *Grease?* No entry. Six years on a hit television series? Barely a word. Going to the Grammy Awards and the Tony Awards? Nada. Making *The Fog, Escape From New York, Back to School, The Cannonball Run?* Zip.

Instead, I wrote about what I was feeling and how I was being in the world. Relationships and love affairs, emotional highs and lows, friendships and loss—that's what I wrote about. Complete conversations, descriptions of feelings (emotional *and* physical)—all detailed down to the last quiver.

I wrote because I wanted to understand myself. I wrote because I wanted to grow. Growth is what interested me more than anything else and I figured relationships were how I grew so that's what I wrote about. The journals were my therapy.

I began in 1955 and I wrote every day for the next forty years. In 1984, when my first son, Cody, was born, I started a separate journal for him, and in 1997, I added two more, for the twins Walker and William. I keep them in the basement in a huge safe—my favorite gift from a man I loved in the mid-'70s. It's three feet tall and two feet wide. There's nothing in it but thirty-year-old traveler's checks and sixty-three journals.

On September 19, 1963, I wrote, "Maybe when everyone has passed away, I can write a book about my life."

Well, they're not all dead yet but . . .

# Mostly Armenian

I'M ARMENIAN. AS FAR AS I'M CONCERNED, THAT explains it all. Well, except for my nose. My nose is French Canadian, from my father's side. But the rest is Armenian: the curly hair, the big breasts, the ability to survive forty-five years in "show business," passed down from my ancestors who survived the Turks during the genocide in 1915.

So truthfully I'm only half Armenian but it's the half I was raised in. My mother's parents had a twenty-acre grape farm near Fresno in Selma, California, "The Raisin Capital of the World," and that's where I spent all my summers, sitting under the water cooler listening to Grandma's 78s on the record player. She had Eartha Kitt singing "Uska Dara" in Turkish and Frankie Laine doing "Mule Train" in Armenian.

I can count to twenty in Armenian. I can also say, "I don't want it," "I don't know it," "I don't like it," in Armenian. And

"What are you doing?", "What do you want?", and "You wild son-of-a-bitch dog, do you want me to hit you?"

I've heard all the stories of the Turkish massacre and I've read Raffi's *The Fool* and Franz Werfel's *The Forty Days of Musa Dagh*. I can make pilaf and stuffed grape leaves and baklava. I know the owners of most of the gas stations in Southern California. But that's pretty much where it ends. My mother married an *odard*—a white man—and his job kept us moving so we didn't live in Fresno near all our relatives. I never really learned the language and I wasn't raised in the Armenian church. Instead, I spent my teenage years using Kix Kinks on my hair and trying to flatten the bridge of my nose.

But when I was growing up, I loved telling people I was Armenian. Outside of Fresno, it seemed like no one knew what an Armenian was. We were unique and exciting and mysterious. And we sure knew how to dance.

My father quit school at age fourteen to pump gas and support his eight brothers and his sister. He went back and graduated from high school when he was fifty-two. By that time he was an executive for Mobil Oil. He was transferred a lot when I was growing up so by the time I was in seventh grade, when my parents divorced and my sister and I stayed with my mom, we'd lived all over California. My mother settled in San Jose in 1957 but the only real home I remember was Grandma's, "on the ranch." It wasn't a ranch really, no cows or horses, just a couple of turkeys and a lamb or two. A lot of chickens, and no indoor plumbing. Grandpa used to chop the chickens' heads off right outside the kitchen door and we'd have to jump over the blood to get to the outhouse. We weren't supposed to use the outhouse to pee anyway, just hide behind it to squat in the sand. That was okay in the daytime but at night, in the pitch black, I was sure some frog was getting rained on.

It was lonely there all summer. Having a sister six years younger didn't help much. I spent my days writing thirty-five-page letters to my friend, Loren Allen. I also sent him plays I had written, like *The Secret Life of Kenneth Turner* (Kenny had a crush on a sixth-grader) and *That Calypso Beat* (dancing in P.E.), and he sent me back critiques: "*On the whole I thought it was very good and not just okay.*" The highlight of the day was when the dogs started barking. That meant company—either the mailman was at the mailbox a quarter mile down the road or my cousins were coming to play Monopoly. On Saturday nights there was always a "gathering," as in "Where's 'the gathering' this week?" or "Who's having 'the gathering'?" The men in the family sat in the living room and played pinochle and slapped the table and yelled while the women stood in the kitchen cooking and serving and washing dishes and putting them away. Sometimes the big square wooden phone, hanging on the wall above the oilcloth-covered table, would ring. It was a party line and we had to count the rings—two long and one short—to know if it was for us.

One Saturday night before the gathering, the phone rang.

It was my uncle Ralph calling from Fresno to say it had started to rain there and it was coming our way, we needed to get out in the fields. The grapes had been picked; they were drying on paper trays up and down the rows of vines. If they got wet, the entire crop of raisins would be worthless.

Relatives arrived by the carload and the men headed out into the darkness to start "cigarette" rolling the trays. If the raisins were completely covered within the paper, they could be saved. I was twelve years old. I'd just seen *Tammy and the Bachelor*—the scene where she saves the tomato crop—and I was determined to be a hero. The Miss America Pageant was on TV in the house and my aunts were making hot chocolate and Turkish coffee. There were yalanchi, sarma, dolma, soubereg, basterma, and baklava, too, but I didn't care. I was going out into the cold, rainy blackness to save the raisins. I'd come in every half hour or so to check on Miss California.

Of course, I got lost. It really was black out there and I wasn't tall enough to see the lights from the house over the vines. The rain was torrential. I couldn't hear Grandpa's voice or any of my uncles or cousins. I was only twelve and I wanted to save my grandparents' farm, but my flashlight battery went dead and my teeth started chattering and it wasn't like the movie at all. Grandpa found me by the levee and we got back to the house in time to see Miss South Carolina win the crown.

We saved 85 percent of the crop and no one ever knew I'd been scared shitless.

When we didn't have company, I helped Grandma cook and clean. She got up before dawn with my grandfather. If I was lucky and woke up early enough, I could catch her getting warm on the metal heating grate in the living room floor, brushing her waist-length hair before it went into a bun at the nape of her neck. Grandpa worked in the fields until noon when the 103-degree temperatures forced him into his rocking chair in front of the TV. Then we watched *The Lone Ranger, Wild Bill Hickok, The Cisco Kid,* and *Sky King.* When Grandpa went back out, Grandma and I watched *Queen for a Day* and *It Could Be You. It Could Be You* was a game show in which they reunited someone in the audience with some long-lost relative from the "old country" who was waiting in the wings. Grandma and I cried through the whole show. I still cry today through *The Price Is Right.*

I must have watched *I Love Lucy,* too, because when I got back home for the school year, I played Lucy and Desi with my next-door neighbor. No one wanted to be Fred or Ethel so we took a little poetic license. I was Lucille Ball and I was married to Desi Arnaz. She was Lucy Ricardo and she was married to Ricky. We only had two dolls between us so they passed for all the kids.

The other thing I played in school was the Black Stallion. Inevitably, whenever my father was transferred, it was the beginning of summer. I always had three months alone in a new town before I could start school and make new friends. I spent every other day at the library, checking out dozens of books at a time. It was the beginning of my love affair with series novels: I read Walter Farley's *The Black Stallion* books, *The Black Stallion Revolts, The Black Stallion Returns, The Son of the Black Stalion, The Black Stallion's Sulky Colt, The Black Stallion and Satan,* and *The Black Stallion's Filly.* When September came around and I started school, I *was* the Black Stallion. All my new friends were organized into a herd of ponies and I led them to the safety of certain school benches we'd designated as "home free." I had the best whinny on campus.

My life sort of stopped and started again when my parents separated. I have very few memories from the time before my father left. I remember one night when we were staying in a motel right after he'd been transferred from San Mateo to San Jose. I woke up because my parents were fighting and my father was heading for the door. I begged him not to leave. It didn't work. He closed the door behind him and I vowed never again to ask for something I didn't think I could get.

On the day he walked out for good, several months later, I put three *X*s across that page of my diary and wrote, "Nothing much happened today." I was twelve years old, it was 1957, and *no one* was divorced. People just didn't do that. It was too shameful to write about but I didn't want to forget the date, either, so that's how I dealt with it. That and twenty-five years of therapy.

# Richard

**My boyfriend sent me a package from Germany.**
There was a picture of him sitting on his bunk with his sleeves
rolled up. I could see the new eagle tattoo and his name on his
bicep. Once he'd transferred from regular Army service to the
National Security Agency, they'd let him grow his hair and it
was perfect again, with just enough grease to keep the pom-
padour in place and the curl down on his forehead. On the
back of the photo he'd written "Your tattooed lover."

Well, "lover" was stretching it a bit. This was 1960 in San
Jose, California, and I was the girl who was going to be a
virgin until she got married. I was fifteen. We met in Sacramento at the Capitol Inn, where my sister and I had stayed
with my father for two weeks. Johnny was the sexiest guy I'd
ever seen. He was nineteen, and he drank beer and kept his
Lucky Strikes in the rolled-up sleeve of his white T-shirt. I
was still wearing white gloves with white patent leather high

heels and getting my hair done in a French twist. I read Ayn Rand and went to ballet class. He read Louis L'Amour and took me to drag races. We made out to the Shirelles singing, "Tonight's the Night." He joined the Army, and we carried on our romance long distance.

Along with the picture he sent were color brochures for Noritake china. It was on sale at the PX. He wanted to get married as soon as he returned to the States. By then, I'd be eighteen.

Packed under the picture and the china ads was the real present: a purple angora sweater with a boat neck. It was absolutely perfect and I put it on immediately with the one straight skirt I owned.

I'd made the skirt in home economics class in eighth grade, right after we learned the correct way to boil eggs. I was a nice girl; I wasn't allowed to wear straight skirts. Or maybe I should say I had a strict mother, I wasn't allowed to wear straight skirts. Rebellion wasn't an option. But to get our grade, the teacher insisted we wear the straight skirt we'd made to class. I *definitely* wasn't allowed to wear a straight skirt without a slip, and the only slip I owned was the crinoline I wore under my round poodle skirt. I went to school with three layers of circular starched lace under a gray wool sheath skirt. I looked like I was hiding huge popcorn balls between my legs. The teacher had met my mother. She knew we pinned the top sheet to the blanket to keep the bed neat when we made it. I got an A minus.

Johnny stayed in Germany while I wore his sweater in California. I was wearing it a year later when I met Richard. I was sixteen and a half, he was twenty-five. He'd been married and divorced and he had a daughter with a woman named Penelope who was a dancer with the San Francisco Ballet. He was sharing an apartment with a man named Leslie whom I had met six months earlier when he directed me in my first musical for the San Jose Light Opera.

I had started acting in school plays and children's theater. I didn't really know how. I just did it. I'd been taking ballet since I was three so I already knew how to stand up straight. I took an acting class in third grade and they taught us how to sit in a chair without turning around to see where it was. I started voice lessons when I was ten because someone told my mother I could sing. Having grown up poor on the farm, she wanted to give me the opportunities she never had. She took me to the Burlingame Conservatory of Music, an hour's drive from our house. I learned how to pronounce my *T*s, *D*s, and *N*s and sang a song that went:

My mother says that babies come in bottles
but last week she said they grow on special baby
  bushes.
I don't believe in the stork either.
They're all in the zoo busy with their own babies.
And what's a baby bush anyway?

Lessons were expensive and the drive to Burlingame cost a lot in gas. My mother worked full-time at Macy's and I'd been working part-time as a receptionist in a beauty salon since I was twelve. One of our patrons at the salon was on the board of directors of the local community theater, the San Jose Light Opera. When my mother raved about my singing, the woman suggested I audition for *The King and I*. By this time I'd done musicals with the Conservatory and in junior high and high school, so I didn't hesitate. I was hired to play Tuptim, and Leslie was my director.

Now Leslie was directing *West Side Story,* again for the San Jose Light Opera. Rehearsals were in the evening, and since I was starring in *The Boyfriend* for my senior class play, Leslie cast two of us to alternate playing the role of Maria and I juggled my schedule. On my off nights, I played Velma, which was primarily a dance role. Richard was the choreographer. I thought he was one of the most beautiful people I'd ever seen. You could cut paper on his cheekbones. He had a dancer's body and gorgeous hands. My diary read: *I could watch Richard dance and dance and dance for years and never tire of it. Ever.*

I imprinted on him like a duckling. He was my Henry Higgins. He introduced me to Rimbaud and Verlaine and Baudelaire. We went to City Lights Bookstore in San Francisco and bought books by Mary Renault and Lawrence Ferlinghetti. I memorized Jacques Prévert's *Paroles* and Diane diPrima's *Dinners and Nightmares* because he loved them. He gave me James Ramsey Ullman's *The Day on Fire* and I found it so shocking, I knew I'd never forget it. (I haven't; the 1958 edition still sits on my bookshelf.)

We played Nina Simone and Carmen MacRae on the hi-fi. Nancy Wilson, Annie Ross, Edith Piaf, Charles Aznavour, Anita O'Day, Morgana King. He took me to hear Bobby Short and Mabel Mercer. We sang "The Thrill Is Gone" and "This Time the Dream's On Me." He ate cubes of Jell-O with his fingers and wrote everything in lowercase letters. I stopped capitalizing anything I wrote and never started again. I was a straight-A student and a cheerleader, but he was *artistic* and that's what I craved. I wrote in my diary: *Goal—Education. I must fill my mind, exercise my intelligence to its fullest. I want to know so much more than I do about the theater and dancing and English. I'm afraid I'm stagnating. My world is getting too narrow. I must do something lasting. Create. My only outlet is this book and it is nothing. I wonder if being a success in my home and my family will be enough for me. I'm thirsting after knowledge, spurred on by Richard whom I have come to call a "genius." Imagine, my knowing a genius!*

I didn't know men lived with other men unless they were roommates so it took me a while to understand that Richard and Leslie were lovers. I didn't know firsthand what "lovers" meant either, because, aside from some heavy petting with Johnny, my sex education consisted entirely of what I'd read in medical books checked out from the San Jose Public Library and biology books from my freshman year in high school. My friendship with Richard gave me a new understanding of love. *Broadmindedness is important to me,* reads the diary. Pretty progressive thinking for a teenager in the mid-'60s.

My mother liked Richard but she didn't like him around me. He was nine years older than I was and I was barely allowed to date. She was watering the plants outside the triplex we rented when he brought me home late from dance class one afternoon. She turned the hose on him. Sprayed him with water and told him not to be late again. I guess it didn't cross her mind that I was safer with him than with any of the panting, pimple-faced boys in my junior class.

I fell in love with him but I didn't admit it, even to myself. He was gay, after all. I knew he cared for me, we were together all the time, but nothing was going to come of it. We were just best friends. I never expected anything else. In my yearbook he wrote:

> *adrienne-*
> *the words, the song, and*
> *the movement have been*
> *more than life if less*
> *than love*
> *catapulted into the future*
> *somewhere (not far away)*
> *adrienne-girl becomes*

*adrienne-woman*
*those of us who have*
*given our hearts to you*
*will know that when you*
*are not here, you*
*are somewhere*
*(not far away)*
*the worlds overlap-rebellion*
*stimulating*
*added chaos, new growth and-*
*renewed courage.*
*the worlds, now strange and now*
*familiar*
*will welcome you*
*will treat you with respect*
*for you are a child of*
*the gods-on-the-hill*
*and*
*somewhere is*
*(not far away)*
*-richard*

It was enough just to be his friend.

We did *Flower Drum Song* together. I went to school during the day, worked on the weekends, and saw him at night at rehearsals. He choreographed and I played Mei Li. He left

Leslie and moved in with Ron, another dancer in the company. I didn't mind; how could I compete with another man?

I graduated high school and left for a two-month tour in a musical revue, *Showtime On Broadway*, again sponsored by the San Jose Light Opera. We had been performing at local Army bases and were chosen by the State Department to entertain G.I.s overseas. My mother was excited; all those lessons hadn't been for naught.

This was 1963. Southeast Asia was still "the Orient." The biggest city I'd ever visited was San Francisco, forty miles north of my home. I'd never been on a plane. My first flight was nonstop, Travis Air Force Base in Sacramento to Yokota, Japan. It was a Pan Am jet and they flew us first class. I was fascinated with the lavatory. Imagine being able to go to the bathroom thirty thousand feet in the air. My grandparents didn't even have one inside their house.

From Japan we took military air transport to Seoul, Korea, and then a bus north toward the DMZ. I was fascinated with the toilets in Korea, too. They had metal covers to protect them from the rains leaking through the roof. Our first two performances were done less than a mile from the Communist border on the night the Korean War truce agreement ended. We played in the camp mess hall, with red lights sitting atop the refrigerators. If the lights started flashing during a performance, it meant the North Koreans had come across the border and were shooting at our troops. When we returned to our billets—over a bridge that we later learned had been rigged with dynamite—we were told that three G.I.s who had attended our show had been killed by snipers waiting under the bridge.

I'd lived for eighteen years in middle-class white suburbia with a mother who listened to Elvis Presley on the car radio while she drove me back and forth to rehearsals. We never discussed politics or world affairs. I didn't even know what party she voted. I never saw a newspaper in the house. I'd never witnessed poverty, never known violence. I knew my relatives had fled from Armenia to escape annihilation but that seemed like hundreds of years ago. I don't remember even learning about the Holocaust until I moved to New York. Korea was the beginning of my loss of innocence. Three hundred Koreans were dying from starvation each day in the city of Seoul alone. I watched villagers brushing their teeth in the same gutters they urinated in. I kept my arms inside the bus so the "schlickie boys" wouldn't steal my watch or rings as we drove by. I saw the Korean prostitutes giving the clenched fist of hatred to us "round-eyes" because they needed the G.I.s to make money off of and were afraid we would sleep with them instead.

I did my best to counteract the resentment we were met with. One day four of us from the show walked six miles into downtown Seoul, smiling and waving to everyone we saw. I was the first American woman most of the villagers had ever seen. Thirty children followed us, begging us to take their pictures. We ended up on a sidewalk where American rock and roll was coming from a storefront, and we started dancing in the street. People stood six deep on every corner to watch. It was a huge accomplishment to have several elderly people smile and say hello.

With the hatred in the eyes of the Koreans and the loneliness on the faces of the G.I.s, I spent a lot of time crying in Korea. And I started drinking: one Grasshopper, two Brandy Alexanders, two Planter's Punches, a Singapore Sling, a Ramos Fizz, and a Sloe Gin Fizz—all in the space of eight weeks. I wrote home to my mother after each one with a report on how they affected me. I didn't want her to worry that I couldn't handle my liquor. Besides, I didn't like the taste of it; I never drank again.

We covered 900 miles by bus in Korea and then went on to Okinawa and Taiwan, getting out of the Lucky Hotel in Taipei eight hours before it was completely submerged by a typhoon. I loved Okinawa, where filet mignon dinners were $1.75, movies were a quarter, and our "maids" ironed our bras after scrubbing them on the stone floor. Then it was on to Johnston Island, an atomic testing site in the Pacific. Johnston Island was just a coral rock with barely enough room on one side for a runway. We changed costumes in the liquor closet and performed on an outdoor stage with planes taking off right next to us. We couldn't hear the music and the men couldn't hear us.

They didn't care. There were no women on the island. We could have picked our noses and they would have loved us. The G.I.s besieged the stage, shoving gifts in our hands: Army pins, self-portraits, jewelry, even a toothbrush.

The tour ended in Hawaii, where we were billeted right on Waikiki Beach. I'd spent more time writing about the relationships that were constantly changing among the cast members than I had writing about what I'd seen, but it was the beginning for me of a lifelong love of exploring new places. *And* I'd earned $7.00 a day for two months—my first "professional" job.

Three weeks after I returned home, Johnny returned from Germany, where he'd fathered a child, and Richard returned from Los Angeles, where he'd married a woman. Her name was Nancy Denise and he wanted us to be friends. I buried myself in schoolwork, tried to figure out how Johnny fit into my plans now that I'd discovered the theater and he had a relationship in Germany, and wondered how it might have been different with Richard if I'd been older and my mother had actually let us date.

I had a scholarship to San Francisco State University but I hadn't taken the entrance exams and the semester had already started by the time I got home. Richard's ex-lover, Leslie, was the head of the Drama Department at Foothill College in Menlo Park, not far from where we lived. He helped me with a late application. I took Stagecraft, Philosophy, and English two days a week from 9:00 A.M. til 9:00 P.M. and worked the other four as office manager for a termite exterminator. I was going to get a degree and teach drama. It never crossed my mind I could act for a living. I didn't know a soul who did that. In 1963, in my family, if you were interested in acting— and no one was, except me—you taught it.

All of that changed six months later when I did another production for the San Jose Light Opera. It was *Carnival* and I was playing Rosalie. Once again, Richard was choreo- graphing. Nancy Denise was no more; rumor had it she was living with a famous symphony conductor in L.A. Richard had moved back in with Ron, and he and I settled into our friendship once again.

I also became friends with the actress who was playing Lilly. Jeanette had just moved to San Jose from New York, where she had appeared off-Broadway in *Little Mary Sunshine.* We had a conversation in the dressing room one night that changed my life.

"You ought to go to New York, Adrienne," she said. "Everyone thinks they should get ready to go to New York but the truth is, you should go to New York to get ready. That's where all the good teachers are."

I'd never thought about it before but suddenly it made all the sense in the world. That's what I would do. I would finish my freshman year at Foothill College and then move to New York to try the professional stage. If nothing happened by the time I was twenty-five, I'd go back to college, get my degree, and teach. Simple.

*May 4, 1964* [age 18]

*A really good review for me as Rosalie. I knew I deserved a good review but not because of me. Rosalie is Richard's creation. Remember how I began the show with no idea at all of Rosalie? Even now, there is no name, no one word for her. But she is there—alive and vital.*

*One all overpowering striving looms large in my life—the theater. I have made my choice and am closing the door on an easy, good, normal, happy life. The road in front of me is only one of pain, nervous breakdowns, emptiness, hollow success, if any. And yet, I have no choice. I am consumed with the theater. What will become of me? Will I lose my sight or be physically kept from the theater by an accident or act of God. Or will I continue secondhand and frustrated 'til the end. Or will I succeed and yet never know success? Will I ever be fulfilled—if I am not, does it even matter?*

*I must go on. I must succeed. I will not be fulfilled until I am on Broadway in lights. What does the future hold?*

*I must be able to say, "I told you so, I knew it." I must have people say, "I used to go to school with her." As ugly or glory-ridden as it is, it is true. I also must be in a position to help other people, to make my mother comfortable for life and make up to her for the terrible personality I am becoming.*

The school year ended and I started planning my departure. In August, Richard called to say he'd just been hired to choreograph two new musical productions: one in San Francisco and one in San Jose. We made a date to meet that night to celebrate but when I got to the theater, he wasn't there. Instead Ron showed up. He was crying. Richard had disappeared, and it had been reported that someone matching his description had jumped off the Golden Gate Bridge. I was terrified. For three days, we waited to see if it was true. I called everywhere, trying to track him down: his first wife, his ex-girlfriend, Nancy Denise, even the Gene Marinaccio Dance Studio in Los Angeles where he used to study.

Which is where he turned up. Taking dance classes in L.A. Unable to face the possibility of succeeding as a choreographer. Not afraid of failure, afraid of success.

My mother loved the idea that I might become an actress but she worried about my moving to New York. She suggested Los Angeles. It was closer. She arranged an interview with an agent named Meyer Mishkin, a friend of a friend. I had no intention of moving to Los Angeles. I wasn't interested in making movies; except for a few European films with Patricia Gozzi (*Sundays and Cybele*) and Rita Tushingham (*A Taste of Honey, The Leather Boys*), I rarely went to see them. I didn't watch television. All I knew was musical comedy. Besides, I thought, L.A. is a flesh market. I didn't know what a flesh market was but that's what all the books I read said and I knew I didn't want to be in it.

So, on the pretext of going to meet the agent, I went to Los Angeles to spend the weekend with Richard. Johnny from Germany was long gone, smoking and drag races having lost out to ballet and theater, and I was no longer determined to be a virgin when I got married.

I remember the weekend as if it were yesterday.

Richard had a one-room apartment with a Murphy bed that pulled down from a pale green wall and rested in front of a long wooden trunk he used for a coffee table. There were three fat bayberry candles sitting in white saucers on the trunk. He kept them lit, day and night. He'd placed two wicker chairs with pale yellow seat cushions at either end of the trunk. Beneath the only window were a small pine dining table and two mismatched wooden chairs. There was a half-refrigerator with a hot plate on top of it and a small porcelain sink with the same pale yellow fabric draped below it. He had fresh daisies in a mason jar on the table. He took me out to dinner and to a gay bar called The Klondike. When we came back to the apartment and the Murphy bed, I had my speech all prepared.

"I want you to be my first lover, Richard. Will you make love to me?"

He called me Adrienna in those days, especially when he was emotional. "Oh, Adrienna, I can't. My heart still belongs to Leslie and I really can't. I'm sorry."

He held me instead and somehow I got through the night.

I moved to New York later that year. It was 1964 and I was nineteen years old. I didn't know a soul in Manhattan. I put all my things in two big boxes and told my mother to send them to me when I had an address. I took $300.00 cash in my purse and had the Bank of America transfer the rest of my savings, all $700.00 of it, to a bank in midtown Manhattan. I didn't know enough to be scared.

The following March I got a letter from Richard: " If you don't have a lover by the time I get there, may I be your lover?"

He arrived five months later.

# Getting Started

**WHEN I WAS IN FIRST GRADE, MY TEACHER WROTE ON** my report card, "Adrienne thinks she's better than the other kids."

I was humiliated. I didn't know what she meant but I knew it wasn't good. I definitely shouldn't think I was better than other kids even if I was. I mean, I was a good tetherball player and I was a good speller and I got all "fours" on my report card, which was the best you could get.

But you shouldn't get the teacher writing something like that about you. That was wrong. That was embarrassing. It made me cry.

I vowed that no one would ever have reason to say such a thing about me again. No one would ever say I was "conceited," which was just about the worst word I could think of to be called. I set about making myself *less* than everyone else. I did such a good job that when I first entered therapy and the shrink asked what I wanted for myself, I couldn't admit I wanted to be a "star" because that was egotistical and "people wouldn't like me if they knew."

The thing that amazes me now is that I succeeded in my career at all.

*Excerpt from ninth-grade term paper entitled "To Be or Not to Be: Acting as a Vocation," written January 5, 1960, by Adrienne Barbeau. Age 15.*

*Courage, will, persistency and perseverance, without these a budding young actress will never succeed. Directors will not come looking for you. Though some fortunates can sit on a bar stool or ride in an elevator and be discovered like a lost diamond brooch, the rest must fend for themselves. Hours turn into days, days turn into weeks, weeks into months, and soon you realize you're spending the best years of your life in the outer office of a producer's studio. It takes downright stubbornness and doggedness to keep trying until that lucky break comes along.*

I was moving to New York to be an actress. Well, to try, at least.

But first, I needed photographs. You had to have photographs and a résumé to send to all the people who might hire you. I wasn't sure who those people were but there must be a way to find out; I'd figure that out when I got there.

I put on a low-cut spaghetti-strap dress, had my dark

brown hair styled in six huge French curls that rose three inches above my head, wore long, dangling black earrings and thick black eyeliner, and drove from San Jose to San Francisco to have my eight-by-ten glossies taken. I loved the way they turned out. They didn't look like me but they sure were glamorous. They were so professional, they even had the photographer's name and city printed on them.

This was 1964. Every girl selling soap on TV had straight blonde hair and blue eyes and a blouse with a Peter Pan collar.

It took me years to figure out why no one ever called me to audition for a commercial.

My plan, once I got to New York, was to find a place to live, get a job, and start auditioning. The only time I'd ever auditioned for anything other than school plays and the San Jose Light Opera was when I drove to San Francisco to try out for the role of Luisa in a professional production of *The Fantasticks.* I'd never seen the show. I didn't know Luisa is a sweet young girl who sings sweet young songs full of romance and delight. I didn't know it would be smart to sing something that was sweet and young and full of romance and delight. I sang a song I thought would show off my eighteen-year-old lyric soprano voice. I sang "My Man's Gone Now" from *Porgy and Bess;* you know, the deep, dark, turgid ballad written for a forty-year-old black woman.

It took me years to figure out why I didn't get a callback.

So I arrived in New York . . .

*September 21, 1964*
*Today is my third day on my own in New York. I love it here.*
*There are trees and shrubs and the freeways are sided with stone*
*instead of concrete. I saw the World's Fair on my way in from the*
*airport and a lot of cemeteries and a complete billboard adver-*
*tising "Hello, Dolly!"*

It was too expensive to call home so I placed a person-to-person call for myself at my mother's house to let her know I was okay and then I checked into the Barbizon Plaza, which was known as a hotel for young women. It was decorated in pale pink and green with gaslit candles and chandeliers and a balcony, and even had a room called The Recital Room with two grand pianos and an organ and a television. It was very impressive. Expensive, though: $8.25 a night. I couldn't afford that for long. On the third day I moved to the YWCA. I had to pay cash every day but it was cheaper.

*Cash on hand:*
*$220.00 in traveler's checks*
*$ 20.00 cash from mother*
*$ 15.00 my own cash*
*Total: $255.00*

I spent the first three days answering rent ads in *The New York Times*. I'd already spent $1.18 on a taxi drive from the Barbizon to the Y, so I walked from one apartment to another:

Fifty-first Street and Eighth Avenue down to Ninth Street and over to Avenue A and up to Ninety-third and York and then back down to the Y at Fifty-first.

I found two girls who had a one-bedroom apartment on Fifty-sixth Street and Lexington Avenue. They were looking for a third roommate. They wanted something called security, which I'd never heard of, in addition to the rent, and didn't want me to move in until the first of the month.

One of the girls was an alcoholic who "borrowed" things, as I later found out on Christmas Eve when my only coat disappeared. The other had "friends" who left money on the dresser on the nights I'd come home to find myself locked out of the bedroom. But I didn't know that at the time. It seemed like a safe neighborhood, so I gave them all my cash, made arrangements to move in October 1, and called my mother to ask her to telegraph me more money.

> *Expenses upon arrival:*
> *$1.75 bus to East Side Terminal from Idyllwild Airport*
> *$ .50 tip to porter at bus station*
> *$ .95 taxi to Barbizon Plaza*
> *$ .55 tip to very nice cab driver, Mr. Jung*
> *$1.75 lunch*
> *$ .40 tip to obnoxious Barbizon Plaza porter*
> *$ .30 onion soup*
> *$ .10 orange juice*

I'd had my entire life savings, the $700.00 I'd earned at the termite control, transferred from the Bank of America to a bank in midtown. By mistake, they deposited it in someone else's account. I spent the next two weeks waiting for them to find it while I slept on the couch of friends who had recently moved to New Jersey from San Jose.

Time to get a part-time job, find an acting teacher, and start auditioning.

# Matty's Mardi Gras

*New York City*
*October 19, 1964*

*Dear Mom,*
*I have found a good—no, better than good—position in a restaurant/cocktail lounge. The owners have been there 15 years and own most of the places on the street but they recently remodeled this place and last night was their grand opening. We had furs, full-length gowns, and Rocky Graziano came in, as did the "Copacabana Girls." They expect more celebs all week. The emcee is Steve Condos—Martha Raye's brother-in-law. It is a small place. They serve Italian-American food and there is a full-time disc jockey in the recording room who plays albums all evening long for dancing. In fact, my bosses hired a professional exhibition dance duo to do the samba, twist, and cha cha cha just for last night.*

*My hours are 7 P.M. to 4 A.M., six days a week. Waitresses are* *paid a tiny salary like $5.00 a week or so and then they keep all tips. Tipping in N.Y. is different than in San Jose—i.e., if a man checks his coat or hat, he is expected to tip at least twenty-five cents to get it. Last night one man tipped $9.00. So the girls average about $100.00 a week on a slow week and $6.00 minimum salary and a percentage of hatcheck tips if they work coatroom, and their dinners. Last night I had a club sandwich, roast beef later and then baked clams even later.*

*My duties vary from singing to hat checking to waitressing to dancing with the emcee or other employees. We wear red, high-necked, long-sleeved leotards with skirts and black mesh tights. You wouldn't believe it but in New York women of forty dance together— ballroom dancing. Two couples will come in for a drink and the women will get up and dance together. I dance alone because I can't follow another girl and refuse to become that New Yorkized.*

*The place is legitimate. We are not allowed to talk, dance or, especially, drink with the patrons. This is a very strict rule. If we have any trouble with a patron—just tell the hosts. No one allowed without coat and tie. The owners are two brothers and they are very nice, very watchful for the girls. Most of the girls have been with them for about three years. My boss owns the Peppermint Lounge in Miami Beach and is a "big man" in New York—although not a member of the Mafia, they are good friends. He owns several clubs in New York. Made all his money from running clip joints in the 1950s but nonetheless, a good man to know in case I ever need help. He is already securing me a stereo for 1/3rd the list price.*

*Now dear—you mustn't get upset. It is a good place. A*

*reputable, SAFE place and it is a necessity. You see, my days must be open. I am getting calls now from agents and directors and producers for interviews because of the résumés and photos I have mailed. I must be free to see them on THEIR time; they can't be bothered if I can't make it at their convenience. Also—there are auditions. And more important—I MUST HAVE TIME FOR DANCE AND VOICE CLASSES.*

*Now, I may continue my market research job for two days a week because I like the people and of course, any extra money is convenient. My third job—the service which places me in the good places—had me hat checking at Basin Street East Monday and Buddy Greco was performing. A good show but small audiences. I will give up that job or perhaps only do it on weekends during the day.*

*And here's the big news . . . I bought a mink stole. First, because I couldn't afford to pass up the price—$100.00. Second, because I know sooner or later in this game of New York I'm going to have great use for it. Bought it from a very nice guy who works with me. His wife is too tall for it and she's buying another. Do you believe it? 19 and a mink stole! Ha! Ha! Ha!*
*Love, Adrienne*

The first full-time job I had in New York was at a restaurant called Matty's Mardi Gras. Matty's was on Forty-seventh Street near Broadway, directly across from a large Armenian restaurant called the Golden Horn. Matty's was about a third the size of the Horn but did almost as much business. Armenians eat Armenian food at home.

Matty ran his help-wanted ad in *Back Stage* magazine. I stopped in one afternoon around four o'clock. There was a long bar on the right with a mirrored wall behind it. The liqueurs sat against the mirror—Gallianos, Drambuies, Courvoisiers, and B & Bs. Jameson, Pinch, Johnny Walker, and the rest of the hard liquors crowded a lower ledge in front. Across from the bar was an eight-by-ten-foot raised platform set up with a piano and drums. You could look in the mirror and watch the band playing behind you. Past the bar, separated by a waist-high oak partition, was the dining room. Red vinyl booths, shiny brown tables.

Matty was sitting at the end of the bar by the window to the street. He had a Coke in his hand. He introduced himself when he heard me ask the bartender about the job. He looked about five-nine, 210 pounds, late thirties. Wearing what I later came to recognize as a Louie Roth suit—the preferred designer for men of a certain Italian social class.

"Whattaya been doin' before this?" he asked.

"Nothing really. I just moved here a week ago. I was going to college in California and working as an office manager for a termite control."

"Termites, huh? Well, sometimes we get bugs around here, don't we, Vinnie? Only they ain't the four-legged kind."

"Actually, I need to work at night 'cause I need my days free to take classes and go to auditions and stuff. I'm trying to be an actress."

"You ain't a pro, are ya?"

"A pro? Well, I did get paid to go to the Orient to entertain the armed forces but I'm not a member of Equity yet, if that's what you mean. I mean, I just go to open non-union chorus calls right now."

"Yeah . . . well . . . that ain't quite what I meant but . . . how old are you?"

"Nineteen."

"Yeah, okay, that's okay. See, the one thing you gotta know about this joint is I can't have any trouble with the cops. Y'know what I mean? I mean, you can talk to the customers as long as you're servin' 'em and there's a bar between youse or you're just standin' at their table with a tray but nobody fools around with my girls, ya get it? It's like a family here. We take care of our girls."

I started working the following night. Waited tables during the dinner hour and when things got quiet, one of the night bartenders taught me to pour drinks. I worked six nights a week from seven to four. When my shift was over, one of the bartenders put me in a cab. I didn't have to pay for dinner, I was earning $125.00 a week cash, and I thought it was more money than I'd ever make in my life.

Matty's full name was Matty the Horse. I never asked why. It didn't dawn on me until years later that I was working for "The Syndicate." No one said "Mafia" out loud in those days. There was always the fear you wouldn't live to say anything else. No one said much of anything, really, except, "You want to buy a full-length mink?"

It took me a while to figure that out, too. The second week I was working there, I asked Matty where I should go to buy a hi-fi.

"Don't worry about it," he said. "I got a friend."

Two nights later, just as we were closing, he told me to take a cab to Thirty-second and Broadway and wait in front of the Smiler's coffee shop for a guy in a brown El Dorado. Twenty minutes later, a man in a black, full-length alpaca coat stepped out of a brown Cadillac, opened the trunk, and held out a large box with the words Magnavox printed on the side.

"You Matty's girl?"

"No, no, I just work for him. How much do I owe you?"

"You ain't worked for him long, have you? You don't owe me nothin'."

"Are you sure?"

"Hey! Just don't ask no goddamn questions. You're a friend of Matty's, Matty's a friend of mine. Capeesh?"

I capeeshed. I capeeshed my way to a TV, a vacuum, and a set of copper cookware. I passed on the diamond ring.

(It wasn't until last year when I read Joe Pantoliano's autobiography that I figured out the word "swag" meant stolen without a gun.)

Matty had a younger brother named Sal. Sal was a bigger version of Matty. Five-eleven, 240 pounds, same suits two sizes larger. He put milk in his scotch. Sal had a tic: Whenever he got nervous or upset, his neck would snap down to his right shoulder. Sal had a girlfriend who worked in the club. He also had a wife who visited the club. We could always tell when his wife was coming in because his tic got violent. If he was pouring drinks, scotch went flying everywhere.

Right after I started working there, Matty got the idea that the place needed entertainment. He put these motorized mannequins on the stage and dressed them up like musicians. The drummer moved his sticks on a drum set, the guitar player strummed a guitar, and the piano player plunked at the keys. All this while a disc jockey was playing records. If you looked in from outside, you thought there was a live band. People came in, sat at the bar, ordered a beer, and then turned around to enjoy the show. Only there was no show, just musical dummies. And they still had to pay for the beer.

After the third night of dealing with a bunch of pissed-off patrons, Sal told his girlfriend and me to get up on stage and dance. We did. Pretty soon we were making more money in tips from dancing than from waiting tables or tending bar.

Years later, Sal's girl wrote a book about her experiences as a mistress to the mob. In it she claims Matty's Mardi Gras gave birth to discotheque dancing and that we were the first go-go girls in existence. I don't know if that's true. All I know is I quit before we went topless.

One night Matty introduced me to a friend of his at the bar. The guy sat down and wrote out an entire scene from

*Goodbye, Columbus* on a cocktail napkin. I was very impressed. I'd just finished reading the book and here I was meeting the author, Philip Roth. Wow. He was a good-looking man, too: dark hair, square jaw, strong features. He was probably twenty years older than I was but that didn't stop me from saying yes when he asked me out.

We started dating. Richard was still in L.A. and I was still a virgin. I took myself down to the Margaret Sanger clinic on Eighteenth Street and got fitted for a diaphragm: something the heroine in *Goodbye, Columbus* was hesitant to do. We drove out to the Montauk Inn and Philip Roth became my first lover.

In the spring I got my first Equity contract for a summer stock job. I told Philip good-bye and headed for the Midwest. When the job ended, I flew to California to visit my family. As soon as I got there, I called my friend Eve. We'd been best friends since seventh grade and had seen each other through every boyfriend and every breakup.

"Come on, I gotta take you to the bookstore and show you a picture of the guy I'm dating. Have you read *Letting Go?*"

I picked her up in my $400.00 1955 Plymouth and drove to the Valley Fair Mall. We found the bookstore, found the fiction section, and I pulled down a copy of *Goodbye, Columbus*. There on the back was a picture of Philip Roth. Only it wasn't the guy I was dating. I'd never seen the real Philip Roth in my life.

• • •

Michael was a regular customer at Matty's. He came in every Tuesday in the early evening, ordered a Budweiser for a dollar, tipped another dollar, and then went across the street for dinner at the Armenian restaurant.

As soon as he walked in, the girls scrambled to wait on him because they knew he was good for the dollar tip. I thought that was terrible and tried to make up for it by carrying on a conversation with him, which wasn't easy because he was very shy.

I got the feeling he was lonely. He never mentioned a wife or kids. He had thick white hair, which made it hard to guess his age, maybe forty, maybe sixty. He was short, about five-six, and he always sat on a stool at the bar.

One weekend he showed up unexpectedly. He'd been to see the New York City Ballet do *The Nutcracker* at The Town Hall. I told him I'd never seen *The Nutcracker* and he offered to pick up tickets for me.

When he came in to give me the tickets, he opened his wallet and I saw his driver's license. His last name was Sahagian. A fellow Armenian. I told him I was half Armenian and we became immediate friends. I never saw him outside Matty's but whenever he came in and I was working, he made sure he sat at my end of the bar and we kept each other company.

He came in on the Tuesday after I had seen *Nutcracker*, and I told him how much I enjoyed it.

"Well, I'd like to do something else for you for Christmas," he said, "but I don't know you well enough to know what you'd like."

"Oh, no, Michael, really. I really appreciate it but I don't want you to get me anything. You're too generous here at the bar as it is. I really couldn't accept anything. Besides, Matty probably wouldn't think too much of the idea, either. Thank you, really, but don't do anything." I went off to take care of my other customers and he left the bar.

On Christmas Eve he came in and gave me a card. We were so busy I put it in my purse and didn't open it until I got home at four in the morning. Inside the card there was a check made out to me for $300.00 and a stock certificate for $300.00 worth of stock in the J. W. Mays department store. I was floored. I had no idea where he lived or what his phone number was, so I couldn't even call him. I put the check and the certificate back in my purse and kept it with me when I went to work two days later.

Michael didn't come into the bar for a month. When he finally did, I told him there was no way I could accept his gracious gift.

"Please," he said, "when I came from the old country, an Armenian couple took me in and helped me until I got my first job. They're both dead so I can't do anything for them, but I would really like to do something for a fellow Armenian. Use the money for your acting classes. I don't want to take it back. And as far as the stock is concerned, all I ask is that if you ever decide to sell it, you contact me first. That's what I do for a living and I know a lot about it and I'll tell you if I think it's a wise move and whether you should invest in something else." He gave me a card with his address and phone number on it.

I thanked him a thousand times and promised to use the money for my classes. And I did. Two months later I left Matty's for a job as a cocktail waitress at a classier joint called the Spindletop. It was a steak house in the theater district and the girls were making $200.00 in tips on a good night. (Several of them were making $500.00 a night as call girls but I never caught on until they spelled it out for me. It amazed me to think that I knew someone who did that for a living.)

In April I signed my first summer stock contract. I'd earn $75.00 a week and at the end of the summer I'd be a member of Actor's Equity—a professional actor.

I ran into Michael on the street two weeks later. I was so excited to be able to tell him that his faith in me was being justified, I rattled on and on about the job and the shows I'd be doing and the roles they had offered me. It was the only time I'd ever seen him outside Matty's. He was incredibly shy and uncomfortable. I could tell he was happy for me but he couldn't get away fast enough.

Every December after that we exchanged Christmas cards. After I moved to L.A. to do *Maude*, his cards stopped coming and mine were returned, stamped "ADDRESSEE UNKNOWN." I assumed he'd died.

Fourteen years later, in 1979, I was in Boston doing press for *The Fog*. One of my appearances was at a department store, signing autographs. As each person came up, the press rep asked for a name and I personalized the photo. One of the men in line refused to give his name.

"She knows me, I think."

*Oh brother, what's this?* I wondered. I didn't know anyone in Boston. I looked up, expecting to find some crazed fan. Instead, I saw Michael. He still had his beautiful white hair.

I gave him a big hug and a kiss on the cheek and asked him what he was doing there. He said he was retired and he'd been living in Boston near his sister and her family for quite awhile. I was so happy to see him I started introducing him to everyone else in line.

"Ladies and gentlemen, this gentleman is responsible, in part, for my being here." I started going on about how he'd been so supportive and how I still had the stock he'd given me. He squirmed out of my embrace, said a quick, red-faced good-bye, and disappeared without leaving a phone number or an address.

Another fifteen years went by. In 1995, I received a letter from Michael's sister. It had been mistakenly sitting in a stack of fan mail for several months awaiting a return photo. She wrote that Michael was now in his nineties, living alone in a boarding house in Boston. She saw him regularly and knew he would love to hear from me. He didn't have a private phone but she gave me his address. I wrote to him immediately.

We corresponded by mail for several years. He still followed the market. In one of his letters he mentioned a stock he thought I should buy. I did. I made a lot of money.

Michael died in 1998. I still have the original stock he gave me.

# The Process

NOT ONLY WERE THERE TEACHERS IN NEW YORK WHO taught acting, there were entire acting schools. I was amazed. Stella Adler had the same last name as my voice teacher in California so her school seemed like a good place to start. I didn't have a clue how famous she was and her classes were expensive ($150 a month) and demanding (three mornings a week) but I was committed. I had the job working at Matty's until four in the morning. Somehow I'd get myself to class five hours later.

I lasted three weeks. It wasn't the hours that did me in; it was the teacher. Stella Adler spent every class alone on stage: performing, lecturing, and demeaning her students. She was especially hard on the girls—cold and unfriendly. All I learned was that I didn't want to be there. I walked out for good after she spent twenty minutes upbraiding me for wearing a hat to class.

I didn't have an agent and I wasn't in the union. I bought a book with the names and addresses of all the agents, managers, casting directors, and producers in Manhattan and I sent out photos—yes, the French-curled, spaghetti-strapped glamour shot—and résumés—San Jose Civic Light Opera, USO tour, and Foothill College—to every one of them. On three-by-five index cards I noted each submission I'd made, the date I'd mailed it, the date I'd placed a follow-up phone call, and the response I got—usually none.

*Back Stage*, the actors' trade paper, listed open, non-union casting calls. That meant you didn't need an agent and you didn't need to be in Equity to audition. Most of them were for musicals. I started studying voice with an elderly Italian woman who refused to let me learn any musical comedy material and insisted I sing Puccini's "O Mio Babbino Caro" (from *Gianni Schicchi*) and Ponchielli's "Suicidio" (from *La Gioconda*). I scheduled secretive appointments with a piano-playing friend to practice the last eight bars of "I Feel Pretty" from *West Side Story* and "If I Loved You" from *Carousel*—my up-tempo number and my ballad.

For seven months I went from the basement of one Broadway theater to another, auditioning for musicals, for industry trade shows, for touring shows and summer stock. There were always at least 300 of us vying for the same ten parts in the chorus, knitting away the hours and trying not to show how nervous we were and how desperately we wanted the job. I made a lot of mufflers.

Sometimes I'd get "typed out" (eliminated) before they'd ask me to sing. At least that way I didn't have to sit around all afternoon and then find out I was too short or too dark or not thin enough. When I did get called back, three or four hours later, after everyone had sung, the next step was learning the choreography. I could handle ballet and jazz but if it was tap, I was done for. My mother thought tap was "too masculine" and had never let me take a lesson.

I saw the voice teacher twice a week. She said my voice had been damaged; my E and my F sounded dead. I didn't know what that meant but it upset me. Was she telling me I didn't sound good, I couldn't sing? More often than not, I left the lesson in tears. That, coupled with seven months of not getting hired, and I was starting to lose my confidence.

Finally, in March 1965, I got my first summer stock job. I went to Augusta, Michigan, to build sets, sew costumes, baby-sit the producer's son, and appear in *Mary, Mary; The Threepenny Opera; Camelot; Stop the World—I Want to Get Off;* and some new play no one's ever heard of since. We had four days off in five months and we had to kick back half our salary under the table to the producer, but at the end of the summer, I had earned my union card. I was a member of Actors' Equity.

# Richard Redux

**RICHARD ARRIVED IN OCTOBER 1965. I HADN'T SEEN** him for a year. I was still in love with him, only this time it seemed possible he was also in love with me. His card had asked if he could be my lover when he arrived and I was more than willing.

I had a studio apartment at 535 Hudson Street in the West Village. I'd left my alcoholic, money-for-sex roommates and signed a year's lease on it as soon as I'd seen it one evening in February. It never dawned on me I should look at it in the daylight. I came from the sunny California suburbs. Who knew that if you had a five-story building right across the air-shaft from your second-story window, no light could get in? It was pitch black in there, morning, noon, and night. I came back from Michigan that fall counting the days until my lease expired. But I loved the Village. It was as close to living in California as I could get, casual and informal. I didn't have to put on makeup to take out my garbage. I knew my neighbors, I knew the shopkeepers. I hung out in the antique stores on Hudson Street and bought Li-Lac chocolates on Christopher Street and ate falafel at the Keneret on Bleecker Street. I visited with Kaye Ballard's nephew, Paul Bellardo, who had a gallery of his blown glass pieces and owned a royal poodle who carried his cigarettes for him. I bought French roast espresso beans from McNulty's and saw Bernadette Peters in her first off-Broadway role at the Theatre De Lys. And sometimes I stood on the corner of Tenth Street and Sixth Avenue and watched girls shout up to their girlfriends incarcerated in the Women's House of Detention.

Having Richard there made the apartment bearable. I sewed curtains by hand out of green fabric that cut my fingers and shed little shards of fiberglass every time we opened them. That didn't matter because we never opened them; there was nothing to see but a brick wall. We put soap on a sponge to wash one dish at a time because the sink was too small and we drained the dishes on top of the refrigerator. I spray-painted wire milk crates silver, stacked them one on top of another, and filled them with record albums and books of poetry. We listened to Shawn Phillips, Donald Byrd, and Villa-Lobos, and we read Allen Ginsburg, Edna St. Vincent Millay, and e. e. cummings. We slept in a single bed.

*Slept* was the operative word. Days went by without our making love, sometimes weeks. I loved him so much I told myself it didn't matter, even when I came home late from work that Thanksgiving eve and found him asleep on the sofa, with his friend Dennis in our bed. I covered them both and made a place for myself on the floor.

Days later, when I finally got up the nerve to ask him if they'd slept together, he said, "I don't think that's a good question for you to ask, Adrienna."

In spite of what may have been going on with Dennis, he spent New Year's Eve telling me how much he loved me. That was all I needed to hear. I hadn't expected our romance to last even that long. He was happy and that made me happy and we were having a great time together. No one made me laugh like he did. I loved him more than anyone in the world.

Five days later I came home and opened the closet door to find it empty. Richard's clothes were gone. It was only a one-room apartment and I couldn't see him, but I couldn't believe he wasn't there. I called out his name in the emptiness. Then I turned to the small built-in shelf next to the closet and found the note he'd left: "Adrienna . . . *alone* I have moved to 250 West Tenth Street. Please don't have the vapors." I walked back out the door and vomited in the gutter.

We continued to see each other, to spend almost all our days together. I forced myself to go to auditions occasionally but if I had the choice of sitting in the basement of a theater all afternoon or walking in the Village with Richard, I chose Richard. I had an agent who was booking me into New Jersey clubs as a go-go girl. At night while I danced, Richard saw other men.

He turned me on to grass for the first time. I was twenty years old. Sitting in his apartment on Tenth Street, smoking, I got so stoned I couldn't go outside because I couldn't open my eyes. I was blind, literally, and I was freezing. Richard wrapped me in blankets, pulled a space heater near me, and watched me shake. I hallucinated for eight hours.

When I woke up the next morning, I knew it was time to get into therapy. I'd had images of myself acting out my feelings of abandonment by my father and my mother's unexpressed rage. I needed to find out why I was attracted to someone who couldn't really be with me.

I had friends who knew a psychiatrist who was working with a new drug designed to facilitate the therapeutic process. They gave me a book called *Myself and I*, written by a woman named Constance Newland. In it she described how she suffered for years with a problem that seemed to have an emotional basis but which manifested physically as a tic: an odd clicking sound in her throat and neck. She also suffered from depression and an inability to experience orgasms. She had undergone Freudian analysis, gestalt therapy, and conventional therapy, all to no avail. When finally she took this new drug and was able to regress to an early childhood trauma that uncovered the source of the problem, she was freed from the tic and the depression and "achieved transcendent sexual fulfillment." The drug was LSD.

I wasn't clicking and I didn't think I was depressed but I

did see a pattern developing in my relationships and although it didn't seem like a problem at the time, I knew that if I eventually wanted to marry and have children I would need to make some changes. I needed to find out why I was only attracted to men who were gay, married, old enough to be my father, emotionally crippled, or all those things at once.

The psychiatrist whom my friends recommended was working under a government grant, researching the effects of LSD. He gave six-year-old children a tab of acid, sat them in front of an aquarium, and studied their responses. I didn't know anything about LSD but if it was good enough for six-year-olds, it was good enough for me.

I made an appointment for a consultation.

We talked for a while and the doctor thought I would be a good candidate for the drug. He wanted to see me three times a week for two hours at a time. I would drop a tab of acid at the beginning of the session, he'd guide me through the experience, and then send me home with a nurse who would stay with me until midnight. I'd have to pay $35.00 for the first hour and the government would pay the rest.

Well, three times $35.00 was more than I could afford, especially when it meant I'd be out of commission three days a week. I was only earning $35.00 a night dancing and I sure couldn't do it on acid with a nurse at the bar.

I needed a major source of income with a minor expenditure of time. Al Capp, the creator of the *L'il Abner* comic strip, was looking for girls to promote his new drink, Kickapoo Joy Juice. The job paid $150.00 a day, with a total of forty days' work over a period of three months. I could get stoned and healed on Monday, Wednesday, and Friday, and advertise a soft drink the rest of the time. It was perfect.

The interview was at Mr. Capp's office. I wore my white gloves to go with my white patent leather heels and my blue pique dress. It was a proper job interview and my mother had taught me how to dress properly. He started out asking me my measurements. I thought he must have the costumes made already and wanted to be sure I could fit into one before he hired me. Then he asked whether or not I had a boyfriend. I thought he wanted to be sure I didn't have any responsibilities that would keep me from traveling. Then he said, "Kiss me good-bye and you can go." I thought that seemed rather inappropriate but I still didn't catch on. It wasn't until I got home and his assistant called to say Mr. Capp would like to spend the evening with me that I finally figured out what the job really entailed.

I was pissed. And disappointed. No Kickapoo Joy Juice job, no money. My LSD therapy went down the drain. I took myself to St. Vincent's Hospital and applied for outpatient therapy instead. They put me in a group because they didn't think I was neurotic enough for private sessions, love affair with a gay man or not. I stayed eight months . . . until the doctor tried to seduce me.

I never did try acid.

In April, four months after I'd found my closet empty, Richard announced he was moving back to L.A. to be with Leslie once again. It was Richard's birthday and I'd just finished buying groceries for a surprise celebration. Instead I took a taxi to Port Authority to say good-bye. Again I was crying but this time my food stayed down. Therapy was helping.

I started another acting class, this time with Bill Hickey at the HB Studios.

Most of what I knew about acting I'd learned from Richard's lover Leslie who had directed me in four musicals. Leslie's approach to acting in musicals was to tell us to "pick up our cues." He didn't want any empty spaces between the speeches. I knew how to do that. Someone else finished speaking, I picked up my cue and delivered my line.

The first scene Bill Hickey assigned me was from *The Days and Nights of Beebee Fenstermaker.* My scene partner and I rehearsed for days and when time came to do the scene in class, I did what I'd been taught was good acting: I picked up my cues. It was a very dramatic scene and whenever my partner finished speaking, I didn't let a beat go by. I spoke up right away just the way I had in *West Side Story* and *Carnival* and *Flower Drum Song.*

There was dead silence when we finished the scene. Then Bill spoke. "You know," he said, "sometimes in life, we THINK before we speak."

I was mortified.

But now I knew three things about acting: pick up your cues, don't wear hats, and think before you speak.

Seven months passed. I continued to discotheque at night and audition during the day. Richard called often and wrote often, and one day he announced he was returning to New York. I didn't know what that meant in terms of the two of us; I tried not to think about it. By then I had moved into another West Village apartment down the street, at 496 Hudson. This time the kitchen was a converted closet. I still washed dishes in a tiny sink, but the living room had high ceilings, dark wood floors, a wood-burning fireplace, and lots of sunshine. I even had a bedroom, just wide enough for my single mattress and long enough for a desk at the end of it. Every twenty minutes I could hear a bus stop right below my window.

I met Richard at the airport and we spent the night together in my apartment. The next morning he said he'd like to stay.

Seven months of therapy went right out the window.

We bought furniture for him. He rented a piano. He had his trunk delivered from Las Vegas where he'd been working as a dancer. He resumed his old job managing Joe Allen's restaurant on West Forty-sixth. We spent our days playing and singing and dancing and yes, finally, making love. We shopped on Eighth Street, cooked elaborate meals for our friends, hung out at Joe's after hours. We never went to bed before 4:00 A.M. We laughed all the time.

I'd just finished another summer stock job in the Poconos and had been accepted into Lee Strasberg's acting class. Getting into "Lee's" class was a real coup—You couldn't just pay your money and sign up, you had to be invited, and I was excited about that. Until I took the class. I couldn't understand a word he said. All I remember was holding an imaginary cup of coffee to feel the imaginary steam on my face. The classes were very exclusive (although I didn't recognize a soul) and no one offered to do a scene with you if you weren't performing on Broadway. I wasn't. I stayed for three months and never got to do a scene. Now I knew four things about acting: pick up your cues, don't wear a hat, think before you speak, and lie about your credits.

I was still dancing at night in New Jersey and at the 8th Wonder on Eighth Street in the Village. I did a stint as a tarantella dancer for "Carnavale Italiano" at Mamma Leone's restaurant in midtown. I signed as a regular dancer on *The Miguelito Valdez Show* on Channel 47, the local Spanish-language television station. That lasted three weeks before the show was canceled. During the day I went to therapy, took voice lessons, and went to auditions, but the more fun I had with Richard, the less energy I put into my career. It was the beginning of a lifelong pattern for me of caring more about love and romance than work. I didn't care if I wasn't getting hired; I was loving my life.

And then one night, it all went to hell.

It was four o'clock in the morning when the doorbell woke me up and I heard Richard's voice over the intercom. He'd lost his keys. I buzzed him in and went back to bed. The doorbell rang again and this time I heard screaming on the street below. When I looked out the window, I saw Richard lying on the sidewalk with two police officers standing over him. They were beating him.

I ran down the stairs and got outside just as they put hand-cuffs on him and started dragging him away. They wouldn't tell me what he'd done; just put him in a squad car and said they were taking him to jail.

I took all my savings—$425.00, my emergency abortion fund—and hired a lawyer and got him out on bail. He'd been charged with felonious assault.

Richard had finished work at 2:00 A.M. that night and had stayed at the bar at Joe's, drinking. He took a cab home. When he went to pay the cabbie, he couldn't find his wallet. He told the driver to wait while he came upstairs to get some cash but the driver thought he was going to get stiffed and hailed two police officers. The cops said when they followed Richard into the foyer, he turned around and drop-kicked them. That's when they dragged him into the street and started beating him.

Richard remembered getting out of the cab to get money from the house. He remembered vomiting in a jail cell. He didn't remember anything else.

I'd been raised to believe the police were the good guys. They were the protectors, the caretakers. If you had a problem, you went to the police. They righted wrongs and corrected inequities. They punished the bad guys. Well, Richard wasn't a bad guy. He was the gentlest soul I'd ever met. He didn't have a violent bone in his body. I'd never heard him yell. He was never aggressive. When he got drunk, he got funny. He made people laugh. I will never believe he attacked those two cops. I think they saw a gay man and they went after him.

The lawyer we hired told us he could take care of everything for a thousand dollars. Richard got him the money and a hearing date was set. Three days before the hearing, the lawyer called to say he needed more money. He'd paid off the cab driver and paid off the cops but he needed a thousand dollars more to pay off the judge.

That was truly the end of my innocence.

We didn't have a thousand dollars. Richard jumped bail and disappeared.

For days and weeks I lived in a nightmare. I was frightened for Richard, scared for his safety, and worried about his state of mind. Hurt that he wouldn't contact me and eventually angry that he could be so selfish as to leave all his friends so concerned for his well-being. The lawyer wanted me to perjure myself with the judge to try to get a continuance of the case. I didn't know what to do and I had no one to ask. They finally issued a bench warrant for his arrest. I was terrified he was somewhere in New York and they'd find him and throw him back in jail. I lived in a constant state of nervous anxiety, waiting for a phone call, a letter, some communication with him.

Which didn't come. Gradually I got used to living with not knowing where he was or how he was. I was lonely and I was depressed but there wasn't much I could do about it. One day, after a week of hot water leaking in my bathtub, and after I'd begged the super for the tenth time to fix it and finally screamed at him in frustration, I lay down on the bed wishing I could die. I didn't have the energy to survive in New York alone. I fell asleep, woke up, and realized I didn't have a choice. I was still alive and I might as well make the best of it.

Three months passed before Richard made contact with anyone. Three months to the day he disappeared, I had a letter from him in my mailbox. He was living in Chicago with a new lover. "Your state of being is a question in my mind," he wrote.

My state of being. Well, I'd gone from pissed off, lonely, sad, frightened, and depressed to being a little wiser, a little stronger, a little more resilient. I'd survived.

I loved Richard in the way that only a young girl can. In the way that felt like, if he left me, I'd die. My mother never got over having my father leave. She didn't speak to him for more than thirty years after their divorce but I don't think she ever stopped loving him. She never remarried and she never again let anyone get very close to her. She was bitter and distrustful. "Don't marry them, Adrienne, look what they do to you" was the mantra I heard repeatedly. Something good in her died when my father left. Well, I loved Richard more than I'd ever loved anyone in my short life but Richard left and I didn't die. And I knew, having learned that lesson, I would never love someone quite that way again.

A year and a half later I was sitting in a theater getting ready to go on stage when Richard's face appeared in my dressing-room mirror. He had moved back to New York with his boyfriend and had gotten his sentence dismissed. We continued to see each other and care for each other but were never again lovers. He moved to Paris to run Joe Allen's there and by the time he returned to the States, I had moved to Los Angeles. He died of cancer in 1986.

So much of who I am has to do with having had him in my life. From my taste in music to my understanding of human nature. He was my teacher and my mirror. Even the woman I set out to become in the aftermath of our love affair: the woman who could love a man who would love her and stay with her. That transformation came about because I recognized my part in our attachment—my insecurities, my diminished self-worth, my need to be with someone who withheld himself—and worked for years to change all that. I have learned from many people in my life but from Richard most of all.

# The Mob Revisited

**IN 1966, I WAS EARNING MY LIVING AS A DISCOTHEQUE** dancer. The term go-go girl hadn't caught on yet. No white vinyl boots. Just the same black leotard and fishnet stockings and black high heels I'd worn at Matty's, only this time the leotard was two-piece and I'd sewn fringe and sequins on the top. I had an agent in Manhattan named Killer Joe Piro who booked me four nights a week at the clubs of my choice. I got $35.00—cash—for five hours a night and he took his commission directly from the club.

Most of the clubs were in New Jersey: Hoboken, Harrison, Secaucus, and Newark. Occasionally I'd go to the Salem Inn in Port Washington on Long Island to dance on top of a baby grand. That ended on the night I kicked a scotch-and-soda all over some jackass who was giving me trouble.

I didn't like the jobs but I didn't mind the dancing. I wasn't acting enough to support myself and this was better than waitressing. I was in demand enough that I could pick my favorite places to dance—the ones where I felt safe, where the management was decent, the clientele was decent, and no one complained if I sat in the ladies' room reading *Tai-Pan* between sets.

The owner of one of these places was an Italian named Vinnie. Vinnie wore dark, pin-striped suits with blue shirts and subdued ties. He was married, had a couple of kids. He also had a mistress who was constantly trying to kill herself. He told me this one night when he was driving me home. He wanted my advice. He'd never known a college girl, he said, and since I'd gone to college he could tell I knew a lot about psychology and why people act the way they do.

What I didn't know, at first, was why there was never anyone in the club. It was a very nice supper club with a bar running the length of one side. Plush blue carpeting and gray linen table-cloths with black French provincial style chairs. The raised dance floor was at the back of the room. Whenever someone came in I'd do a set, but most of the time I was the only one at the bar, drinking coffee and talking to Mike, the bartender.

"What's the story here, Mike? I don't understand it. It's a nice club, the food is good. How come nobody ever comes in?"

"Well, somebody got snuffed here a year ago. Took two in the gut sittin' over there havin' sausage and peppers with a lady wasn't his wife, ya know what I mean. Business ain't been the same since."

Vinnie occasionally had business associates visit the club. One night, he asked if I'd mind serving coffee to them in the back room. Twelve huge Italian men in shiny suits walked in. No one said a word. They just sat there smoking cigars and rubbing lemon peel on the rim of their espresso cups until I left the room.

Afterward, Vinnie offered to drive me all the way home again. He said he had a problem and didn't know what to do. He was a member of an organization, he told me, and he was up for a promotion. He'd been in this organization for twenty years and he really wanted the promotion. The problem was, in order to get it he was going to have to tell the truth about someone else in the organization, something only Vinnie knew. This man was a friend of his and he'd done something wrong and if Vinnie told the truth, the man would have to pay the consequences. He had a wife and three kids and they might lose their husband and father if Vinnie spoke up.

It wasn't the kind of problem we dealt with in college—at least not freshman year. I told him maybe he should talk directly to this friend and that if he were absolutely certain no one else knew what the guy had done, he should keep his mouth shut. No promotion is worth that kind of guilt.

I was a little more helpful with his mistress, I guess, because she kept herself alive long enough to get pregnant. Vinnie "took care of it" and said if I was ever in trouble, I should call him. This was years before *Roe v. Wade*.

Several weeks later a friend of mine who was also working

as a dancer called to tell me she was pregnant. She was single, alone, and broke. She'd been using birth control, but it hadn't worked. She'd given money to someone to help her get an abortion and the guy had disappeared. I told her I'd see what I could do. That night when I went to work, I asked Vinnie for help.

The following night I brought her with me to the club. Vinnie's doctor arrived a little after we did. My friend paid him $400.00 in twenties and they got in the car and drove off. They were back in an hour. He told her she couldn't have any booze and no painkillers, and that she'd probably miscarry within twenty-four hours.

I still had two hours to go before my shift was over so she sat at the bar, sipping a Coke, and waited for me to finish dancing. Within minutes she was in incredible pain, having violent cramps. Vinnie told me to knock off work and asked Mike to drive us back to Manhattan. The doctor had said no painkillers, not even aspirin. The ride home was brutal. She was screaming, digging her nails in my hands as I held her. By the time we got to my apartment, she was hemorrhaging. There was blood everywhere: the hallway, the kitchen, the living room floor. She finally passed the baby in my bathroom an hour later.

I was horrified by what she went through: the pain and the blood and the emotional trauma. Especially since there was nothing I could do to help. I had nightmares about it for weeks. Years later, when we did the two-part abortion show on *Maude* and I found myself a vocal pro-choice advocate, I realized it was that incident that set the groundwork for my belief. Until we have birth control that is 100 percent safe, 100 percent effective, 100 percent available and easy to use, and until we have no rape in the world, we need to provide safe, legal, low-cost abortions.

A few years after that, when I was no longer dancing and had lost touch with Vinnie, I called him at the club to ask for help for another friend. He wasn't there.

"Well, if I could leave my name and number, could you have him call me back?"

"I don't think so, honey. Vinnie's not comin' back any time soon. He gets out in ten years."

# Broadway

I'D COME BACK FROM MY FIRST SUMMER STOCK JOB A member of Actors' Equity. A year later, I still didn't have an agent—I couldn't get an actual appointment for an audition—but at least I could go to union calls. So now there were only 150 of us in the basement with our knitting, instead of 300. And sometimes we got to sing a whole song.

Which is what I did in the summer of 1966 when I auditioned for a production of *The Pajama Game.* I belted "Where Is Love?" (from *Oliver!*) and "I Enjoy Being a Girl" (from *Flower Drum Song*) and was called back to sing "Mr. Snow" (from *Carousel*) and "My Lord and Master" (from *The King and I*) and then called back to dance. Then they narrowed their selection to eight of us and matched us to the guys they'd already hired. Fortunately I looked like I belonged with one of them and I got the job. A month in the Poconos singing "When You're Racing with the Clock."

The following summer I did a tour of *Half a Sixpence*. We played Skowhegan and Ogunquit, Maine; Wallingford, Connecticut; again the Poconos; and Elitch Gardens in Denver, Colorado. It was great fun because we vacationed all day and performed at night, but it still wasn't a career. Three years of auditioning in New York and the closest I'd gotten to the Great White Way was across the river in Paramus, New Jersey.

Which is where I was in January 1968. I'd just finished a production of *The King and I* at the Paper Mill Playhouse in Paramus and had stayed on to dance in *This Was Burlesque*, starring Ann Corio and Pinky Lee. They wanted me to continue with the show when it went on the road but that was definitely not a "career" move. I wasn't a "gypsy," one of the singers or dancers who goes from musical to musical: Broadway, national tours, bus and truck tours, summer stock. I was an actress. I wanted to act. On Broadway.

I was losing faith in myself. I'd left the Italian voice teacher but not soon enough. After two years of listening to her tell me my voice was damaged, I didn't think I could sing. It didn't matter that my mother thought I could. It didn't matter that the musical directors of the shows I was doing thought I could. It didn't matter that I'd entertained G.I.s all over Southeast Asia and I'd been getting paid to sing ever since. I didn't believe I was any good. On top of that, I'd auditioned to replace Connie Stevens in *The Star-Spangled Girl* on Broadway (not a musical), and I'd lost out at the final audition to one other actress.

Instead of taking that as an acknowledgement of my talent, I'd begun to believe I was never going to get where I wanted to go; I wasn't going to succeed. I'd been talented enough for the San Jose Light Opera but maybe I didn't have what it takes to compete in New York. I knew I was going to defeat myself if I didn't change the way I was thinking, but I was having a hard time maintaining my optimism.

And then, on a Friday afternoon in February 1968, I got a call from Hal Prince's casting director, Shirley Rich. We'd never met but she had my photo and résumé on file, thanks to my three-by-five index cards, and she wanted me to audition for *Fiddler on the Roof* on the following Tuesday. They were replacing an understudy to Tevye's second daughter. There was another actress already in the show who would also be auditioning for the understudy role.

For the first time ever a complete sense of certainty settled over me. I knew this was my job. I hadn't seen *Fiddler* and I didn't know the role, but I knew I was going to be hired. And it wasn't anything I was doing to myself. I wasn't convincing myself or pretending to be positive to try to overcome my nerves. I just knew.

I believe now it was my grandmother watching over me. She had recently died and I think she decided to make things happen for me. She didn't want me to worry.

And I didn't. It was a grueling audition but I never lost the feeling that I was going to get the job. Twelve of us auditioned, one of whom was the actress who was already in the show in the chorus. That just added to the stress. For five hours we heard one another sing and watched one another dance and then saw the scenes as we each did them. I stayed calm throughout. I was exhausted when it was over.

On February 7, 1968—three years and four and a half months after I arrived in New York—I signed my first Broadway contract as a chorus member and understudy in *Fiddler on the Roof.*

*I must never forget this freshness,* I wrote in my diary. *This gratefulness and excitement. Never become so jaded or take my success for granted without humbleness or thankfulness. I cannot describe my excitement or happiness or sense of accomplishment. New York has me by the throat now and I'll not get away for a long while!*

I called everyone I knew. I wanted to thank the world!

Instead, I took my contract, which showed I was employed for the next whole year, and my first paycheck and I went directly to the customer service department at Bloomingdale's and applied for a credit card. I was a working actress in a long-running show and I was going to buy things.

My downstairs neighbors, who were my best friends, came to see the show on my opening night. Wyatt started applauding as soon as I stepped out singing "Tradition." Even though all the women on stage were wearing babushkas and you could barely see our faces, she said she knew which one was me. I walked out so proudly, my breasts preceded me on stage by half a chorus.

I loved doing *Fiddler.* It was so much more than a musical to me. In the first place, it was about Russian Jews escaping the pogroms and having to leave their homes and loved ones. The same history my Armenian ancestors shared. Maybe that's why my grandmother got involved. There were forty-three of us in the cast so I had an instant extended family of friends. And *Fiddler* was not some lightweight, frothy pastiche of unimportant songs, like *No, No, Nanette.* It required emotional honesty and depth to perform.

The first two weeks before I joined the cast, I rehearsed during the day with the stage manager and understudies and watched the show at night. Every night for two weeks I sat in the theater and wept. Bette Midler was playing Tzeitel, Tevye's oldest daughter. She had yet to create the "Divine Miss M" and was just beginning to work as a singer in small clubs after the show. Every night I watched her beg Papa to let her marry Motel, the tailor, and not Lazar Wolf, the butcher, and every night I was overwhelmed by her performance. When we shared a dressing room and became friends, there was never any question in my mind that she would become a major star.

She used to come in every night with a new list of songs she was considering for her nightclub act. It always started with "Am I Blue." On the days we didn't have matinees, Bette would go shopping in thrift stores in the Village looking for dresses from the thirties and forties for her to wear when she performed. She'd come to the theater and show me what I thought were god-awful old rags, but somehow, on her, they worked. She was brilliant and single-minded. On one night, her boyfriend showed up at the theater in a rage because she had been so involved rehearsing her act, she'd forgotten to meet him somewhere or leave a key for him to get into her apartment. She didn't really care. Nothing was as important as her work. By that time, I was back in therapy, hoping to solve some of my relationship problems and feelings of insecurity. I thought to myself that I might achieve personal happiness before Bette did but she would become a much greater success much sooner than I ever would.

Seven months after I joined the chorus, I took over the role of Hodel. No more climbing four flights of stairs to a dressing room; I joined Bette and Tanya Everett (Chava) on the second floor. We even had our own dresser, a wonderful Irish woman who spent her time between scenes knitting one sweater per week. From my apartment on Hudson Street I rode my bike up Eighth Avenue to the theater every night. I loved walking to the stage door through the alley that separated the Majestic from the Royale. I was so proud that I belonged there. My mother was, too. She told everyone she met that her daughter was costarring in a hit Broadway musical.

*October 2, 1969*
*Perhaps I am on my way toward being a success—toward being a*
*pleasing actress, a special actress. Because it isn't enough for me to*
*be an actress, I must be an actress of whom the audience talks*
*favorably and remembers. I want to be exceptional—any less*
*would eat me alive.*

    *I am going to accomplish what I set out to do*
    *I am going to be*
    *I am an actress*

I never missed a performance. I was supporting myself doing
what I loved to do. I didn't have to audition anymore; I didn't
have to discotheque anymore. I could afford to buy the juicer I'd
always wanted, the kind they used on Fifth Avenue at the orange
juice stands where you cut the orange in half and pull down hard
on the steel arm. I was on Broadway and I had a juicer.

And, finally, I even had an acting teacher I was learning
something from. Warren Robertson taught a combination of
Lee Strasberg's techniques and a variation of Reichian therapy
called Bio-Energetics. I'd been having trouble with the scene
in *Fiddler* where Hodel gets angry at Perchik. It didn't feel
honest to me; it didn't feel real. I'd never been allowed to
express anger in my own life and, now, when I had to be angry,
I was acting what I thought anger was like. The exercises in
Warren's classes helped me get in touch with my emotions and
express them in the characters I was portraying. He'd ask us to

think of a time in our lives when we'd been hurt or rejected or relieved or overjoyed and then act out with our scene partner what we were feeling. Alternately, I'd imagine Richard or my father in place of my scene partner and wail away with my emotions. The exercises were as much therapy sessions as acting classes and I was learning a lot about myself.

At the end of the year, my contract reverted to a standard "two-week out" stipulation. That meant I could leave the show after giving two weeks' notice. There were three actors who would remain in the show through its entire eight-year run. One of them had put his children through college. One was a talented painter. One had used the show to support his real love: singing opera. *Fiddler* was their job. I'd had the job for a year and I loved every minute of it but I didn't want just a job, I wanted a career. The Divine Miss M had appeared at the Continental Baths, and Bette's career as a singer/comedienne was taking off. She left the show. It was time for me to leave as well, and move on to something new, something in which I would be seen by members of the theatrical community and reviewed by the media. I needed to open in an original production, to be noticed by critics and agents and producers.

But after a year and a half of not having to audition, my nerves were worse than they'd been before I'd started work. I was singing the dramatic solo ("Far From the Home I Love") in a Broadway show and I still didn't believe I could sing. Katharine Hepburn came to see the show one night. I was a wreck. It didn't matter that she came backstage afterward to say how much she enjoyed my performance. Harry Goz, who played Tevye, didn't understand me. "Why should she make you nervous? She can't give you a job."

I couldn't overcome the damage the singing teacher had done to my self-confidence. I remember leaving the theater one night and running into a friend of Bette's who grabbed my hand and said, "Oh, your song was absolutely beautiful. It brought tears to my eyes." I walked away thinking, "Why did he say that? He doesn't owe me anything. He didn't have to say a word. Could he possibly have meant it?" What little belief I had in myself came from other people. In my guts I didn't know.

Years later, when I was working hard to overcome my insecurities about singing, I asked myself why I thought people had hired me over and over again to work as a singer. They must have felt sorry for me, I thought. Given me the jobs out of the kindness of their hearts.

On top of feeling I needed to leave the show for my career, I was having trouble with my costar, the fellow who had replaced Bert Convy as Perchik, the revolutionary. He was a lovely man who unknowingly mouthed all of my lines as I was saying them. It drove me nuts. He also threw me around the stage during our dance together, wildly out of control. The more it happened the angrier I got, but instead of saying something to him, I withdrew and shut down. When I finally did screw up my courage and tell him what was bothering me, he said, "Oh, I'm so glad you said something, Adrienne. You'll feel so much better now that you've got that off your chest." And went right back to mouthing my words and slinging me around. I needed to leave the show.

I still didn't have an agent. I started buying the trades, circling the audition notices, and then staying home. When I did get myself to an audition, I couldn't get through a song without losing control of my muscles. My knees shook. My lips trembled. Peg Murray, who was playing Golde at the time, knew I was having trouble. She encouraged me to go back into therapy. "The more you know about yourself," she said, "the better off you'll be as an actor."

I started seeing a psychologist who smoked during my sessions and sometimes fell asleep while I was talking. Didn't make a pass at me though, which would have been doubly distressing, since she was married with two kids, and she did teach me the rudiments of the therapeutic process.

The first thing she asked me was what had happened at my last couple of auditions. Well . . . one of them had come down to me and another actress and after three days of waiting for a decision, I lost the role. The other one had been for Hal Prince, my current boss. I'd gone in to audition for the role of the Leader in *Zorba* and Hal had yelled at me from the back of the theater: "What are you singing that song for? You're not right for that role, you should be auditioning for the widow!" I was mortified. Not only had he ridiculed me, he'd yelled at me. At least that's what it felt like. I stopped auditioning.

Therapy helped me get a handle on my audition anxiety and finally, in September 1969, two years after I'd taken over the role of Hodel, I was hired to star in an off-Broadway musical farce called *Stag Movie*.

*Stag Movie* was a show within a show about a group of down-on-their-luck performers who decide to make a musical version of the classic stag film *The Grocery Boy*. I was playing the innocent young actress who gets cast as the housewife in the X-rated film. I would be singing and dancing my way through thirteen numbers—in the nude.

This was 1971. *Hair* had opened on Broadway three years earlier and *Oh! Calcutta!* (starring my future stepfather on *Maude*, Bill Macy) was selling out. My boyfriend was playing drums in the pit of *Let My People Come*. Terrence McNally's *Sweet Eros* had Sally Kirkland bare on stage and Sylvester Stallone was undressed in the movie *Score*. Brian De Palma's film *Dionysus in '69*, which featured simulated nude orgies, opened to good reviews. Musicals, especially, were using nudity to reflect and question sexual attitudes in an entertaining, good-humored way.

I wasn't chomping at the bit to get onstage unclothed but I needed to open a show in New York. I needed to get reviewed. I needed to be seen by agents, directors, and producers.

And seen I was. All 123 pounds of me. But this was New York, not L.A. I wasn't thinking about my weight or my body; I was thinking about hitting the high notes and learning the choreography. Not tap, thank God. Not easy, though, singing upside down in a headstand on a raked platform with your unfettered breasts hitting you in the chin.

I was a bit concerned about what my mother would say when I told her I'd be performing nude in an off-Broadway show. She'd been excited for me every step along the way but she was my mother, after all, and I'd had a fairly strict upbringing. I called her before we started rehearsals.

"Off-Broadway, Adrienne?" she asked. "Won't you be taking a cut in salary?"

I had a friend who'd been in the original cast of *Oh! Calcutta!* He'd told me all about the "sensitivity" rehearsals they'd had, the weeks of emotional exercises they'd done to make themselves comfortable with undressing before they ever appeared nude on stage.

Not us. We learned the songs around the piano, took off our clothes when the time came, and sang the songs. I was red-faced the first day of rehearsal but once I got on stage, I didn't think about it. It was part of the play and had to be done. We hadn't had a man in our house since I was twelve so I hadn't grown up worrying about modesty. I was more concerned with singing well. Upside down. Stark nude.

The show was a farce, it wasn't erotic. I sang songs like "I Want More Out of Life Than This," about what happens when a couple has been married for a long time. I was clothed in that one. But in "Try a Trio," with the lyrics:

It's groovy to be a bisexual—your hunting
    grounds double in size
With no one are you ineffectual—to every
    occasion you rise!

And "Do the Get Your Rocks Off Rock," which went:

Oh the flesh is protoplasmic and the rhythm is
    orgasmic
Just wait, you're gonna heave a sigh, Max, when you
    and the music climax

I was definitely nude. These days there are entire websites devoted to the rehearsal photographs taken while we sang those songs. You can tell it's a farce—my breasts look like casaba melons and Brad Sullivan's eyes are almost as big. I just wish the lighting were better.

Anyway, I got my reviews and they were good. The three major papers hated the show but we got raves on television, in *Back Stage*, and *Cue Magazine*, and in *New York* magazine, John Simon, who rarely liked anyone, was very kind to me. Critic Harris Green said the show was better than anything Lincoln Center had put on in years. The AP reporter, William Glover, wrote, "[The songs] allow Adrienne Barbeau opportunity to exercise her impressive vocal cords in unusual circumstance. Miss Barbeau, a sultry, raven-tress type lately of *Fiddler on the*

*Roof*, may in fact be the first leading lady required to render—and rather beautifully at that—an anthem of joy while simultaneously involved in complicated if simulated amative ecstasy."

The show ran five months. Years later, David Newburge, the composer, gave an interview in which he said, "Adrienne Barbeau was amazing. I had written the show for a down-and-out, forty-year-old hooker. I rewrote it for Adrienne. She was the only one who was any good." I wish I had known that at the time. I may have gained a little confidence from doing the show, but it wasn't enough. I still didn't have a career.

*March 27, 1971*
*I've just finished two leading roles—obviously someone thought I was good enough—and I still don't always believe in myself. I am overwhelmed with a sense of futility. The futility comes from not knowing—having no assurance that any of this will pay off. That the goal will ever be attained.*

And then I got *Grease.*

# *Grease*

*Excerpt from ninth-grade term paper entitled "To Be or Not to Be: Acting as a Vocation," written January 5, 1960.*

*"Acting does not involve just the motion picture industry as most people are inclined to think. The live stage is much more important than the screen though its actors are not half as renown [sic] or quite as rich."*

I received a Tony nomination for singing "There Are Worse Things I Could Do" in the original Broadway production of *Grease*. The song almost didn't make it into the show. Actually, *I* almost didn't make it into the show.

My first audition was just a meeting with the director, Tom Moore. He asked me who my favorite groups were from the 1950s and I told him The Drifters, The Platters, The Shirelles, and Johnny and Jo. I didn't know it at the time, but Tom didn't know a thing about fifties music. He said later he was just looking for actors who seemed to be telling the truth and had a feeling for the period. The producers, Ken Waissman and Maxine Fox, had hired him because they had seen his production of *Welcome to Andromeda*. Tom's strength was getting performances that were so realistic the audience didn't believe they were watching actors. That's what Ken and Maxine wanted for *Grease*. What they didn't want was a cotton-candy musical comedy.

Years later I was introduced to Madeline Kahn as "the girl who played Rizzo in *Grease*." "You're an actress?" she said. "You were so real I thought you were some chick they found on the streets." It was a compliment I've never forgotten. And all because of Tom.

I sang "Over the Mountain" and "Love Potion Number Nine" for my audition and then I left town. It was Christmas vacation and I was visiting my boyfriend's family in Southern California.

A week later I got a call asking me to come in for another audition. They'd been thinking about me for the role of Marty but they wanted to see me again with Rizzo in mind. Once more, romance won out over career. "I can't," I told them. "I'm on vacation." Besides, I couldn't afford to change my plane reservation.

Two days later they called and asked again. I was still on vacation.

Three days later they called once more. Could I come in on New Year's Eve?

"Adrienne," I thought, "if you don't want to be unemployed for the rest of your life, you'd better get on a plane and get back there."

Two hours after my audition I got the call saying I'd been hired. It was a great way to start the new year.

We had four weeks of rehearsal and two weeks of previews. The most important job of my life to date and I never wrote a word about it in my journal. I was caught up in a romance with a married man—a well-known actor I'd met on the set of his latest film. I hadn't known he was married when I met him and by the time I found out, I was already hooked. I needed to get over it. It didn't last long but it obviously took precedence over everything else in my life; it's all I wrote about in early 1972.

*Grease* had a great cast: Meg Bennett, who went on to star in and produce daytime dramas; Marya (Mews) Small who, among other film credits, later costarred in *One Flew Over the Cuckoo's Nest;* Garn Stephens, who costarred in *Phyllis* with Cloris Leachman and won an Emmy nomination with Mews's sister Emilie, as a writing team; Alan Paul, one of the singers in the group Manhattan Transfer; Carole Demas, who has a long-running children's TV series on the air; Ilene Kristen, also a daytime drama star; Jeff Conaway, costar on *Taxi;* Jim Canning, with whom I later worked in *The Fog;* Kathi Moss, star of *Nine* and *Grand Hotel;* Ilene Graff, who spent years on *Mr. Belvedere;* Walter Bobbie, who became a successful

Broadway director (*Chicago, Sweet Charity*); and Barry Bostwick, star of *Spin City* and myriad TV films and miniseries.

Most of my scenes were with Timothy Meyers who played Kenickie. Timmy was a classically trained Shakespearean actor who was so good as Kenickie that when he went for an interview at the William Morris Agency, the agents got nervous. They thought he was a juvenile delinquent.

My favorite story about Tim took place the night he and Kathi Moss (Cha Cha) tried to help Meg Bennett (Marty) get rid of the mice in her apartment. Because Meg never cooked, a family of mice had moved into her stove. Kathi took her cat over to do some stalking and Timmy spent the night yelling directions to the mice about how to get out of the house.

I loved playing opposite Timmy. We had a scene on a park bench where Rizzo and Kenickie are making out. It was pretty obvious that Tim was enjoying himself and after a couple of days of necking and grinding, I was beginning to think we might become more than just friends. Until the night I drove him home and he invited me in to meet his boyfriend. Didn't stop us from having fun on stage, though.

In 1989, when I was in Pittsburgh filming *Two Evil Eyes* for George Romero, I got a call from Tim's students at Carnegie Mellon. He had been teaching there when he died. His students gave me the honor of signing his panel in the AIDS quilt.

Rehearsals were fraught with problems. The actor playing Sonny had to be fired and Jim Borrelli was brought in to replace him. The main financial backer didn't like anything the production staff was doing; he called a meeting and demanded changes. The initial budget had been $125,000 and twice that had already been spent. Tom Moore wasn't sure we were going to continue. Finally, Warren Casey, who had written the book and music with his partner, Jim Jacobs, lost control and started screaming, "This is wrong! This is wrong! This is bullshit!" He was so apoplectic, everyone just stopped speaking and left the production meeting to go back to what they were doing.

The night before our first preview, we had a final dress rehearsal. The theater was packed with friends of the cast. The show was a mess. "Greased Lighting" hadn't even been staged. "There Are Worse Things I Could Do" wasn't working. Word went out that the show was a disaster. People were calling it the worst turkey they'd ever seen. Walter Bobbie had tears in his eyes. "I can't take another flop," he cried.

We redid everything in the next forty-eight hours. Songs were cut, songs were moved, blocking changed. Ilene Kristen (Patty Simcox) lost her only solo, "Yuck." "Magic Changes" was pulled from the second act and put into the first. Pat Birch, our choreographer, worked like a madwoman to make everything flow together. Tim Meyers hadn't expected any changes at all; true to his bad-boy character, he'd smoked a joint before rehearsal. He didn't have a clue what we were doing, let alone could he remember it for the performance.

"Worse Things" was on the chopping block. The song was

the reason Ken Waissman and Maxine Fox had produced the show—the entire story of fifties' morality in its lyrics—and it wasn't working. Ken's heart was breaking at the thought of having to cut it. I didn't know any of this at the time but I owe a big debt to a woman named Sylvia Herscher. She worked for E. H. Morris, the people who were publishing the music, and she happened to be in the theater the night they were making the decision to cut the song. She told Ken the problem wasn't with the song; it was with the scene that preceded it. Rizzo wasn't getting any sympathy from the greasers; she had nothing to reject and so the audience couldn't see the vulnerability under her tough-guy exterior. Without the vulnerability, no one cared about her or her song. Jim and Warren rewrote the scene and "There Are Worse Things I Could Do" became the dramatic high point of the second act.

I loved singing it. I loved the moment I finished the last note, before the applause started. That's when I could hear people crying in the audience.

I've never seen the movie version of *Grease*—Stockard Channing's manager, Allan Carr, produced the film but at the time, I was doing *Maude* and once again involved in a relationship and not paying attention to my career. And by the time they were casting, I assumed I was too old to play Rizzo. I heard part of the soundtrack once though, and that was enough for me. They'd recorded "Worse Things" as sort of a Muzak-style jazz waltz. I couldn't face seeing it sung that way.

The first preview went much more smoothly than the dress rehearsal except for the scene where the Pink Ladies sing "Summer Nights" while they dance on the cafeteria table. With all the changes we'd made since the night before, the stage-hands forgot to put the table on stage. When the curtain came up, Frenchie and Marty and Jan were seated on a cafeteria bench with their food trays on their laps and no table in front of them. Tom and Pat and Ken and Maxine were standing at the back of the theater freaking out because there was no way we could do "Summer Nights" if there was no table to dance on. They were going to have to bring down the curtain and reset the furniture in the middle of the scene. Pat started running toward the stage just as I made my entrance. I had my food tray in one hand and the entire cafeteria table in the other. A full-size cafeteria table. In one hand. After the show, when the stagehands asked me to try it again, I couldn't pick it up with both hands. I told Tom, "I knew it had to be out there and I just did it." I don't remember this happening at all.

The show opened on Valentine's Day, 1972. Halfway through "Worse Things," my dramatic number in the second act, a woman fell down sick in the middle of the aisle. Tom Moore wouldn't let anyone touch her; he didn't want a distraction during my song.

*Grease* was a major turning point in my life. Not just theatrically but personally. Four of the cast members became my closest friends, my extended family, and the others became good friends for life. We were all about the same age and at the same place in our careers. We have remained friends for more than thirty years. We hold annual reunions, and everyone from the original production who happens to be in town attends.

In those days, if you got panned by Clive Barnes in the *New York Times*, you could pretty much plan on closing the next day. Clive Barnes panned us, big-time: " . . . the show is a thin joke . . . Not even Elvis Presley himself could ever have thought it an interesting story—and it still isn't . . . Most of the so-designated teenagers look trustworthily over thirty, perhaps they were meant to be playing their past." He did, at least, single out Tim and myself as being good and tough (as did *The New Yorker*) and he mentioned that the first-night audience seemed genuinely to enjoy it.

Richard Watts in the *New York Post* hated it even more. He thought the title of the show was taken from the name of the car. He just didn't get it.

But three out of five television reviews were raves and Douglas Watt's review in the *Daily News* was a rave.

Pressure was on to close the show immediately but Ken and Maxine refused. There was a "pilot light" in the box office based on word of mouth from the previews; the audiences were loving it. They had enough money to stay open for a week and they went out to investors to look for more.

At that point, they offered each of us in the cast the opportunity to buy a point. Barry Bostwick and I talked about splitting one but it would have cost me my total savings: $500.00. I passed. Tom Moore was so sure the show was going to close that he turned back his points for the certainty of cash instead.

We would have made millions if we'd invested.

Betty Lee Hunt was our publicist. She and Ken and Maxine came up with a great ad idea. They took the rave review that Doug Watt had written for the *Daily News*, waited until the end of the day when the likelihood of it being scrutinized was lessened, and sent it to the *New York Post* as a paid ad. Because the *Post* reviewer was *Richard Watts* and no one caught the fact that this ad was quoting *Douglas Watt*, it looked like the *Post* had given us a rave as well.

Ken and Maxine managed to raise enough money to keep us afloat. By the time the second wave of reviews came in, we were a hit. (It was Jack Kroll's review in *Time* magazine, singling out Barry, Tim, and me, that led to Norman Lear calling me in to read for *Maude*.)

I had my head under the sink, washing my hair, when a girlfriend called to tell me I'd been nominated for a Tony Award. I couldn't take it in at first; it just didn't make sense to me. I'd won a *Theatre World* Award for the show but it had never crossed my mind that I might be eligible for a Tony. I was overwhelmed.

Again, Ken and Maxine and Betty Lee Hunt were partly responsible. Alexander Cohen was producing the Tonys that year and he didn't believe *Grease* should be eligible. We were playing at the Eden Theatre, which was downtown, not on Broadway. But the Eden had 1,100 seats and the actors and musicians were earning Broadway scale, so Ken and Maxine were sure we met the requirements. Betty Lee wrote a letter to every member of the New York theatrical press, stating that the producers of *Grease* intended to sue CBS and the League of New York Theatres for ruling we did not qualify. Alex Cohen capitulated but not before swearing that since we'd aired our dirty laundry in public, the only way we'd ever win a Tony would be over his dead body.

*Grease* was nominated for seven awards. Tim and I were both nominated in the best supporting actor category and Barry was nominated for best actor in a musical. I went down to SoHo and bought my first pair of expensive shoes: $34.00 Yves St. Laurent ankle straps. I didn't have the budget to spend money on a wrap so I crocheted a stole out of shiny gold yarn. I still have the shoes and the stole. Linda Hopkins has the Tony.

Alexander Cohen didn't die and *Grease* won not one award.

# *Maude*

THE ONLY TV SHOW I REMEMBER WATCHING, ASIDE from *I Love Lucy,* my grandpa's westerns, and my grandma's tear-jerking game shows, was *Adventures in Music* with Korla Pandit. Korla Pandit was an African American from Missouri named John Roland Redd who had started his musical career playing Latin tunes as "Juan Rolando." Reinventing himself as Korla Pandit, he became an ersatz East Indian with a jeweled turban on his head. He stared straight into the camera while he played the electric organ. For a change of pace he stared straight into the camera while he played the organ and the piano at the same time. He never spoke. It was like watching the televised Yule log at Christmas.

That was the extent of my experience with television. When you're doing eight shows a week on stage, you're not watching prime time. I didn't know anything about TV, least of all the impact it could have on my career.

All I knew in 1972 after *Grease* opened, was that I had accomplished what I'd set out to do: I'd originated a role on Broadway. I was ready for the next step. I wasn't sure what that was, but I knew I didn't want to sit in another Broadway show for a lot of years. So when Norman Lear's casting director approached me about a new sitcom called *Maude*, I was interested. My friends were talking about a show called *All in the Family*, which Norman Lear and his partner, Bud Yorkin, were producing, and they said it was really funny.

*All in the Family* starred Carroll O'Connor as the bigoted, working-class Archie Bunker and Jean Stapleton as his dingbat wife, Edith. When Norman Lear needed an actress to go up against Archie's conservative, right-wing politics, he begged his friend Bea Arthur to leave her New York home for a week to play Edith's liberal cousin, Maude. Bea was a Broadway star best known for her roles in *Three Penny Opera, Mame,* and *Fiddler on the Roof.* Her character on *All in the Family* was literally an overnight success. CBS asked Norman to create a spin-off series called *Maude* and Bea agreed to relocate to Los Angeles to give it a try.

The pilot for *Maude* had already been filmed and the actress playing her daughter was being replaced. She was a wonderful comedienne but the producers felt her style was too similar to Bea's and they wanted more contrast. The role had been established as having a seven-year-old son, played by Brian Morrison. I met with Norman in an office in New York

at the request of Jane Murray, his casting director, who had
seen me in *Grease*. Norman was very gracious but word came
back he felt I looked too young to play the part. I was not
going to get the chance to audition. I stopped thinking about
television and went back to doing *Grease*.

A month later, on a Saturday between the matinee and the
evening show, my agent came to the theater.

"They've auditioned hundreds of girls in L.A.," he said,
"and they haven't been able to find anyone to play Maude's
daughter. They want to see you on Monday. In Los Angeles."

I didn't have a day off and my understudy wasn't available.
*Grease* was moving from off-Broadway to Broadway that week,
changing performance schedules. My understudy was on in
one of the other roles.

Our producers agreed to let me go as long as I could teach
Rizzo to Joy Rinaldi, who understudied the lead role of Sandy.
If they hadn't said yes, I have no idea what path my career
would have taken. I am forever indebted to Ken and Maxine
and Joy.

I flew to Los Angeles Monday morning, June 12, 1972,
the day after my twenty-seventh birthday. My mother met me
there for moral support. I'd never auditioned for a television
show and I was terrified I'd blow it.

The audition was that afternoon. I think I was terrible. I
know I wasn't good. I was shaking so badly I couldn't hold the
script still. After the audition Norman and Bud took me into

a screening room and showed me the pilot with the original actress. They thought it would help me understand what they were looking for. Then I read for them again. Still nervous, still shaking. They thanked me and told me they'd let me know by Thursday if they were going to use me so I could give my two weeks' Equity notice to *Grease* and be back in L.A. in time to start work.

Thursday came and went. No phone call.

Friday came and went. No phone call.

Saturday morning at 1:00 A.M. I got the call saying I had the job.

*Excerpt from ninth-grade term paper entitled "To Be or Not to Be: Acting as a Vocation," written January 5, 1960.*

*"Bodily poise and self-confidence, along with an agreeable speaking voice, are probably the three most important articles show business people look for. Though, as they say, most of the best enter-tainers are always ill before they go on; if they didn't have a large amount of self-confidence, they would never go on. To apply for an acting job a large amount of confidence in yourself is needed."*

If Maude had been created today, I wouldn't have lasted a week. Today, if an actor doesn't hit a home run with every joke at the first read-through of the script, he's fired. Network exec-utives won't wait even for the first rehearsal; you've got to be funny from day one.

I may have been funny, I don't know. It was too traumatic to remember. All I remember is that I showed up on the set, fresh from a Tony-nominated performance on Broadway, and I froze. There was Bea Arthur, a Broadway star, towering over me at five-ten in her leather sandals, and Bill Macy, Esther Rolle, and Conrad Bain, all twenty years older than I was, each of them with twenty years' more experience in the theater. I immediately felt they were all more talented than I was, more educated than I was, and funnier than I was. Once again my insecurities overcame me.

We had a scene in the first show of the season where I had to butter some toast on a breakfast plate. My hands were shaking so hard I couldn't hold the knife still. The soundman complained that someone was hammering backstage. It was my knife hitting the china.

It didn't help that none of us had had much experience with television sitcoms. Bea, Conrad, and Esther were all primarily stage actors. Bill had just come from doing *Oh! Calcutta!* off-Broadway in the East Village. And our director had never directed a television show in his life. He had directed Conrad in an off-Broadway play and when Connie walked into the rehearsal hall and saw who had been hired to direct, all he could think was, "This show doesn't stand a chance." We rehearsed ninety hours that week and then they fired the director.

By the time we did our first run-through I was questioning

why *I* had been hired. Why was I there? I felt untalented and wrong. Not only had I never done television before, I'd never even done a straight play. I'd been on stage for nine years, all of them in musicals. I'd just come from doing *Grease* where I'd created a character a million miles away from me: a defensive, sarcastic street chick with a different walk and a different talk. And I'd been studying acting in New York with a teacher who taught us to use moments from our lives to bring up the *real* emotions we needed. So I was going to create this character of Carole (she finally got a last name in the second season— Trainor) and she was going to be Maude's daughter and she was going to be a lot different from Adrienne Barbeau. When she got angry, she was REALLY going to be ANGRY and when she had to cry, she was REALLY going to cry. I didn't understand that wasn't funny. It wasn't comedy. I didn't understand the medium. I was going to ACT.

I didn't understand that I'd been hired to play myself. That's the way television worked. There was something in my personality that the writers thought was perfect to play opposite Bea. I could stand up to her without being abrasive. I could set her up for her jokes, and I could get laughs with mine without imitating her. If only I'd be myself and *stop acting*.

I couldn't do that. I couldn't be myself. I was sure I was going to say something unfunny so I stopped talking during rehearsals. I was very serious. The writers in turn didn't know how to write for me because they couldn't get a sense of my humor, so Carole started getting straighter and straighter on screen. Walter, Maude's husband; Florida, our maid; and Arthur, our next-door neighbor, took on more of the jokes and Carole started delivering the straight lines. My friends complimented me on how good I looked on the show; no one said anything about how funny I was.

*July 18, 1972*
*Oh, I just want to go home. I feel so defeated in this role, I just don't think I'm right and I just wish . . . well, no, of course I don't wish they'd fire me . . . but I just feel so discouraged. I haven't found the secret yet.*

Time to go back to therapy. Because I'd been introduced to it in Warren Robertson's acting classes, I thought Bio-Energetics might help. Bio-Energetics deals with an individual's life energy, how it may flow freely or be physically blocked by defenses that are the result of traumatic life experiences. I was interested in the verbal/physical integrative approach to therapy. I got the numbers of the only two Bio-Energetic therapists in the Los Angeles area and called the first one, in Beverly Hills. His secretary scheduled a consultation for me. I spent an hour and a half with the shrink and left his office thinking I should just shoot myself. He'd criticized me brutally. Then he sent me a bill for $180.00 (in 1972!) for a double session. When I called to complain that I hadn't requested a double session, he said he was sorry to hear that I thought I was only "worth half."

I persisted and called the second therapist. Kaj Lohmann was a wise, gentle, loving man who drove an old Volvo from his native Sweden and was usually late to our appointments because he couldn't read his own handwriting in his date book, when he could even *find* the date book among the research papers, empty soda bottles, and fast-food wrappers that littered the backseat of his car. I spent eight years with him, learning and healing and growing. I'm sure the work I did with him is responsible for much of the happiness in my life today.

But it took a while for me to find my way on *Maude*. I think if anyone other than Bud and Norman had been producing, they would have fired me. I wasn't "bringing anything to the table" as an actor. Norman kept telling me to relax and trust myself, that I was really good; and if I couldn't trust myself then to trust him because he knew I could do it and he wouldn't have hired me if I couldn't.

It wasn't until early in our second season that I started doing good work. We shot our first "telethon" show, the plot of which involved Maude raising money for some cause and insisting that everyone in the household perform. Suddenly I was back in my métier, singing and dancing, and I *knew* how to do that. Finally I was comfortable and no longer self-conscious. My confidence returned, my insecurities disappeared, and Maude's daughter became a character people remember.

Not always clearly, though. People recognized me but they weren't sure from where. "Hey, Kate Jackson, right? I love you on *Charlie's Angels.*" Or "Didn't we go to school together? You look familiar." My favorite was the day I stopped in a deli in Encino and the owner said, "You know who you look like?" I bowed my head in a semblance of humility and replied, "Yes, the girl on *Maude.*" "No, no. Anne Bancroft. She comes in here all the time."

I dread seeing those early episodes of *Maude.* What were those clothes I was wearing? To this day, I refuse to put on a surplice top where one side wraps over the other across the bust. And my hair? I never wore the same style twice. First, the producers asked me to dye it because it was so dark and the network didn't want us all to look too "ethnic." They sent me off to a place on Sunset Boulevard called Cinema Hairstylists, where there wasn't a hairdresser working who was under sixty. They put something called a soap cap on my head and my hair turned orange. Then they dyed my eyebrows to match. I looked like a short, chubby hooker with curly orange hair. They finally sent me to Beverly Hills to a "celebrity hairstylist" named Hugh York. Every tape day, Hugh did Suzanne Pleshette, Rue McClanahan, and me. He charged the production company $95.00 for a shampoo and set. In 1972.

But I loved doing the show. I loved working with Bea and Bill and Conrad and Rue and Esther and later John Amos, Fred Grandy, Brian Morrison, Kraig Metzinger, Hermione

Baddeley, and J. Pat O'Malley. Fred went on to become a congressman in the Ohio House of Representatives and then president of Goodwill Industries. Brian became a special effects designer. Esther and John left us for their own successful series, a spin-off of *Maude* called *Good Times.*

Bea had been the original Yente in *Fiddler* but she'd left before I joined the cast, so we'd never met. I was intimidated by her at first—she was the star, after all, and a lot taller than I was—but that lasted all of ten minutes. She was incredibly giving with all of us. If she had a line that would be funnier coming from another actor, she was the first to point it out. She was the ultimate professional and, with her photographic memory, an amazingly fast study. Never once did she miss a rehearsal or refuse to say a line or to try a piece of business. Since this was my first experience with TV, I came to expect Bea's behavior from every series star. I was appalled years later when I guest-starred on other sitcoms where the stars couldn't be bothered to rehearse.

Audiences confused Bea with her character, but she wasn't as loud or as opinionated as Maude. She lets you know what she's thinking, though. One night when we attended the opening of a play at the Westwood Playhouse, an intimate 500-seat theater, Bea stood up at intermission and announced, "This play is a piece of shit. I'd leave but I've got to go backstage afterwards." I doubt that she minced any words when she got there.

Success didn't change her, either. She remained generous

and loving throughout all our years on *Maude* and, later, during her success on *The Golden Girls*. Even today, as she travels the world performing in her one-woman show, Bea is still the down-to-earth working actress who hates wearing shoes and loves her kids and her dogs more than anything else in her life. She's a great cook, too. She's the one who taught me to put Tabasco sauce on my hard-boiled eggs.

Conrad was my surrogate father. When I bought my first house and was sitting in the empty living room terrified I'd made a huge mistake, Conrad was the friend I called to come over and tell me otherwise. He taught me how to negotiate a contract ("You can't bargain unless you're willing to walk away from the job") and which car to buy (we both drove diesel Mercedes until they stopped importing them). He's a man of great integrity in an industry where integrity is in short supply and I am forever grateful that *Maude* brought us together. And he always makes me laugh.

Norman Lear was the first genius I'd ever met. He knew how to tell a story. He didn't always write great comedy but he rewrote great comedy. He came to work every morning at 5:00 A.M. and worked on what the writing staff had produced the day before. When we sat in that rehearsal hall on Wednesdays, reading the script scheduled to begin taping the following week, Norman always knew what was going to work, what wasn't going to work, and how to fix it. He must have had an ego but I never saw it. If he suggested a joke that died, he was the first to admit it. If his writing staff came up with something funny that meant losing something he'd suggested, we lost it. He listened to everyone and he was willing to take a good gag from any source without being threatened. He was a master at understanding structure and setup, and timing and delivery.

And Bea, of course, was just as masterful in *her* timing and delivery. Several years ago, we did a charity show together, which was the first time we'd worked together since *Maude* went off the air. When we met at the podium, she looked at me in her deadpan way and said, "You never write. You never call." The audience loved it. No one can hold a take longer than Bea Arthur and make it work like she does. Fans still come up to me and repeat her classic line: "God'll getcha for that."

Bill Macy played Maude's fourth husband, Walter. He and Bea lived close to each other so he often drove her to work, but on tape day they had different call times. On those days, Bill always stopped at "the best deli in Los Angeles" and brought Bea a pastrami sandwich. The look on her face when she saw it was worth every minute of the trip. "She's *kvelling*," he always said.

That didn't stop her from unleashing her brutal wit on him, though. On one occasion, they were in the elevator after a difficult day's rehearsal with a script that wasn't working. Bea turned to Bill and said, "Bill, you are a rock and I love you. Despite your lack of humor."

Bill was sometimes late for rehearsals. He called one

morning to say he was stuck in traffic and wouldn't arrive for at least half an hour for the first read-through of that week's script. Rod Parker, our executive producer, sent one of the writers' assistants up to the office to change the name of the episode on the title page. When Bill walked in and sat down to open his script, it read, "Walter's Fatal Heart Attack." He was never late again.

Bill had performed in the nude in *Oh! Calcutta!* and he loved to drop his pants. He thought it was funny. The first time he did it in rehearsal, I took one look at his penis and yelled, "Props!" Even that didn't stop him. Early on in our first season, the Writer's Guild had a big, black-tie affair honoring Bud and Norman. We were all seated at large round tables in our evening gowns and tuxedos, facing the stage where celebrity after celebrity stood to tell funny, scripted stories about our two bosses. Bill downed a bottle of wine and jumped up on the stage to grab the microphone. "Cocksuckers of the world, unite!" he yelled and proceeded to unzip his fly.

There was dead silence in the room. Then some low-pitched mumblings. Then the entire gathering headed for the doors. Within minutes not a person was left in the room except Conrad, Bea, Esther, and I.

The next day CBS held closed-door meetings to decide whether or not Bill had violated his morals clause and should be released. The Television Academy insisted that Norman fire him. Norman refused. The Academy struck back by telling

Norman not to expect any awards for the show in the future. In the six years we were on the air, always in the top twenty of the Nielsen ratings and most often in the top five, *Maude* was never nominated for best comedy. It wasn't until 1977, five years later, that Bea won for Best Actress.

Bill called it his act of professional suicide. The more visibility the show brought him, the more frightened he became of succeeding. This was an unconscious act designed to undermine that success. Fortunately for us, it didn't work and he stayed with the show.

These are the great talents I learned from. I never consciously set out to be a comic actress, and believe me, it's a lot harder to do comedy than drama—timing is not something you can learn in an acting class. However, working with Bea and Norman, Bud Yorkin, our team of writer-producers (Bob Schiller and Bob Weiskopf, Rod Parker, Charlie Hauck, Thad Mumford, Arte Julian, Budd Grossman, and Elliott Shoenman), our director, Hal Cooper, and our brilliant cast, I became one.

There are times, though, when I hear myself deliver a comic line and I think, "My God, that's Bea's timing." And I thank her all over again.

We had a great time working together, all of us. They were my family for six years and we laughed for six years straight.

Not everyone stayed with us though. In our first season, Norman fired three directors, including Broadway choreographer

Michael Kidd (*Hello, Dolly!*). Later on he had to fire Anne Jackson, who was a fine actress but just couldn't find her way in a guest-starring role.

The show was a challenge for guest actors because we performed and filmed it like a half-hour stage play. We started our week on Wednesdays with a table reading of the following week's script and the one we were filming that week. Then, while the writers went off to fix anything that needed fixing, we blocked and rehearsed what we had. Thursday was another full rehearsal day and on Friday we did a run-through for the writers and producers. Over the weekend we got a rewritten script to memorize. Mondays we did a run-through on camera for the network executives and then on Tuesdays we did our first performance at 5:30 on camera in front of an audience. Dinner was served immediately afterward and during that time whatever parts of the script which hadn't worked were rewritten and we talked through any blocking changes the rewrites necessitated. That was the hard part because it sometimes meant losing entire pieces of dialogue, forgetting what you'd memorized, and memorizing new lines, new jokes, and new movements. We had until 8:00 to learn the changes, redo our makeup, and start again with a second audience. We did pickups as we went along; if someone fumbled a line, we'd just start back a little earlier in the script and continue on. Bea didn't like to stay late. When the show was over, she wanted to have a nightcap and go home to her two sons and her German shepherds.

The work was hardest on our guest actors who had never done theater. M-G-M star Van Johnson guested on our first season, wearing his trademark red socks. He needed cue cards for his lines and let loose with a tirade when anyone interrupted his concentration by walking behind the cards. John Wayne used his double to stand in for him and only came to rehearsal on tape day. He was charming and genial and had trouble with one line only: "Cohen's Cowboy Corral." It may have been the case of Wild Turkey the producers had delivered to his dressing room, but he just couldn't get it out. He used a cue card for that.

Henry Fonda was absolutely wonderful and adapted to the rewrites like he'd been with us for years. The show he did was a two-parter in which Maude decides to get Henry Fonda nominated for President without him even knowing it. She campaigns hysterically and becomes very depressed when he turns her down. Walter consults a doctor for her and the diagnosis is manic depression. This was in 1976 before the term bipolar was widely known and very few people understood the illness. Norman Lear's then wife, Frances, suffered with it. Frances's doctor had written a book about the illness, titled *From Sad to Glad,* and he served as our technical advisor.

A year later I began dating a record producer from Nashville. He was very charismatic. It was a long-distance relationship, so it took me a while to realize he was also very troubled. He had enormous bouts of energy followed by migraine headaches and black depressions. He rarely slept and never without sleeping pills. There were times when he was in such physical pain he was suicidal. It dawned on me one day that he was exhibiting the same symptoms we'd dealt with on *Maude*. I contacted Frances's doctor and he agreed to see my friend if we could get him to New York.

We flew there Thanksgiving weekend. The doctor prescribed lithium and, overnight, the symptoms began to disappear. My friend wept for hours on the plane back to Nashville. For twenty years he had been asking doctors for help because he thought he was crazy and for twenty years they had been telling him there was nothing wrong with him, he just needed a little Valium. A television show helped save his life.

Those were the shows I loved and the shows I remember: the socially significant episodes that dealt with important issues: malpractice, abortion, cosmetic surgery, gay rights. Norman was the driving force behind *Maude*'s liberal advocacy; he went on to found the People for the American Way, an organization devoted to protecting democracy, diversity, and liberty in our country. With his sitcoms, he understood the power of using laughter to temper his message. *Maude* broke ground in television on a lot of controversial subjects, so much so that it was never widely syndicated; broadcasters felt it was too controversial for daytime television.

We were in the top ten Nielsen ratings for our first four years, along with *M*A*S*H, Sanford and Son, Laverne and*

*Shirley, Hawaii Five-O,* and, of course, *All in the Family.* But by our sixth year, Bea was tired. She was going through a divorce. She wanted to leave the show while it still had the same high-quality writing it enjoyed from the beginning. I was ready to leave, too. I loved going to work every day but it was time for the next step, whatever that was going to be. *Maude*'s final season ended in April 1978.

In the 1970s, if you were on television, no one would hire you to do films. The prevailing mind-set was that audiences wouldn't pay to see someone in a movie who they could see at home for free. So, as much as I might have liked to do a feature, I never really thought about it. I had a steady job from July through February every year, I was earning a living doing what I love, and I was happy. I spent my hiatuses volunteering at a low-cost women's health-care clinic. *Roe v. Wade* had just passed and the clinic provided counseling and contraception and first-trimester pregnancy terminations. The memory of my friend's back-alley abortion was always with me. I wanted to do whatever I could to help other women avoid that.

Although I had worked in New York for eight years, I never had an agent until after I was nominated for the Tony. Then I signed with Marvin Josephson at the Agency for the Performing Arts, and he negotiated my deal for *Maude.* When I made the move to L.A., Marvin turned me over to Hal Gefsky in the West Coast office. Hal was a great guy who invited me to his home, called me on my birthday, and booked me to appear on cerebral palsy telethons. At the end of each season of *Maude*, he got me a $250.00-a-week raise. I thought that was fantastic.

It wasn't until our third year on *Maude*, when Cleavon Little took me to his agent's home for dinner, that I found out I should have been doing other things. "Who are you auditioning for?" the agent asked. "What movies-of-the-week have you done? Why aren't you doing guest-star roles on other series? This is the time, when you're working on *Maude*, that you should be furthering your career. What's going to happen when the show goes off the air?"

It hadn't crossed my mind. My close friends were either New York stage actors or they weren't in the business at all, so they never said anything. My agent had never said anything. As far as I was concerned, I had a great job and when that ended, I'd look for another one. Wasn't that how it worked?

Cleavon's agent, David Wardlow, asked me to leave APA and sign with him. Two weeks later David got an offer to produce a film and closed his agency. He turned me over to five friends of his who had just left the William Morris Agency to start their own firm. Suddenly I was with Creative Artists Agency, one of the first clients of the talent agency that was to become the most powerful in the industry.

I was lost. And intimidated. I didn't really know anyone there. I never knew which agent was handling which projects or whom I should talk to when I had any questions. Ron Myers and Bill Haber were both very nice to me but I was uncomfortable calling them to ask about work. I wasn't some major star who could get away with making demands. They wouldn't like me if I bugged them, I thought. The same inability to ask for what I wanted that had colored my earlier career was still in play. I figured if there was something I was right for, they'd call me.

The first job they got me was *Houdini*, a TV movie with Paul Michael Glazer and Sally Struthers. I was to play Houdini's mistress. After I accepted the offer, the agent called back to say they wanted to do a seminude scene for European release. I was so concerned about being shot only from the waist up and no one seeing my big butt that it never dawned on me to ask for more money. The agent didn't, either. My boyfriend was outraged, not because of the nudity but because I wasn't getting paid for it. He blamed the agency.

Mike Ovitz was one of the partners in the firm. This was the 1970s; I was a strong believer in the Equal Rights Amendment (and would eventually be invited to meet President and Mrs. Carter at an E.R.A. reception at the White House several years later) and I was hypersensitive about women's liberation. I thought Mike Ovitz was a major chauvinist. He talked about women as though they were chattel. Every time we spoke on the phone, I hung up enraged or in tears. He didn't have a clue, of course.

Then in 1976, during my hiatus from *Maude*, I called the

agency to tell them I would be in Reno for three weeks, opening for Roy Clark at Harrah's. This was a job that had been offered me directly by Roy's manager, Jim Halsey. Creative Artists said they wanted a commission on it. I wasn't signed to them for singing engagements, they hadn't done anything to get the job for me or negotiate the contract, and I didn't think I owed them a commission. It was just one more reason why I didn't feel comfortable being with CAA. I changed agencies.

Creative Artists went on to become the biggest agency in town. They represent, among others, Tom Hanks, Nicole Kidman, Julia Roberts, and Bruce Springsteen. They package their clients, putting actors into projects written by their writers and directed by their directors. Oftentimes, these projects are cast without actors from other agencies ever being auditioned. Agencies that package talent are very influential in making an actor's career.

Occasionally I think I might have had a much different career had I been less insecure when I started on *Maude* or had I stayed at CAA in spite of my discomfort at being there. I might have gone right from television into big screen comedies, perhaps. Or onto a Las Vegas stage with tuxedoed boys dancing behind me. But I didn't because that's not who I was at that time in my career. Instead, I went from being a musical comedy performer to a sitcom actress to a scream queen to a mother and a TV talk-show host and a book reviewer and a voice-over performer, and then back to the stage and back to musical comedy and back to television and concert halls and more films, and even into the recording studio for a CD and into my office to write this book. I can't complain.

# The Sex Symbol

I'M SHORT. I'VE ALWAYS BEEN SHORT. FIVE-THREE ON A good day. People think I'm tall because I spent six years standing next to Bea Arthur, who's seven inches taller, but this was the seventies—I was wearing platform boots and spike heels.

And I'm thin. I haven't always been thin. I was thin in junior high. I was a short, thin girl whose mother made her take a bath in Tide so she wouldn't leave a ring around the tub. I had cat's-eye glasses and really ugly curly hair. I bought hairstyling magazines and tried a different look every week. My favorite was the "Butterfly." It involved a center part and a lot of pin curls. When that didn't work, I wore a "Brush Up." That meant shaving the sides of my head to a quarter-inch length and brushing the back up from the nape of my neck to the crown.

When I was a freshman in high school, I dated a junior who said he'd played in the orchestra that had visited my junior high.

"I was the eighth-grade class president," I told him. "I introduced your orchestra to the assembly."

"No, you didn't," he replied. "It was a guy. With dry skin and weird glasses and no hair."

When I got to high school I bought contact lenses and Vitabath. I was still short and I still had ugly hair but I no longer looked like a boy. I had large breasts. I carried stacks of medical books to hide them, used four-syllable words whenever possible, and wanted the boys to like me for my mind.

I also had a thyroid problem but I didn't know it. I was so busy with school, cheerleading, dance classes, voice lessons, working part-time at the termite control company, and rehearsing theatrical productions that it didn't seem odd that I was tired all the time. And no longer thin.

It wasn't until I went off to do summer stock the summer after I'd moved to New York that I realized I had a problem. I kept falling asleep on our five-minute breaks. I went on my first diet: grapefruit for every meal. I got canker sores from the acid and never lost a pound. Made an appointment with the only doctor in town. He hit my knees with a hammer to measure my reflex reaction. I had none. He put me on thyroid pills and I lost seven pounds in two weeks.

I still wasn't thin. Full-figured, maybe you'd say. But it was New York and it was the theater and no one seemed to care if you didn't look like Twiggy. I obviously didn't—my favorite dessert was half a Sara Lee chocolate cake.

It wasn't until I got to L.A. to do *Maude* that I started worrying about how I looked. No one ever sat me down and told me to lose weight for the role, but I got the message. The old "camera adds ten pounds, you know" message. I tried. I went off to some diet mill on Sunset Boulevard where they shot me full of pregnant-horse urine and put me on a 500-calorie diet. Told me if I even used certain kinds of hand lotion I'd gain weight. (Yep, the oil would go right through my skin.) I was religious about it for a month. Went from 122 to 106. Looked like I was dying. The day I went off the diet, I left rehearsal and went straight to the Farmers Market next door to CBS. Bought a pound of roasted cashews and a pound of pineapple-carrot salad, went back to my house, lay on the middle of the bed, and ate until I had cramps.

In three weeks I was back up to 118.

Then I went to a hypnotist. That worked, actually. Not right away, nothing dramatic, but over the years I lost my taste for sweets and fattening foods and one day I woke up realizing I had completely changed my eating habits.

Somewhere in the middle of the horse urine and the hypnotist, I became a "sex symbol."

I didn't know I was a sex symbol. I never meant to be one. I still don't think of myself that way. But other people seem to.

What I was, in my mind, at least, was an actress delivering straight lines in a comedy series. If the producers needed information related in a scene, my character was the one to do it.

"But Mother," I'd say, "women all over the country have the choice to terminate a pregnancy, it's legal now." Or, "Walter, Mother's behavior seems like manic depression. We should get her to a doctor." Stuff like that.

What I didn't know is that when I said those things, I was usually walking down a flight of stairs and no one was even listening to me. They were just watching my breasts precede me.

I guess that's what made me a "sex symbol." But I didn't know it. I actually thought CBS asked me to be on *The Battle of the Network Stars* because they thought I was athletic. I thought that up until a week ago when I started writing this chapter and my husband clued me in: Who cared if I won the race, as long as I bounced when I ran?

It's odd having people think of you in a way you don't think of yourself. I'm a short woman with a pretty good body and large breasts—that's not what I think of as sexy. Sexy is Anouk Aimée in *A Man and a Woman* or Jeanne Moreau in *Jules and Jim.* Sexy is Sophia Loren in *Two Women.* Or Sophia Loren in anything she's ever done. Sexy for me is some inner quality that has nothing to do with the way a woman looks—an earthiness, a freedom, a strong emotional-physical connection. And sexy roles are those with romance and intimacy or flirtation or sexual attraction. I've done close to a hundred roles on television and in film and I can only think of two, *The Cannonball Run* and an episode of *Dream On,* that even come close to being sexy in my mind.

The truth is, until I did the HBO series *Carnivàle* at age fifty-eight, the only love scene I can remember doing was with a green rubber monster. And he may have been naked but I wasn't.

But people think of me as a sex symbol. That's a lot to live up to. Actually these days they probably think of me as an aging sex symbol. That's worse. There are days when I look in the mirror and wish I believed in plastic surgery. It would be so nice to have my tits on the same plane as my breastbone.

I saw Jeanne Moreau several years ago on *60 Minutes*. She must have been in her late sixties, with dark circles under her eyes and no signs of plastic surgery. She was oozing sexuality. So that's what I really wish . . . that our American culture valued the signs of aging like other cultures do. That laugh lines were sexy and wrinkled skin seductive. Then I could continue to be a sex symbol and I'd know it.

Or maybe I should just move to France.

# Burt

IF IT HADN'T BEEN FOR THE PSYCHIC, I WOULD HAVE laughed in his face. I damn well wouldn't have slept with him, joining the long list of women who had. Well, that's what I told myself later. Blamed it on the psychic.

Because the psychic had predicted him exactly.

"You're going to meet someone you already know," she said. "I don't know what that means, how you can know someone without having met him, but that's what I'm picking up. This is going to be a major romance. I see him lying on a rug, an animal skin of some kind. He's got dark hair and he's lying on this rug, smiling. I see the initials B. R. This could be the one."

The psychic worked with the LAPD finding missing persons. She had an 85 percent success rate. I didn't have anyone missing; I just hadn't found anyone yet. *Maude* was in its second season and we were on hiatus. I kept busy at the clinic and entertaining friends but I would have liked someone special to spend time with. The last ongoing relationship I'd had was before I'd left New York to do the series. He was a drummer who lived in Queens with a huge xylophone in the living room and a stash of grass in the hall. He played percussion in the pit for *Jesus Christ Superstar*. Sometimes he got so stoned he forgot to make the whipping sounds during the crucifixion.

A week after the psychic made her prediction, I met the man she talked about, the man I already knew. I'd been asked to fly to Nashville to appear on a telethon for Easter Seals. He was the host. He hadn't achieved superstardom yet but he was on his way. He fit the psychic's description perfectly. I knew him from his appearances on *The Tonight Show* but we'd never met. He had dark hair and he'd just posed for a *Cosmopolitan* centerfold lying on a bearskin rug. I think that's the rug she meant. Or it could have been the one he was wearing on his head. His initials were B.R. . . . for Burt Reynolds.

He was witty. He had a ridiculously high-pitched laugh and was very self-deprecating. It wasn't until years later I learned that a lot of his material was written by his friend Jimmy Hampton. I found him, and Jimmy, very funny.

We broke for a commercial. He put his arm around me and asked what I was doing after the show. I was going back to the hotel to eat dinner and pack . I had to fly to Jacksonville the following day to visit friends and I wanted to get ready. He invited me back to the house he and Jimmy were leasing while they filmed *W. W. and the Dixie Dance Kings*.

From what the psychic said, he could be the one.

I accepted.

The house was in the woods outside of Nashville. It had just been built on spec, wasn't even in escrow yet. The movie company was renting it for him. Very modern. Lots of marble and glass. Completely furnished down to the coffee grinder and bread machine. There was a baby grand in the living room so he could prepare for his next film, a musical called *At Long Last Love.* The bathroom had a radiant-heated black slate floor with a huge, square, black marble tub on a raised platform in the middle of the room. Floor-to-ceiling windows looking out on bare gray trees. Nothing else in sight. It screamed romance.

Jimmy ordered Cajun food and then left us alone after dinner. Burt started talking and didn't stop.

He knew I was a singer, had been nominated for a Tony. He sang for me, asked my advice. I thought he was charming. Not a singer maybe, but appealing nonetheless. He talked about his childhood. He talked about his brother and sister, how they both had the kind of fantasy marriages he longed for.

We talked late into the night. When I said I had to go, he asked Jimmy to drive me back to the hotel. Then he asked me to return and stay with him when I was finished in Jacksonville. I heard the psychic's voice. I agreed.

Three days later I returned. Too excited to sleep. Too nervous to eat. *Why couldn't this happen more often?* I thought. *I could lose weight.*

I was frightened. I was nearly thirty years old. I'd dated nine men in eleven years, not one of them interested in a long-term commitment. I didn't care about getting married but I was ready for a relationship and I wanted children. He was a single man. A single, successful man who wanted children. He seemed like a good man. There had to be a hitch, I thought. Can something that starts out so exciting and romantic and seemingly free of complications sustain itself? Disappointment has to follow, right?

He was a romantic. I'd never dated a romantic before. He talked the way I talked, the way I believed only other women talked. It was incredibly seductive.

"What do you want from me?" I asked him on our second night together.

"Honesty, vulnerability, loyalty, and love."

He told me he'd wanted to meet me ever since he'd read a *TV Guide* article about me that had appeared a year before. He quoted it, for God's sake, from memory. He even knew which page it was on.

He told me he was going to make trouble for me.

What he didn't tell me was that he was still in his much-publicized relationship with the famous singer Dinah Shore.

He told me he'd never felt the feelings he was feeling for me and he would miss me terribly when I flew back to L.A.

What he didn't tell me was that when I turned on the Academy Awards two weeks later, I would see him with her.

I stayed in Nashville for three days. By that time, he'd told me that he was still in a business partnership with Dinah and he needed some time to extricate himself. He couldn't break it off overnight.

"I want you to call me tomorrow," he said, as I was packing to leave. "I'm going to miss you." Earlier he had asked me to return.

"Shall I stay now?"

"I'm really confused. Everything in my head is very foggy and you're no help. I mean, having you here is no help. I love it but I've got to figure out what I'm going to do. I want you to come back. You'll be hearing from me. I'm not going to say good-bye."

I called him the next day.

"I miss you terribly," he said.

"Well, I have plenty of time and no commitments until we start filming again."

"I'll call you later in the week and let you know what I want you to do," he said.

He didn't call. I had friends over for dinner, went to a benefit, had friends over for brunch. Went to the movies. Sang on *The Tonight Show.* Did *Hollywood Squares.*

Saw the psychic again.

"Well, he's extremely involved in haggling over a business deal," she said. "It's taking all his thought and concentration. There's a woman in New Jersey, a real bitch, who's involved in this deal. And someone named Cybill. Your friend has a pounding in his head. He's taking red pills to ease the pain. He's thinking of you, he has good feelings towards you. I feel as though you're special to him. Thursday will be a good day to call him if you haven't heard from him before that." It was Saturday.

I couldn't wait that long. On Tuesday I called. Jimmy answered.

"He's in a meeting. Says to tell you he'll call you back."

On Thursday, I called again.

"I miss you," he said. "I wanted to call. I should have called. I needed to call but, believe me, right now it's very difficult for me."

"I understand," I said. I didn't understand at all but I was smitten and he'd said he missed me, that was the important thing. Strange, though, if he missed me why couldn't he just pick up the phone, even if only for a minute?

Sunday was the Oscars. He and Dinah on camera together. Not looking like business partners at all. And the Oscars, of course, are held in L.A.

I called Nashville the next day, not really expecting an answer. He was back there and happy to hear from me. He never mentioned the night before.

"When are you going to be free to get on a plane and come to Nashville?"

"I'm free whenever you want me there."

"You'll be getting a phone call momentarily, so keep your sneakers on."

Eight days passed. I dreamt one night that he had called to say he wanted me with him but when I tried to call the airline to make reservations, the pay phone wouldn't work. I kept putting in money and handcuffs came out.

On the ninth day he called and asked me to join him the following week. I was on my way to Philadelphia to do *The Mike Douglas Show.* I changed my return flight to Nashville instead.

I stopped eating, stopped sleeping. Copied my favorite recipes in the back of my journal so I could have them on hand in case he wanted me to cook for him.

Which he did. He and Jimmy were filming during the day. I went shopping, made lemon chiffon pies, and played house. He was tired most of the time, didn't want to go out. Sick a lot of the time. He took a lot of pills. I thought they were for his aches and pains.

One night he handed me one of the pills. A big white one. A Quaalude. I didn't know what it was. I didn't drink and I didn't take pills. I don't like the taste of alcohol, never have. Didn't like the idea of pills, either. I smoked grass occasionally but never in public and only with very close friends. I trusted him. I took half the 'lude.

The room went black. Depression pushed down on me. I couldn't move, could barely talk. I kept hoping I'd pass out to escape it and finally I did.

A few hours later I awakened to find Jimmy standing in the doorway to the bedroom. Well, not standing exactly, bent over and clutching his stomach.

"I'm going to the hospital. I don't know when I'll be back."

"What do you mean?" I asked. I could barely think. "What's wrong?" Burt was asleep beside me. He never moved a muscle.

"I don't know. I think I've got an ulcer. I've been taking milk of magnesia for a month now but the pain just keeps getting worse and now it's really bad and I can't stand it. I'm gonna go to the emergency ward."

"You can't drive like that. I'll take you." I stood up and immediately fell backward and hit my head on the bathroom counter. The Quaalude hadn't worn off.

Somehow we got to the car and got to the hospital. I got out of the driver's seat and an emergency attendant raced over to me with a gurney. "Not me," I said, "him." He didn't look as wasted as I did.

But he was. A lot worse. He had a burst appendix. If we'd waited even a few more hours, he would have died.

Burt arranged a screening of the movie he'd just completed, *White Lightning*. His parents flew up from Florida to see it. He introduced me to them at the airport and then he went back to work while Ned Beatty joined us for dinner and a show at the Opry. We met back at the screening room at midnight.

The entire cast and crew of *W. W. and the Dixie Dance Kings* had been invited. I was there as Burt's date, our first time together in public. We sat in the middle of the third row with all eyes upon us. Halfway through the film I realized I was in trouble. I'd just had an IUD put in before I'd left L.A. and something was wrong. I needed to get to a bathroom.

"I think the closest one is across the street in the bus station," Burt whispered. "The rest of this building is locked."

Well, what could I do? He was the star of the film. He was in every scene. I was, perhaps, his girlfriend, albeit a fairly new one. If nothing else, I was his date for the night. I couldn't walk out of the movie for fifteen minutes unless I held up a sign that said, "Sorry, it's an emergency!"

I stayed. The longest film I've ever sat through. Finally the lights came up and everyone stood to applaud. There was blood running down my legs and my gray seat cushion was red. Burt was the only one who saw it.

"Why didn't you tell me you had to go that bad?" he said.

I stayed in Nashville a week. The night before I left, Burt told me he loved me. I went off to Michigan to appear in some parade. He finished filming and flew to his ranch in Florida.

Three days later, Dinah was there with him. When we spoke on the phone, he told me he was sorry, her presence had been unexpected.

He came back to L.A. two weeks before I was to begin rehearsals for a production of William Inge's *Bus Stop* at a theater in San Diego. He had encouraged me to take the job, said he'd come down to visit me. But when he got to L.A., he never called. Jimmy told me he was in town. He's exhausted, I thought. Probably drained of energy and overwhelmed with all the things that have to be taken care of when you've been away for a while. And he doesn't know me well enough to know he doesn't have to entertain me, I'd be happy just being with him. Or maybe he feels we have our entire lives to spend together and a day or two won't make a difference.

Once again, I called him. We made a date for two days later. I was shaking when he arrived. And then it was as though we'd never been apart.

Weeks went by like that. We saw each other when he could get away. He was a "movie star," after all. With business meetings and voice lessons and dance rehearsals. Personal appearances, magazine interviews, photo sessions. I would have liked to have been invited to observe but I wasn't. One night he asked me to come to his house, and while I sat in the kitchen, he sat in the red and black living room, doing script revisions with Robert Aldrich. I never saw either of them. Sometimes I waited hours for him to return a call because he said he'd get right back to me. It's business, I said. Something must have come up, I said.

One night he asked me to cook dinner at his house in the Hollywood Hills. When I got there, he was out of butter. I grabbed my purse and was heading out the door to the deli on Sunset when he stopped me. Instead he called his secretary at her house who then called the deli who delivered a *case* of butter. I didn't know whether to be impressed with his fame or appalled at his inability to take care of himself.

I started rehearsals in San Diego. Drove home to see him on my days off. He drove down to visit. We'd been seeing each other for three months and I still couldn't get over my initial nervousness every time he showed up. How long will we last, I wondered. I spent the hour before his arrival changing all the light bulbs in my hotel suite from bright white to soft pink. He wanted the curtains closed and he needed the heat in the room up very high. I ignored the thought that I couldn't live like that forever. We didn't make love because he had a splinter in his finger and it took a while for me to get it out. Then he wasn't feeling well. He came to the theater to see the show but left immediately afterward.

For my birthday, he took out a full-page ad in *Variety* with my picture and reprints of the reviews I'd gotten for the show. There was nothing in the ad to indicate it was a gift. I wondered whether people would think I had paid for it myself.

*Bus Stop* closed on a Sunday afternoon after a three-week run. I raced back to L.A. to see him. He was supposed to meet me at my house at 8:30 that night. Nine o'clock came and went and then 9:30. At 10:00 I called his house. The line was busy. At 10:30 it was still busy. At 11:00 I called the operator. The phone was off the hook. He never showed.

The next morning I went out to get in my car and found a pale blue envelope under the windshield wiper. It was addressed SWEETHEART. Inside was an eighteen-page letter telling me what a "gutless hero" he was. "I am in the middle of the biggest picture of my career, trying to cope with how much I love you but unable to pull the plug on my relationship with Dinah. I care too much for her to tell her the truth, she'll fall apart. I need time. If it's right for us . . . well . . . I can't ask you to wait. I won't call you until I'm free but I love you and I always will."

I went back into the house to call him. This time I got a recorded message. "The number you have called is not in service at this time. There is no new number."

Two days later he collapsed and ended up in a hospital. Somehow I got a call through to him.

"I want to see you," I said.

"I want to see you, too, but every time I do, I get sick. I can't handle it. I can't face myself in the mirror."

"I understand. I really do. I love you. I'll wait as long as I can for you to work things out with her. But I hope we can at least talk to each other."

A week later I got a call from Renee Valente, then head of casting for Universal Studios. She was a friend of Burt's. I assumed he had asked her to call me, maybe about a job offer.

We met for lunch. Burt had asked her to call, all right, but not about a job. He wanted her to make sure it was clear to me that our love affair was over, that I had joined the ranks of women like Susan Clark and Brenda Vaccaro—women he had fallen in love with and then walked away from. Like the actress he was living with who came home one day to find his lawyer waiting for her with an edict to clear out that afternoon. He loved me, yes; he just wasn't going to see me again.

The next time I spoke to him was six years later. He called to say he was doing a production of *Grease* at his theater in Florida and he'd love to have me direct it. I turned him down.

# The Sex Symbol in Action —Or Lack Thereof

HE WAS A COMEDIAN ON THE BORSCHT BELT. THE FIRST man I met when I moved to New York. We took a dance class together at Madame Danilova's and afterward he invited me to this really neat place on Fifty-seventh Street that had food in glass cubbyholes in the wall. You put in twenty-five cents and opened a glass door and got your coffee. It was called the Automat. I was very impressed.

I reciprocated by inviting him to a small dinner party at the home of the only other person I knew in New York, my friend Jeanette. He brought her flowers. I thought I might fall in love.

He offered to cook dinner at his place for our third date. He lived on Avenue D in one room with a bed and a metal table. The bed was covered in black-and-white fake animal skins with red satin pillows. The table had aluminum legs and matching chairs with red checked seat covers. He kept offering me wine but I don't like it. He fixed salad and barbecued chicken. I was very impressed.

After dinner, I went to the bathroom. I thought it was sort of weird, really, because the walls were papered in his reviews from the Catskills. No wallpaper at all, just reviews. Some of them weren't even very good. I wasn't quite as impressed.

When I came out of the bathroom, he was sitting on the bed in his jockey shorts. Dingy white jockey shorts. On black satin sheets. Definitely not impressive. I thanked him for dinner and ran out the door.

Two days later I saw one of those barbecued chickens roasting on a spit at Smiler's deli. Son of a bitch. He hadn't even cooked that chicken.

He owned a cocktail lounge on Sixty-fourth and Lex called The Loser's Club. He was looking for a waitress to push a Sabrett's hot-dog cart through the club during happy hour. He told me I had the job if I could fit in the uniform and to come back that night to try it on.

I reported for work and followed him upstairs to his office where he kept the uniforms. I didn't want to go in but he said that was the place where I could change. He locked the door behind me. There was a bearskin rug on the floor. Within seconds I was on the floor, too. "You don't understand," I kept saying, "I'm a virgin! I'm a virgin!" That's all that saved me. I didn't get the job.

He was a well-known actor. I met him on the set of a movie. I was an extra and he was one of the stars. He liked my legs. I didn't. I'd been a pom-pom girl in high school and had the calves to prove it: muscular and thick. My friends wore falsies, I wore high boots. Whenever I could find a pair that fit. And long skirts. Anything to disguise my legs. But he liked them. He thought they were great. No one else ever had. And I liked him. I figured if they were good enough for him, they should be good enough for me and I never thought about them again.

He made me laugh and he gave me back my legs and I could have fallen in love with him but he was married. Whenever I see him now, thirty years later, we smile and say hello and I remember every moment we spent together. That's enough.

He was a twenty-eight-year-old Italian who lived with his mother and taught me the term "muff-diver." He owned a cocktail lounge and he made book. He drove a white Lincoln Continental and wore matching Piaget watches and diamond pinkie rings. Every time he changed his watch, he changed his ring. He took me to the track and to the Copacabana to see Trini Lopez. I took him to see *Man of La Mancha.* He took me to Bookbinder's in Philadelphia for clam chowder and lobster. I took him to my apartment for shish kebab and pilaf—the first time he'd ever eaten at a girlfriend's house. The night I got hired to do a summer tour of *Half a Sixpence,* he stood me up. When he finally called, he said he couldn't see me anymore. It was for my own good, he said. I deserved to have a career and he would just hold me back.

He was a shrink. My shrink. My first shrink. It was group therapy at St. Vincent's Hospital in Greenwich Village and he ran the program. He said he'd been a professional boxer and appeared in the *Our Gang* comedies. He told me it was a grave error to date only one man at a time. When the group disbanded for the summer, he invited me to his office for a private session. His office was in his apartment. He took me into his living room to show me "his etchings" and then he took me into his arms and kissed me. He said he wanted to see me when I returned from summer stock. When I phoned him from out of town, he never returned my call.

He was a daytime soap star. I interviewed him when I was cohosting *A.M. Los Angeles.* He was my first date after my estranged husband and I had separated, a year earlier. I was alternately excited at the prospect of going out and depressed that having a date meant one more concrete sign my marriage was over. I spent the afternoon crying on the bed and shaking while I got dressed. He took me out for a lovely dinner and, when we came back to my place, explained he was madly in love with another soap star and wanted my advice on how to fix their relationship.

He was an actor. Trying to be. I met him when he spilled red wine all over my dress at a party and insisted on driving me home to change. We started dating. Months passed and he moved more and more of his things into my apartment. I was his "favorite go-to-bed-with person," he said. When I mentioned how much money I was spending on groceries for the two of us, he told me to cut down on my eating. When I told him I was falling in love with him, he told me my sinuses were infected.

He disappeared over the Fourth of July weekend. When he called four days later, it was to tell me he'd fallen in love with someone he'd just met and they'd gone to the Caribbean and everyone thought they were on their honeymoon because they were so happy together. He wanted me to talk to her, though, because she had trouble having orgasms and maybe I could help. He didn't know I'd faked half of mine because he was such a lousy lover. When he came over to get his stuff, he tried to take me to bed. That's when I told him.

Years later I ran into him outside the office of my then husband, John Carpenter. He had just auditioned for a part in one of John's films. He didn't know it but he didn't stand a chance.

# Sex in '77

IT'S FEBRUARY 1977. A TWO-YEAR ROMANCE WITH A loving man has grown into a friendship instead, and I've been alone for a while. I don't drink so I don't go to bars, and I don't do cocaine so that eliminates a lot of parties. I'd rather read a good book than go out on a date just for the sake of dating. So in spite of what you might think about the glamour of a TV star's life, I don't meet many men I'm attracted to. Maybe I'm just picky.

It's a Tuesday night. I'm driving home from the studio where we've just finished taping *Maude.* Halfway up Lookout Mountain, just before it splits off to Wonderland Avenue, my tire blows out. I live on Wonderland; I could walk if I want to. It's a straight shot up a steep hill about a mile away.

I'm one of the first people in L.A. to have a mobile phone. It's a big, unwieldy thing that plugs into some clunky box that's installed under the dashboard on the passenger's side.

There's no direct dialing. I call the operator and ask her to call Triple-A. When they come on, I give them my location and sit back to wait.

A few minutes go by and a pickup truck stops in front of me. The driver leaves his headlights on, gets out, and walks toward my car. He's tall, six-two, at least, and he's slender. He's got cowboy boots on. I can't see his face but his walk is sexy.

He bends down to my window and I'm not disappointed. He's got a great face and his eyes are smiling. It's hard to tell in the dark but I think his hair is sort of sandy red.

"Hey. You having some trouble?"

"It's just a flat. I've already called Triple-A."

"I could change it if you'd like. I'm good at that kind of stuff." I'll bet he's good at a lot of stuff. And he knows it.

"Oh, thank you, but that's okay. They're on their way."

"You're Adrienne Barbeau, aren't you? You live around here?"

"Yep. I'm just up Wonderland close to the top."

"I'm James. I'm just up Lookout. Are you okay sitting here alone or would you like me to wait with you?"

"I'm fine, really. Thank you, though, that's very nice of you."

"No problem. Good-night." He starts to go and turns back. "I like your work, by the way."

"Thanks. That's nice of you to say. Good-night."

Four weeks later I'm in Houston working on a TV movie about a nuclear meltdown. William Devane, Michael Brandon, and I are shooting inside NASA headquarters.

When I get to the hotel after the first day's work, there's a bouquet of flowers waiting in my room. The card reads, "I hope Triple-A showed up. James. P.S. I'm working on the film."

I see him on the set the following day and thank him for the flowers. He's playing one of the NASA scientists. We don't have any scenes together but he's waiting when I finish work and he asks me out to dinner.

When we return to L.A., we continue to see each other. On our ninth date, we fly to Ireland. James has lived with a family there for a short time and he wants to visit them again. We land in Shannon. It takes him an hour to decide which rental car he wants but eventually we arrive at Dromoland Castle and our room, which is the size of a small football field. Twenty-foot ceilings, three sofas, two desks, and assorted oil paintings to match.

James lies down on the canopy bed and tells me about the cold sore.

"Cold sore?"

"Yeah, you know, like a virus. The herpes virus. I get them when I get tired or nervous."

"I don't see it. Where is it?"

"Oh, underneath my cock. It's tiny, just starting. Nothing to be worried about."

This is 1977. I don't know enough to be worried.

"Does it hurt?"

"Nah, not really. It might sting a little when we make love."

"Well, Jesus, what are we supposed to do about it? Do you have any medicine? Should we be making love?"

"Sure. We just need some rubbers."

"You mean you don't have any."

"Right. Not the kind of thing I carry around, you know. I'm not real comfortable going into a drugstore and asking."

Isn't that sweet, I think. My preppie cowboy is shy. This is 1977. I'm not evolved enough to think he's an asshole.

So he takes a nap and I take the car and set out for the town of Ennis. I've never driven a Renault and I can't find the release for the emergency brake, but the car is driving okay so I stop worrying. It's hard enough staying on the left side of the road.

A half mile from town, the car starts smoking. I pull over. There's a local boy sitting on a barrel by the side of the road, completely absorbed in watching the fumes.

"I think I've got a problem," I say.

Speechless, he points to a garage mechanic about ten yards away. The mechanic releases the brake, says I've burned the lining a bit but it should be okay once it cools off and he can check it for me then.

I leave the car there and walk to the chemist's. The girl behind the counter is fifteen if she's a day.

"I'd like some prophylactics please," I say in my best matter-of-fact voice.

"Ah, sure, here ya go. Is it sunny out there then?" She hands me a tube of zinc oxide.

"No, no. I'm sorry. Prophylactics."

She bows her head and starts to blush. "Oh, a laxative, ya mean."

"No, not a laxative. A prophylactic. You know, for birth control?"

Now her skin is bright red. "Oh . . . oh. Well, you need a doctor for that, you know. And he's not here right now."

"In Ireland, you mean? You need a prescription?" This is 1977. I don't know enough to realize it's a Catholic country.

"Yes. You might try another chemist."

I thank her and head for the next chemist. I ask for a doctor but they don't have one. This time I'm prepared.

"My husband and I have a slight problem. He has a fever blister and I'd like to purchase some prophylactics."

The girl behind the counter goes into a back room and returns with an older woman, the chemist. I mention herpes simplex.

"Oh yes, yes, I have medication for that."

"Well, it's on his genitals."

"Yes, this will be all right for that." She hands me a tube of cod liver oil ointment.

"I also think we should have some prophylactics if you can sell them to me."

"Yes, yes, of course. Something you can drink."

I thank her and walk across the street to a doctor's office. He's willing to see me right then but when I explain my situation, once again playing the part of the loving wife with the ailing husband, he says, "Well, I don't know what to tell ya. I think you'll be getting cancer of the cervix." No condoms.

I am determined to have sex. I walk back across the street and buy some band-aids. This is 1977. I don't know enough to realize this relationship won't be saved by Johnson & Johnson.

# Meeting John

**I MET JOHN CARPENTER IN 1978 WHEN HE WAS CASTING** his first network television film. The original title was *High Rise;* it aired as *Someone's Watching Me.* It was based on a newspaper article about a woman whose belief that she was being spied upon in her home led her to commit suicide. Warner Bros. hired John to write and direct. Lauren Hutton was playing the woman, David Birney was playing her boyfriend. John was interested in having me play Lauren's lesbian friend who gets thrown off her apartment balcony while Lauren watches helplessly through a telescope in a high rise across the street.

My agent called to say that this hot, young feature film director wanted to meet me. I hadn't heard of him but that still didn't keep me from getting nervous. Then I read the script and liked it a lot. Wanting the role just increased my nerves. My stomach started doing flip-flops.

I drove to Warner Bros. and found his temporary office, a

trailer with dark wood paneling and not much light. He was barely visible in a cloud of cigarette smoke.

*Oh, jeez*, I thought. *He's good-looking.* Tall, slender, hazel eyes, a mustache, dark shoulder-length hair with some gray running through it. Dressed in jeans and a plaid shirt and tennis shoes. Nice hands and a great smile.

I liked him immediately. He was funny and relaxed and he put me at ease. Months later he told me he'd been just as nervous as I was. He had watched me in *Maude*, liked the character I played, and was hoping I had her same sensibilities. It was the kind of character he wrote, the Howard Hawks-type woman. Strong, smart, quick, witty. Lauren Bacall in *To Have and Have Not* and *The Big Sleep*. He was also nervous because this was his first studio film and he was having to answer to "the suits." He'd wanted me for Lauren's role but they wanted a bigger name.

We talked about the character he wanted me to play.

"How do you feel about her being gay?" he asked. It was 1978, I couldn't think of another gay woman character on television.

"I love it. I think it's great the way you handled it. Not hitting people over the head with it, just keeping it very matter of fact."

"Well, I just figured if I were going to tell my friends, that's how I'd do it."

*Oh shit*, I thought, *he's telling me he's gay.* Well, so much for finding him attractive.

The first day of shooting he gave me the best direction I'd ever had.

"Do less," he said.

"Less?"

"Yes. The scene where you and Lauren are establishing your friendship. You don't have to act at all."

I knew what he meant instantly. Up until that time I'd done years of musical comedy and a TV sitcom. The only experience I'd had with film was in *Houdini*. We finished the master shot of the first scene—a wide-angle framing of all the actors—and I went off to change clothes for the next scene. I had no idea I was supposed to shoot coverage—the close-ups and various angles the director needed to cut into the master to make the scene interesting. I learned fast doing subsequent TV movies and dramatic guest-star roles but I wasn't wise in the ways of film acting. Fortunately I hadn't embarrassed myself yet. Those two words of John's made all the difference to me in terms of the work that followed. He was talking about keeping things real, keeping the performance intimate for the camera, not overacting, letting the camera do the work. He didn't say any of that, he just said, "Do less," but I understood. It was my first day working with him but already he'd earned my trust.

We had lunch together that first day. Somehow he ended up next to me in the food line and we took our trays to the makeshift tables near the set. No one sat near us. I had salad.

He had fried pork chops. We talked about ourselves. His gray hair was misleading; he was twenty-eight, three years younger than I. He'd attended USC where he won an Academy Award for a short film called *Bronco Billy*. He never graduated because he wouldn't finish French and the school didn't let him keep the Oscar because they deemed it a school project.

Using USC equipment, and with a budget of a thousand dollars, he started on a science-fiction film called *Dark Star* in collaboration with Dan O'Bannon, who went on to write *Alien.* An investor came along with more money. John completed *Dark Star* for $60,000 and entered it in Filmex, the prestigious L.A. film festival. That got him an agent and a series of screenwriting assignments. One, *Blood River,* was being developed for John Wayne. It was eventually done years after Mr. Wayne died, with Wilford Brimley, Rick Schroeder, and myself. Another script, *The Eyes of Laura Mars,* had been bought by Jon Peters for Barbra Streisand. John spent weeks driving out to Barbra's home in Malibu to do the rewrites she demanded. He was supposed to direct the film if Barbra starred. During one of the rewrite sessions John began to feel Barbra found him attractive. He didn't pick up on it. Suddenly she was no longer available for rewrites. Jon Peters called John's agent to say they didn't believe Barbra's audience would accept her in the role. John retained screenwriting credit but he was out as director.

He made a second independent film, *Assault on Precinct*

*13.* It was a modern-day western, *Rio Bravo* in a ghetto. A huge success in Europe (in Germany alone it played in one theater for a year), it didn't do as well in the States.

He told me most of this during our first lunch. He also told me he was living with a woman named Debra Hill. She'd been his script supervisor on *Assault* and they'd been together about nine months. They were planning another collaboration on a script called *Halloween.*

So much for his being gay. And to his being available. I wasn't about to go where I didn't belong. I immediately did everything I could to make him unattractive in my eyes. *He's too thin,* I thought. *He smokes cigarettes. He eats junk food. He likes his broccoli boiled to mush. Forget about him.*

And I did. Consciously, at least. I had a dream about him one night and mentioned it to Lauren. She teased me for days about not admitting my real feelings. I found myself doing personal things like leaving vitamins for him on the hood of his car. Bringing him copies of articles on topics we'd discussed.

We filmed for three weeks and we had fun. Debra came to the set. She was very nice. His friends Tommy Lee Wallace and Nancy Loomis came to the set. I liked them a lot.

On my last night of the shoot, he came into my trailer and kissed me good-bye. It seemed more passionate to me than your basic director-giving-his-actress-a-farewell-kiss but I figured I was just fantasizing. I was leaving for New York the following day and he asked me to call him when I returned. "I have something I want to discuss with you," he said. I assumed it was another job.

On the plane, I found myself writing him a letter. I told myself it was a thank-you note, but when I read it, I knew it wasn't the kind of letter I would normally write to a director at the end of a shoot. It was funny and silly and personal. I ignored the danger signs and mailed it anyway.

When I returned to L.A., I went right into the hospital for some minor surgery. John sent flowers and signed the card "ALL MY LOVE." Not the kind of card I'd normally expect from a director sending a get-well bouquet.

I called to thank him. Debra answered.

"We've got to get together," she said. "Maybe you can come over for dinner. John talks about you all the time." John got on the phone and asked when I'd be able to meet him. We made a date for the following Wednesday night.

He picked me up in his father's old brown Cadillac. It had a GOD BLESS JOHN WAYNE sticker on the bumper. We went to a small place in Santa Monica and sat in a private high-walled wooden booth. He ordered beef Stroganoff. I had a whole-wheat chicken enchilada.

Then he told me he'd fallen in love with me.

He said he didn't know how else to say what he had to say other than to just tell me. He'd been thinking about it for weeks. He'd discussed it with his therapist. He was sure this wasn't just something that happened because he was the director and I was the actress. And he'd told Debra what he was feeling. He didn't want to lie to her.

I was dumbfounded.

"I don't know what to say. I thought you just wanted to talk about work. I'm stunned."

"Well, what do you think?"

"I don't know. The timing is all wrong. I mean, I like you. I was attracted to you from the moment I met you. But when I found out you were with Debra, I did everything I could to make you unattractive to me."

"What do you mean? Like what?"

"Oh, you know. You smoke cigarettes. You eat junk food. Stuff like that. So . . . I don't know. I don't know how good a job I did at convincing myself."

"Well, will you think about it? I'd like to see you again. I don't have a lot of time right now anyway. I'm in preproduction on *Halloween* and, of course, Debra is working on it with me, so. . . . Well, I guess I'm confused, too, but I know what I've told you is true."

He took me home and kissed me good-night and I knew, no matter how much work I'd done to make him unattractive to me, I hadn't succeeded.

# Singing

*Excerpt from ninth-grade term paper entitled "To Be or Not to Be: Acting as a Vocation," written January 5, 1960.*

*". . . an actress, no matter how ravishing or talented, is always a step behind if she can't give a rendition of the C scale or kick up her heels when she's exceptionally joyous. Especially in making guest appearances on television. You can't always do a scene from your latest movie on The Chevy Show and get away with it.*

*I have taken three years of vocal training and through it have developed fairly good diction and resonance. I have learned to keep the nasal tones out of my voice and I think I'm safe in saying it is fairly agreeable."*

Six months after *Maude* went on the air I started making those guest appearances I'd written about when I was fifteen. And not wanting to be a "step behind." I forced myself to sing each time I was asked. I didn't have any qualms about talking on a talk show, but singing, especially as myself and not a character in a musical, brought up all those old anxieties.

I started out with *The Tonight Show.* The first time I sat on the dais, I told Johnny Carson about the fellow I'd dated who passed himself off to me as Philip Roth.

"What did he expect to gain by that?" Johnny asked.

"My virginity, I suppose."

That was all Johnny needed to hear. He leaned over to me in the middle of a commercial and asked if I'd come back to do the show again. I did. Repeatedly. I didn't enjoy doing it like I enjoyed doing Mike Douglas or Merv Griffin but it was an important show to do.

Mike's show was great fun to do. A first-class trip to Philadelphia to spend time with a lovely, caring man who made his guests feel welcome. I guested several times and then co-hosted for a week. It was easy and low-key.

Merv, too. Merv was witty and charming and he loved lighthearted gossip. I never knew what we'd talk about but I always knew we'd be laughing. He turned to me once during a break and said, "My mother is having lunch with your mother next week." I didn't know what he was talking about. My mother lived in Northern California; she'd never met Merv or his mother. Well, it turned out the two ladies lived an hour away from each other and somehow they'd made a date to meet for the first time just because their children had something in common.

(Above) *My grandmother and grandfather, Marine and Simon Nalbandian.*

(Right) *My parents, Armen and Joe Barbeau. 1944.*

*Grandma "on the ranch."*
*And me.*

*My first cheesecake shot.*

*With my parents, in costume for my first operetta at The Burlingame Conservatory of Music.*

*Richard.*

*My mother, my sister, and my cat's eye glasses. 1957.*

*You thought I was kidding? And they still voted me eighth-grade class president.*

*The French curled 8 x 10 glossy. Would you buy soap from this girl?*

Fiddler on the Roof. *1969. Bette Midler, Tanya Everett, and myself.*

*The cast of* Grease.

*Well, it was a paying job.*

*Burt Reynolds, the weekend we met on the telethon.*

*With my TV family from* Maude. *Bill Macy, Conrad Bain, and Bea Arthur.*

*John's dad took this picture at our wedding. Tommy Lee Wallace was John's best man. My dear friend Eva Long stood up for me.*

*On the set of* The Fog *with John, Jamie Leigh Curtis, and Janet Leigh.*

Escape From New York.

Swamp Thing.

*With Roger Moore on the set of* Cannonball Run. *Even here you can see I was star struck.*

*My buddy Tom Atkins. We did* The Fog, Escape From New York, Creepshow, *and* Two Evil Eyes *together.*

*The Masters of Horror with their wives. John and I, Chris and George Romero.*

*With Dennis Adams at the
Kentucky Derby.*

*Atop Mt. Whitney with Alex
Daniels.*

*With Suzanne.*

*My favorite Billy picture.*

*The cast of* Drop Dead. *Billy's partner Jane is between Donny Most and Rose Marie. That's Barney Martin behind her.*

(Right) *The rat movie.*

(Below) *Blowing away nuns in*
The Convent. *Cody and I went
to Belgium when this won a
prize at the Festival du Film
Fantastique.*

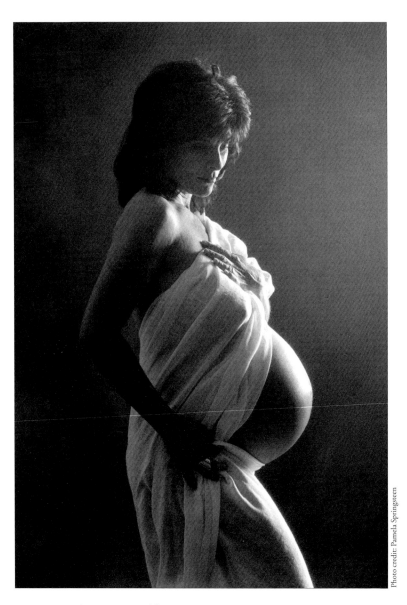

*Pregnant with twins at age fifty-one.*

*My mother and Cody. I love this picture.*

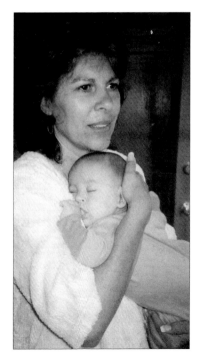

(Above) *My niece Jennifer and William.*

(Left) *My sister Jocelyn and Walker. I love this one, too.*

*Leticia. My lifesaver for the past twenty-two years.*

*Aunty Ruby and my niece Jaime.*

*The funniest man in the world, my husband Billy, with his brother Steven and sister Kathi.*

(Top) *The greatest smiles in the world. Walker's on the left, William's on the right.*

(Middle) *William, Walker, and Cody. Christmas 2001.*

(Right) *Cody. Christmas 2005.*

*Opening night in New York for Billy's play* Silent Laughter.

*Dressing myself.*

Carnivàle.

Johnny's show wasn't fun for me. It was necessary. Appearing on *The Tonight Show* was a career boost. There was an enormous amount of unspoken pressure to succeed: to be entertaining, to be funny, to set Johnny up to be funny. At least that's how I experienced it. This wasn't a relaxing evening sitting around talking. You had to deliver.

A talent coordinator from the show would call to set up a time to do a pre-interview interview. They wanted to make sure you had funny stories to tell or that Johnny knew what he could talk about with you to get laughs. The last time I ever did the show, I had trouble making a time for the pre-interview that was convenient for the talent coordinator. She went nuts. Screamed at me over the phone that they were the most important talk show on the air and I'd better find the time to meet her schedule or I wouldn't be on the show. When I sat in the makeup chair before the taping and she came in to discuss what I was going to say, I broke out in hives.

It was easier doing the show with a guest host. John Davidson gave me flowers before we went on the air. Bill Cosby invited me to his dressing room to chat. Don Rickles became a good friend. Roy Clark asked me to open for him at Harrah's in Reno. George Carlin had me guest on his own series years later. David Brenner and Robert Klein were sweethearts.

The hardest part for me was singing. Except for the *Maude* "telethons," I hadn't sung at all since I'd left *Grease* months earlier, but Johnny's talent coordinators wanted me to and I felt I should. It was an opportunity to let the Hollywood community know I could sing, even though I still didn't think of myself as a singer.

I'd only done musical comedy material in New York and I didn't have a concert act. I didn't have any identity as a singer, so the question was: What was I going to sing? I chose songs I liked. They were always obscure, oddball songs from the B side of some not-so-mainstream album: Harry Chapin, Patti Dahlstrom, Janis Ian, Joni Mitchell. Even the Elton John song I chose was one that didn't get airplay: "Come Down in Time."

I rehearsed with a piano player who then wrote the charts for Doc Severinson's band to accompany me. Doc and the band had been in the audience during my nude foray off-Broadway in *Stag Movie.* They were always happy to see me. I never heard the full orchestration until I sang the song one time at the camera rehearsal an hour before the show was taped. Then I sang it live in front of the studio audience and that's the performance that was seen a few hours later by millions of viewers.

It was terrifying. I went through the same process every time I did the show and every time I was a nervous wreck for days before. I couldn't eat. I couldn't get out of the bathroom. My hands shook so hard I was afraid to hold the mic. I was certain people everywhere were going to spend the next morning at the breakfast table talking about how badly I sang.

I kept expecting it to get easier, expecting to be less nervous each time I did it, but I wasn't. It didn't cross my mind that I was terrified because I'd never sung the song for anyone before, I'd never heard the orchestration before, and I was completely under-rehearsed.

I must have been nuts.

But that's what you were supposed to do if you wanted to succeed. I'd been offered the opportunity to sing on *The Tonight Show*. I had to take it.

Years later, I sang again in *Pump Boys and Dinettes* and *Best Little Whorehouse in Texas* with my friend Glenn Casale directing. I did an original musical based on Nelson Algren's book *Walk on the Wild Side*. I did another production of *Fiddler*, this time playing Golde. They were musicals. I thought of myself as an actress who did musicals. I didn't think of myself as a singer. Linda Ronstadt was a singer; Stevie Nicks, Minnie Riperton, Bonnie Raitt. Not me.

In 1976, I went to Reno to open for Roy Clark. Roy's manager had offered me the job, saying he'd help me put an act together that would showcase the kinds of songs I liked to sing and be appropriate for Roy's audiences. A few days after I agreed, Roy and his manager flew to Russia to perform and I was left to make my own decisions. The show was successful, I got nice reviews, but I still didn't have "an act." I just sang songs I thought Roy's fans would like.

It was an odd experience: trying to get people's attention when they were half-crocked and just wanted Roy to come on stage. I'd never sung onstage without a character and a script to provide a persona. I told a few stories about *Maude,* made people laugh, sang my four songs, and got off stage. The audiences enjoyed it, but it wasn't fun for me.

It didn't help that I was alone in Reno with nothing to do when I wasn't performing. I didn't gamble. I didn't drink. I couldn't work out because the gym was closed to women during the hours I could get there. I decided I wasn't cut out to sing in clubs.

In 1978 I was approached by two record producers from Nashville. They'd heard a demo I'd done for Kelly Gordon, the producer of "Ode To Billy Joe." They wanted to cut four tunes with me and shop for a recording contract.

They surrounded me with some great Country artists: musicians and backup singers. Record execs loved my voice but didn't like the songs we'd chosen. I wasn't known as a singer and we hadn't found a style to identify me with. I loved being in the recording studio but nobody wanted to sign me.

I let eight years go by before I sang again on my own. In 1986 I appeared at the Gardenia Room and the Cinegrill in the Hollywood Roosevelt Hotel, both in L.A. By this time I had some idea of who I was and what I wanted to say musically.

I opened on a Friday night at the Cinegrill. Still nervous, still in the bathroom, but not shaking at least. The audience loved it. Saturday morning I awakened with bronchitis. The first time I'd been sick in ten years. I barely had a voice. Nervousness gave way to terror.

I got through the show with lozenges and hot tea. When I finished, the audience stood up to applaud. I didn't believe it. I thought for sure they were just being nice.

Afterward, I made excuses to friends in the audience.

"Oh, my God, I'm so sorry. I sounded terrible. My voice is just gone."

"What are you talking about?" they asked. "It sounded great. You've got so much emotion in your songs, the way you sing them is fantastic. We couldn't tell you were having trouble with your voice."

It was an important lesson. I actually believe I created that illness to learn from it. It didn't matter what my voice sounded like. Sure, I had to be in key and in rhythm but the sound didn't have to be perfect. People weren't responding to the tonal quality of my voice, they were responding to my connection with the songs. I had chosen material with lyrics that meant something to me and this was evident in the way I sang them. I was moving the audience emotionally because I was moved myself.

It was the first time I understood why audiences love the jagged-edged voices of Joe Cocker and Janis Joplin.

I felt like I'd gotten a little closer to believing I could entertain people with my voice but it still wasn't something I looked forward to doing. I loved the rehearsal process, loved standing at the piano with a mic in my hand singing my heart out for no one but myself and my musical director. But add an audience and anxiety colored my enjoyment. I sang around the house instead.

In 1994 I was sitting at a traffic light on Ventura Boulevard singing along with Aaron Neville's "Arianne" and thinking if I'd been born in Nashville or New Orleans maybe I'd have grown up to be a singer, and how I was going to have to wait for another lifetime to start again and how sad that made me because I really love to sing, but I was too old and it was never going to happen. That's the moment when my car phone rang and someone on the other end said he wanted to book my nightclub act. My nonexistent nightclub act. When I got home, I had a message on my answering machine from someone else asking me to sing at a charity event. An hour later my friend Mews Small called to tell me she wanted me to meet a friend of hers who was a musical director.

Synchronicity. Someone was sending me a message.

I called Mews's friend. He lived six blocks from me. I told him all I wanted to do was start singing again, just for myself. Maybe prepare a couple of songs in case I needed something for a personal appearance or a musical audition. We made a date for the following day.

Wayland Pickard is a musical director, all right. He plays twelve instruments. He's also a composer, an author, an actor, and a humorist. He has his own concert act, a contemporary Victor Borge, and also an act in which he appears as Liberace. He's remarkable. But the thing that made him so right for me at that time of my life is that Wayland is a salesman extraordinaire. Two weeks after we started working together, he sold me on doing an act. He convinced me there were venues all across the country that would love to have me. Once I created the act, he helped me sell it. We booked it into a supper club, filmed the performance, and sent it off to his booking agents.

Within a year, I was singing in concert halls, performing arts centers, and theaters. I was getting standing ovations and requests for a CD, which I eventually recorded while I was pregnant with my twins. My hands weren't shaking when I held the mic. I didn't need the bathroom anymore.

It took thirty years, but finally I know I can sing.

# Marrying John

I WAS THIRTY-THREE YEARS OLD AND I DIDN'T WANT TO get married. Ever. It sure hadn't worked for my parents. Getting married seemed to me like the beginning of the end: the end of youth, the end of romance, the end of excitement. I wanted children, I wanted a partner, but I didn't want marriage.

And then I fell in love with John.

We were staying in his condominium on the beach in Malibu. He was sitting on the sofa in a yellow T-shirt, shorts, and flip-flops, eating a bologna sandwich with mayo on Wonder Bread with a glass of milk and a Hostess cupcake. He announced that he wanted to talk to me after he finished eating.

We'd been together for six months. We'd talked nonstop about everything—our histories, our dreams, our beliefs, our desires—but he'd never made an announcement like this before. I fixed myself some decaf espresso and a croissant and sat on the floor reading a magazine, thinking, *Here it comes, he's going to say he thinks I should stay at my place for a while. Something's happened, I did something to upset him.*

Instead, he asked me to marry him.

I burst into tears and left for the airport. I had to do a talk show in Vancouver. I took my journal with me.

*August 25, 1978*
*The truth, I believe, is I will not meet another man who is as open, understanding, sensitive, intelligent, funny, sexual, talented, creative and all those indefinable things that make someone right.*

He may have been right but I still had a lot of anxiety about the state of marriage itself. I told my father about my fear that marriage might be the end of romance. It was one of the few conversations I remember having with him and the only time in my life he gave me advice, about marriage, of all things: "Well, it's the end of romance with more than one person but it doesn't have to be the end of romance."

I made a list of all the reasons I should marry John and all the reasons I shouldn't. The first list was a lot longer. The second list only had one reason: I was afraid of giving up my freedom.

Love won out over fear. I went to a shop in Vancouver and had YES, JC printed on a T-shirt. I wore it on the plane flying home with another shirt underneath in case I chickened out at the last minute. The actor Dick Gautier sat next to me on the plane. He thought I'd found Christ.

We were married four months later, on New Year's Day 1979, in Bowling Green, Kentucky, by a one-armed judge who years earlier had lost his hand in the mixer at the bakery where we'd gotten our wedding cake. John's two best friends, Tommy Wallace and Nancy Loomis, and my two best friends, Eva Long and Wyatt Harlan, flew in for the ceremony. We spent New Year's Eve cruising downtown Bowling Green and had a country-style brunch the next morning at Tommy's mother's house. Wyatt had her first taste of grits, biscuits, and red-eye gravy. That evening I drove the two girls from our hotel to John's parents' house where we said our vows. Afterward we all went to John's favorite restaurant and had fried chicken, barbecued pork, corn fritters, okra and tomatoes, salad, creamed corn, squash soufflé, black-eyed peas, string beans, candied yams, candied apples, pecan pie, cherry pie, chocolate pie and meal pie. The bill came to $38.00.

It was very romantic.

# The Fog

*THE FOG* WAS MY FIRST FEATURE FILM. APRIL **1979**. SO long ago that they've remade it since I started writing this book. The papers refer to the "Adrienne Barbeau" role of Stevie Wayne. I can't tell you how strange that is for me.

First, it's strange to realize that there's a role I'm so identified with that its ownership is attributed to me and second, to realize that so much time has passed since I did it that I'm too old to do it again.

I didn't have any inkling at the time John was writing it that *The Fog* would become a classic of the genre and that twenty-five years later fans would be clamoring to have me sign their copy of the DVD.

I'd never seen a horror film until John showed me *Halloween*. Not *Psycho,* not *Night of the Living Dead,* not *Texas Chain Saw Massacre.* And I haven't seen many since. I love doing them, I don't like watching them. So when John gave me *The Fog* to read, I was disappointed. I knew it was well written but I just didn't get it. I wanted him to use his artistry to write IMPORTANT films like *The China Syndrome* and *Coming Home.* I wanted to tackle abortion rights and women's rights and civil rights. I wanted to make people think.

John wanted to make them jump. He wanted to get them on a visceral level. No thinking, no message. He wanted to give them the same experience he'd had as a boy when his mother had taken him to see *It Came from Outer Space* and he went running up the aisle in terror only to stop when he realized getting scared like that was the most fun thing ever. That's what he wanted to do for his audiences.

*The Fog* was the most difficult film he'd worked on to date: huge, unwieldy, and demanding. He'd just finished shooting *Elvis* with Kurt Russell but that was as a director for hire. *The Fog* was his screenplay, his direction, his music, and he only had a million dollars to shoot it with, on location with Janet Leigh (who impressed us every morning by jumping rope in a cashmere sweat suit), her daughter Jamie Lee Curtis, Tom Atkins, Nancy Loomis, John Houseman, and Hal Holbrook. And me, his wife.

It didn't help that we'd only been married three months and were both having difficulties adjusting. I was freaking out because I'd "lost my freedom" and he was disappointed because our courtship had ended. On top of that, his career had blown wide open and I was no longer working nonstop; six years of *Maude* had ended and I was turning down work in television so I could establish myself in films. He was exhausted and I was going crazy with nothing to do; I was questioning my talent and wondering if I would ever be a star. I was hoping *The Fog* would lead to other film offers.

We were determined to be very professional during the shoot. I even took my own motel room so we would be seen as director and actress and not husband and wife. We didn't want anyone thinking our relationship would single me out for special attention. That lasted about four hours. After spending the entire morning on the set without speaking to each other except when I was on camera, John finally said, "This isn't any fun," and we went back to being ourselves. John even used my mom in the film; she's one of the town dignitaries on the dais during the unveiling of the statue.

We shot most of the film in the Point Reyes National Seashore just north of San Francisco. I was in Montreal filming a miniseries when John went location scouting and found the lighthouse in Inverness, California. He called to tell me he'd found the place where he wanted to finish out his life. I understood what he meant as soon as I saw it.

As beautiful as it is, it was a difficult location to work in. To get to the lighthouse, the camera crew had to carry their equipment down 365 steps in thirty-mile-per-hour winds. When the winds got too strong, the National Park Service shut us down and we had to scramble to change locations.

We shot one of the lighthouse scenes on a soundstage. I had to crawl in fear to the top of the lighthouse, pursued by ghosts barely visible through the fog. Then suddenly the ghosts disappear and I am left relieved and confused as the fog drifts away.

This was 1979 and no one had a way to control the smoke we were using to simulate fog. They could blow it into the room and around the lighthouse but they couldn't suck it back out again when the ghosts disappeared. I had to act the scene in reverse: start with no fog around me, relieved and confused, and then shift to terror as the ghost was almost on top of me and less terror as he was coming toward me. Or something like that. I still can't explain it. All I know is that when I did it I had to be very careful not to blink because they were going to reverse the film in the editing process, and if I blinked, it would look strange.

John loved Stevie Wayne as much as I did. On the day I wrapped my scenes, he sent me three dozen roses with a note that read, "Being as close as I am to you, I had forgotten what an extraordinary actress you are. Shamelessly I admit, you are still my favorite star and I have fallen in love with Stevie Wayne." After he got home from seeing dailies that last night, I found him playing The Beach Boys' "Good Timing" and weeping with relief that I had worked in the role and that he had found the character he had been looking for all his life—the woman of his films.

But when he put the movie together, it didn't work. Halfway through the first screening, with only six of us in attendance, John asked me to step outside to talk. He felt he had failed; the movie wasn't scary. And the pain of making it was killing him. He asked if it would be all right with me if he quit directing. Of course it would, I said. Whatever he wanted to do was fine with me.

But he didn't quit, he just worked harder. The movie needed fixing, that's all. He and Tommy Wallace recut the second reel and planned some reshoots, which John was going to pay for himself. Avco Embassy couldn't believe he was so conscientious, telling him most directors just turn in their cut and walk away. They volunteered to absorb the cost.

In the meantime, we bought a house in Inverness.

John was sick on the day the realtor called to say she was listing our dream house and she thought it would probably be sold within hours. I got on a plane alone that night. The next morning I called John from Inverness.

"Well . . . how much do you trust me?"

"It's that good, huh?"

"It's our house, John, it's absolutely perfect."

We made an offer without him seeing it. We moved in on Labor Day weekend. He loved it.

The house was built by an architect for himself and his family. It had been featured in the *L.A. Times* magazine section and appeared in one of *Sunset* magazine's kitchen books. It was all rough-hewn cedar and glass: floor-to-ceiling windows, clerestories and skylights with a huge, round, sunken copper bathtub and an outdoor shower. Radiant-heated aggregate floors. All the beds and sofas and window seats were built-in. There was a separate studio with its own fireplace where John could write. It was on an acre of trees in the middle of the Point Reyes National Seashore, surrounded by forest with hiking trails leading down to the Pacific. If you stood on the sod roof, you could see the ocean. If you stood on the toilet, you could see Tomales Bay. If you stood in the kitchen, you could watch the deer eating loganberries three feet away.

I loved that house more than any place I've ever lived. It disappeared in a fire in 1995.

The first night we slept there was the night of the Jerry Lewis telethon. John loved staying up all night to see what kind of foolishness Jerry came up with. I lasted until 1:00 A.M. and then went to bed. At 4:00 A.M. I was awakened by John's voice coming from somewhere below the bed.

"Adrienne, Adrienne, wake up. Wake up."

John was on his hands and knees with a towel wrapped around his head.

"There's a bat in the living room," he said. I could barely understand him through the towel.

"What?"

"A bat. There's a bat in the living room. It's flying back and forth in front of the TV."

"So? Let it out."

"I'm not gonna let it out, are you nuts? It's got rabies! Do something. Call the cops or something." He pulled the towel tighter around his head.

"Oh, Jesus, John." I got up and went into the living room and opened the front and side doors. After a few minutes I saw a tiny shadow, about the size of a monarch butterfly, streak across the TV and out the door. I shut the doors and went back to bed. The Master of Horror was waiting for me, huddled under the blankets. He missed the end of the telethon.

We screened *The Fog* in Phoenix the day after our first anniversary. The audience loved it. Their comment cards singled out Nick Castle (Tom Atkins) and Stevie Wayne as their favorite characters. I thought I was all right. I'd never seen myself on a big screen before and I wondered if I was too dramatic.

Before *The Fog* opened in the States, it was in competition in the Fantasy Film Festival in Avoriaz, France. As producer of the film, Debra Hill (the woman John had been living with when we met) and her boyfriend, Michael Malone (the man I introduced her to several years after he and I had lived together), accompanied us to the French Alps. I'm sure the gossip about the four of us together was fast and furious but we were all good friends and enjoyed each other's company. We started in Paris, staying at the luxurious Plaza Athenée. John hates to travel. He came down with the flu as soon as we arrived and went right to bed. I went walking on the Champs-Elysees to buy him a camel-hair scarf for his birthday the next day. Debra and Michael and I had dinner together that night, astounded to be paying $10.00 for a bowl of onion soup.

Avoriaz was exquisite. A beautiful ski resort in Portes du Soleil accessible only by aerial tram. John spent the days doing interviews while I went shopping for ridiculous-looking fur boots. It was exhausting for him but worth the entire trip just to meet Roman Polanski and Claude Lelouche. Roman joined us for dinner after a screening of *The Fog* and John mustered up his courage to tell him what a fan he was of *The Tenant*. They spent the rest of the evening talking about the pain of directing. John said he could see the hurt in Roman's eyes as he remembered the critics' response to his film.

The demand for *The Fog* was so great, five screenings were scheduled—a first for the festival. They screened John's first feature, *Dark Star,* immediately before the awards ceremony. I was struck once again by his brilliance and I had tears in my eyes as I always did at the ending of that film. Then the announcements were made: *Time After Time* won the Grand Prize to scattered applause. *When a Stranger Calls* and *Mad Max* tied for the Jury's Prize and we were happy for George Miller, director of *Mad Max,* whom we'd just met. The TV Prize was next. Just when we thought the ceremony was over, Alberto Sordi announced *The Fog* as the winner of the Critics' Prize. "*C'est vraiment un film fantastique!*" he said. The audience went wild, standing up and yelling bravos, and the band started playing "Pomp and Circumstance." John stared at me, stunned, and once again I had tears in my eyes. There were fireworks going off in the snow outside the theater.

*The Fog* was a great success. President and Mrs. Carter requested a screening at the White House. John and I went on tour to promote the movie. *The New Yorker* did a profile on him. People began to recognize him on the street. He turned to me in the middle of Francis Ford Coppola's art deco suite at the Sherry-Netherlands, where we were staying, and said, "I never thought I'd be famous."

There was never any doubt in my mind.

# Answers to Frequently Asked Questions

Q: "Are they real?"

A: "Yes. Just sitting a little lower than twenty years ago."

Q: "How do you manage with twins at your age?"

A: "Video games. Lots of video games."

Q: "Did y'all have as much fun doing *Cannonball Run* as it looks like ya did?"

A: "No. But I got to meet Roger Moore."

I'd already met Burt Reynolds. After the way he'd said good-bye, I was pretty amazed when he called to ask me to be in the film. We'd only spoken once in the six years that had passed: when he asked me to direct *Grease* at his theater in Florida. I turned him down because I didn't think I could do a good job. *The Cannonball Run* is a comedy with a huge cast of characters, played by a huge cast of stars, all trying to win a cross-country car race. Burt wanted me to play a girl in a purple spandex jumpsuit who wins the race driving her black Lamborghini. *That* I could do.

Well, except for the driving part. I was too short to reach the pedals. We needed a stuntman for that.

We started filming in Georgia in June 1980. On Friday I was with John at the film festival in Cannes, eating croissants and drinking café au lait at the Hotel Majestic. On Saturday I was alone on a highway twelve miles south of Atlanta, eating orange cheese on white bread and drinking powdered Sanka at a Best Western motel.

I was one of the first to arrive. I sat out at the motel pool and watched this fascinating lineup of celebrities make their way to the lobby: Burt Reynolds, Dom DeLuise, Dean Martin, Sammy Davis, Jr., Roger Moore, Jamie Farr, Farrah Fawcett, Jack Elam, George Furth, Terry Bradshaw, Bert Convy, Mel Tillis, and Jackie Chan. Valerie Perrine, Molly Picon, Peter Fonda, and Bianca Jagger would be joining us later.

Apart from the day he'd invited me to his house to discuss doing the movie, this was the first time I'd spent with Burt since the infamous note on my windshield. I kept waiting for him to talk about our breakup but he never did. He had someone invite me to join him for dinner in his room one night but when I got there, he was ensconced in front of the TV and there was no mention of food. After forty-five minutes of silence while we watched some sports show, I left.

Filming started and everyone was having a good time, but I can't say anyone was thinking about acting. Burt's buddy and stunt double, Hal Needham, was directing. Hal's idea of a good day's filming was one in which we finished by noon. More time to party.

Jackie Chan was already a star in China. This was his second American film. He didn't find out until he arrived on the set that the character he was playing was Japanese. He wasn't happy about that.

I wasn't happy about any of it. I hated that no one took what we were doing seriously. Burt's attitude seemed to be, "It doesn't matter what we do, we can just screw around and the audience will buy it." He improvised most of his scenes with a humor that bordered on being vicious. At one point he struck Dom across the face, supposedly in character and in jest, but he was out of control and he slapped him hard. It took a second before Dom made the decision to laugh and then the ass-kissers on the set followed suit. If you look at the outtakes at the end of the movie, you'll see him do this again and again. And you'll see me not laughing.

I suppose my problem was that I took it too seriously. This was only my second feature film and I approached it the same way I approached *The Fog* and *Maude* and *Grease* and all the television films I'd made since *Houdini* and *Someone's Watching Me.* I had a character to create. I was making choices. Deciding what my motivation was. Everyone else was having a great time, and I was acting. It never once crossed my mind that my character was simply the crux of a running tit joke: stupid male becomes blithering idiot when faced with exposed mammaries.

I was also dealing with the insecurity of feeling that I'd only been hired because I was a friend of Burt's. I'd done *The Fog* because of my relationship with John. I was grateful to Burt but here was another job offer coming out of a personal relationship and not an audition. I needed to prove I was talented.

In *Cannonball Run?* In a purple spandex jumpsuit with a workable zipper? All the talent I needed was attached to my breastbone. But I didn't think that. I was worried about acting.

Farrah was not. She was at the height of her celebrity but she couldn't act and it didn't matter. She had great teeth and nipples that stood up on cue for the scene where she first meets Burt. You couldn't take your eyes off them. Sorry . . . her.

It rained hard the first week of production. We were doing a scene at the beginning of the movie, working outdoors at night with all the cars lined up to begin the race. Hal called "action" and we started for our places. Two of the actors were just feet away from the car they were driving when the huge crane that held a gigantic "moon" light above us sank into the rain-soaked mud and sliced the car in half. If Hal had spoken a minute sooner, they would have been dead. The car was a classic. A Cobra. The last one off the assembly line before they stopped making them. The owner was in tears.

We moved from Atlanta to Lancaster, California. The desert. Roger Moore showed up on the set in his all-white suit, playing a knockoff James Bond character named Seymour Goldfarb, Jr. He spent the day doing stunts in the dirt and I swear to God that suit was as white when he finished as when he started. He just looked absolutely perfect.

Actually, that was the only good part of the movie for me. Meeting Roger Moore and Dean Martin. Dean was a sweetheart of a man who never said one line of dialogue the way it was written. Forget getting a cue from him so you could deliver the right line. He simply went his merry way, making stuff up as it came into his head. He was so delightful it didn't matter. Roger, on the other hand, was very professional. He was also breathtakingly handsome and witty and charming. And clean. I was starstruck. The air conditioner in his trailer broke and he came to mine to hang out. I was dumbstruck, too. I couldn't believe I had Roger Moore all to myself and all I could think to talk about was the poor education in California schools. The spandex jumpsuit should have helped but it didn't. He was very gracious and chatty but for all the interest he paid in me, I could have been wearing sackcloth.

From Lancaster we went to Las Vegas. Sammy Davis, Jr. had a party in his suite and was afraid no one would come. He invited me four times and I was happy to attend but the desperation in his voice didn't give me much option anyway. I didn't want to let him down. Obviously I wasn't the only one with insecurities.

It was in Las Vegas that a second accident took place. This one much grimmer. I wasn't working that day; I was in the hotel when Valerie Perrine found me to tell me what had happened. An Aston-Martin, doubling for the one Roger Moore drove in the race, had been switched from a left-hand drive to a right-hand drive at the last minute and no one had allowed time to install seat belts. They were "losing the light" and in a hurry to get the shot. For the stunt, the car was going sixty miles an hour and heading straight for a van coming from the opposite direction. The stuntman driving the Aston-Martin was supposed to veer off at the last minute. Instead, the steering column locked and he crashed into the van. He and another stuntman had minor injuries but Heidi Von Beltz, a beautiful model, actress, and stuntwoman, who had just gotten engaged to the stunt coordinator, was riding in the passenger seat, doubling the actress playing Roger's girlfriend. Her neck was broken.

We kept on filming. The final scenes were in Redondo Beach. By that time, we knew Heidi was paralyzed from the neck down. Today Heidi is the founder of the Follow Your Heart Foundation for people with severe neuromuscular disorders and she has written a book about her path to recovery, *My Soul Purpose*. She can stand unassisted and is learning to walk. But at that time, her doctors told her she would never move again and would die within five years.

When people ask if I had a good time making *The Cannonball Run,* all I think about is that accident.

The movie got terrible reviews. "A crappy movie made by actors who seem to forget they are on camera . . . it has a complete lack of respect for its viewers." "A movie that should have crashed at the starting line." "AAA calculates better road trips." Farrah won a Razzie Award nomination for Worst Supporting Actress of 1982 for her performance. But it made money and people loved it. Fans still come up to tell me it's their favorite movie of all time. I met a professor who did his master's thesis on it because he loved it so much. And the people who think it's funny are certain I must have had the time of my life filming it. Well, no, but I did get to meet Roger Moore.

# Escape

**WE'RE AT THE CAST AND CREW SCREENING FOR**
*Escape from New York.* It's fall of 1980. A hundred friends
carrying on in a big roller rink at the corner of La Cienega
and Santa Monica Boulevards in West Hollywood.

Everyone is having a great time. We're bound together by
our excitement for the film and the feeling that all our careers
are beginning to break open. Larry Franco, our executive producer, assistant director, and Kurt Russell's brother-in-law, will
go on to great success as a producer (*Batman Begins, Jurassic
Park III, Mars Attacks!*), as will Barry Bernardi, our associate
producer (*The Longest Yard, The Devil's Advocate*). Jeff
Chernov, our second assistant director, will hire me in 1993
when he produces *Father Hood,* starring Patrick Swayze. An
eighteen-year-old production assistant, David DeCoteau,
directs me in 2004 in *Ring of Darkness.* Nick Castle, who has
cowritten the script and music for *Escape,* will continue to

write and direct (*Hook, The Last Starfighter*), and James Cameron, who has done the matte paintings on our film, becomes known worldwide for directing *Titanic* and writing the *Terminator* films. Debra Hill will become one of Hollywood's best-known and most popular female producers.

But tonight we're just a bunch of friends celebrating the end of a seven-week shoot. I look around and realize I can't find John. It takes me a half-hour to get through the crowd. He's in a little anteroom filled with pinball machines and Pac Man. He's not alone. Kelli, the PR girl on the film, is with him. Their heads are together and there's something intimate about the way they're talking. They don't hear me come in. Two crew members are standing across the room. They see me see John and Kelli and the look on their faces makes me uncomfortable. I back out of the room unseen by anyone else.

*Escape from New York* is the third film John and I have done together. It's also our last but we don't know that right now.

We shoot it in St. Louis and L.A. Only one scene in the movie is actually shot in New York: the opening dolly shot passing the Statue of Liberty. The movie takes place in 1997 when Manhattan has been turned into a maximum-security prison. Air Force One is shot down over the island and Kurt Russell's character, an ex-Army officer turned bank robber named Snake Plissken, has twenty-four hours to rescue the President before the explosive the government has injected into Snake's arm dissolves, killing him and his chance for freedom.

St. Louis has had a terrible fire, leaving a downtown area in rubble. There's an abandoned bridge and the city's Union Station is in ruins. They're perfect for the exteriors John needs and for a fight scene that takes place in a massive wrestling ring. My character, Maggie, and her boyfriend, Brain, played by Harry Dean Stanton, live inside a giant library. We shoot that at the University of Southern California.

Once again John has written a Howard Hawks-type woman's role for me. This time she's serving a life sentence in maximum security. She's dressed in great-looking rags and stiletto boots and she knows how to defend herself. I want Maggie to be as authentic as possible. I need a logical reason for everything about her. We're in a prison on an island. Where am I going to get nail polish? Melt down batteries and paint my nails silver. A clip for my too-curly hair? Cook a turkey, clean the breastbone, and put a drumstick through it. That's what I do. As for the stiletto boots, well, I figure some Italian had a shoe store in the Bowery before the government took over.

John wants Kurt Russell in the film. They've just finished working together on *Elvis,* and Kurt was hysterically funny in *Used Cars,* but the studio doesn't see him as an action hero. Charles Bronson lobbies for the role. John thinks he's too old. The studio wants Tommy Lee Jones. John holds out for Kurt and wins. "He's my kind of actor," John says. "He knows what's going on, knows his lines, hits his marks, and there isn't a lot of bullshit."

John has also worked with Season Hubley in *Elvis.* She and Kurt met and fell in love on the set when she played

Priscilla to his Elvis. They married soon after we did and Season has recently given birth to their son, Boston. Season is playing the Chock Full O'Nuts girl.

John has directed Donald Pleasence before, too, in *Halloween*. Donald keeps me laughing through the whole shoot. Years before, when I was doing *Fiddler,* I used to hear him through the walls of my dressing room, screaming from the theater next door as he performed *The Man in the Glass Booth*. Now he keeps up a running commentary sotto voce as we prepare to do our scenes. There are times I'm laughing so hard I have to ask John to wait before he rolls the camera so I can get myself together.

The one thing I'll always remember about Donald, who was one of Britain's most popular television stars, had done close to 200 films and telefilms, and starred on Broadway seven times, was the comment he made to John about his career. "I could have had a totally different career," he said, "a prestigious career, George C. Scott's career, if I hadn't had three ex-wives to support."

We're staying in a very nice hotel near the Arch in downtown St. Louis. The hotel management tells us the neighborhood isn't safe after dark. Donald takes the warning seriously. He hires a cab to drive him to the restaurant across the street.

Ernie Borgnine is playing Cabbie; he's our transportation in the prison. Whenever I run into him in the hotel lobby, he's memorizing lines for the one-man show he's planning to take on the road when we finish. He's worried about being able to remember an hour-and-a-half's worth of dialogue. I suggest hypnosis and self-relaxation techniques. He looks at me like I'm nuts.

We're working nights. John can sleep during the day but I'm an early riser no matter what time I get to bed. I nap in the afternoon and spend my mornings in antique stores. The set decorators are going to have to transport major pieces back to L.A. by truck so I don't have to limit myself to small purchases. I buy a great iron bed (which I still have) and Fiestaware and antique quilts. The set decorators give me an original Morris chair.

I don't visit the set unless I'm working. St. Louis is in the middle of a heat wave. The tar on the streets is so hot it's melting. We have actors who are supposed to drop out of helicopters and hit the street running. They keep landing in the soft pavement, twisting their ankles and breaking bones.

We film my favorite scene on the abandoned bridge. Maggie has a line to Brain as they're careening over the bridge with Snake driving Cabbie's taxi. Brain says, "Slow down a little, Snake. I think they've got mines up ahead," and Maggie says, "You think?" I love that line, it makes me laugh.

Then Brain is killed and Maggie stands her ground to avenge his death in front of the Duke's oncoming car. She turns to Snake, puts out her hand, and he throws her his gun. She stands stock-still and fires repeatedly at the Duke as he's heading right for her. John sees it as a "Hawksian" scene: two people (Maggie and Snake) who understand each other without speaking. I don't have Howard Hawks for a reference, I just know all Maggie's morality and ethics and honor are expressed in that one action.

Months later, when John has put the film together and screens it for a preview audience, we realize that Maggie's self-sacrifice is ambiguous. The scene ends with me firing at the Duke's car. People aren't sure whether I've been killed or not. Production has already wrapped and we're back in Los Angeles. I put on Maggie's costume once again, cook another turkey so I'll have a hair clip, lie down on the cement floor of our garage, and let John pour fake blood around my head. Then he shoots twenty seconds of film of me holding my breath with my eyes closed and Maggie becomes most definitely dead.

John and I always have a great time working together but *Escape* puts a strain on our marriage. I really don't understand the toll directing is taking on him: the physical exhaustion and emotional debilitation. I finish work and I'm ready to play. He's living with the job twenty-four hours a day. He's exhausted and I'm not empathizing. I don't understand how he can stay in the hotel room his entire day off and not even want to go to the dining room for dinner. It feels like he only has energy for his work and none for me. When we first met, he told me taking responsibility was his "raison d'être." I've come to realize he meant taking responsibility as a *director*. I'm angry when he doesn't deal with the responsibilities of day-to-day living. He thinks I'm selfish and demanding. Before we left L.A., we'd just closed escrow on a new house, a fifty-year-old Spanish hacienda on an acre of land in Studio City. He's blaming me for putting him in the position of having to continue to work to pay for it. He feels responsible for me when I'm on location with him. I think I'm being a great wife by taking care of myself alone while he's working. He asks me to leave as soon as I finish filming my scenes. I'm hurt by his rejection. We disappoint each other daily.

We had probably rushed into our marriage too soon. We love each other deeply but we really didn't know each other. In his desire to make it work, John threw himself over when we first met. He did things for me that I took for granted were a part of his personality but they weren't really. John is not gregarious by nature; unless he's working he doesn't like to leave the house. I love people, love to socialize, love to go out. Once we were secure in our love for each other, we discovered we didn't have a lot in common. We believed in therapy, we could talk about our problems for hours, but that's where the similarities ended.

We'd done our best to accommodate our differences. If I wanted to take a walk or shop or swim or bowl or ride a bike, go dancing or go to a nice restaurant, I went with friends. If I wanted to eat with him on the weekend, I waited until 2:00 P.M. when he awakened. If he wanted to watch black-and-white movies on television, he watched them alone. If he wanted to fly his helicopter, he flew alone.

That worked while we were both unemployed or when we

were both working on separate projects. But here on location together in St. Louis, with John under enormous pressure and me feeling unimportant to him, we're in trouble.

The day after the cast party, John tells me Kelli, the PR girl, has asked him to sleep with her. I was right in my interpretation of what I saw in the bowling alley. I'm stunned. I can't believe it. This is a woman I know. We work together. How can she do this? How can she have so little regard for the fact that John is married?

John seems bemused by it and maybe a little bit flattered. He doesn't understand why I'm so upset.

And I am. Extremely so. The next day I fly to New York. By the time the plane lands, I'm so depressed I can barely move. Literally. I don't want to get off the plane. It feels like my entire existence has been threatened. The only thing that keeps me functioning is having to make conversation with my driver and the hotel staff when I check in.

John flies in the next day. He has the dolly shot to film at the Statue of Liberty. I'm a wreck. My reaction is way out of proportion to having some chick make a pass at my husband, especially when he didn't take her up on it. John is worried about me. He points out that I have made him more important than anything else in my life, myself included. He's right, I have. It's a responsibility he doesn't want.

We fly back to L.A. the next day. He goes into the editing room and I go back into therapy.

# Swamp Thing

**I WALK OUT OF A PRIVATE SCREENING OF *SWAMP THING*** and call John in tears.

"It's god-awful," I say. "My hair looks like shit, my costumes look like shit, and I can't even see what my makeup looks like because the lighting is so dark I can barely see the actors. What am I going to do? How can I go on the road and promote this? I can't ask people to spend six dollars on something I don't believe in. What am I going to tell Wes? He's never going to understand and he's going to hate me. But I can't lie!"

A month later, Siskel and Ebert give it two thumbs up. Label it a cult classic.

What do I know?

I love the first draft of the screenplay when I read it. It's 1981 and I've just finished *Escape from New York.* Put a gun in my hand, let me blow away the bad guys, and I'm in heaven. Angelina Jolie and Charlize Theron, future action heroines, are only six. There aren't too many actresses giving Arnold a run for his money. I get to be one of them.

I've only seen one horror film in my life, *Halloween,* and that was under duress—I was engaged to the director. I watched the entire movie screaming and grabbing onto John and praying for it to be over. So I'm definitely not a fan of the genre and I've never heard of Wes Craven, the man who's written and will direct *Swamp Thing.* But John knows his work and raves about him. He's more excited about me doing the film than I am.

Wes is a lovely guy. Very gentle. A quiet man who was raised as a Baptist and never saw a movie until he was a senior in college. He's been making up for it by directing films like *The Hills Have Eyes* and *Last House on the Left.* I haven't seen them but from what John says, I suspect they make *The Fog* look like a Disney film.

The script he's written for *Swamp Thing* is witty and tender and fun. I have high hopes for it. Secretly, I think to myself it could be as successful as *Star Wars.*

What I don't know is that the budget isn't enough to pay for one R2-D2, let alone film an entire movie on location in Charleston, South Carolina, for seven weeks.

I arrive in Charleston, completely enchanted with its old, quiet beauty. The producer meets me at the airport with the concierge from the hotel where I will be staying. They've given me a large suite with a beautiful sunset view. I'm a little disappointed I'm not downtown with the rest of the crew but their hotel is old, the rooms are small and depressing, and there are hundreds of people milling around the lobby. I'll be alone but I appreciate the arrangements they've made for me in this genteel town.

There's a sign on a store window down the street from the hotel: Up for Adoption. Born at Charleston Memorial Hospital. Inquire within.

Maybe it's not quite so genteel.

The first few days are okay. Seems like a lot of the crew has hay fever. A lot of red noses. Wes is very laid-back. His strength lies in getting the performances he wants from the actors. Reggie Batts, the fourteen-year-old who plays Jude, has never acted before and Wes works with him in an easy, non-defensive way. It's fun for me to watch the character I'm playing, Lt. Cable, take shape in a way I hadn't expected, thanks to his direction. I trust him.

The assistant director, on the other hand, is *so* laid-back I can't figure out if he cares at all about what we're doing. We start falling behind schedule. He doesn't take control and he doesn't communicate very well. No one ever seems to know what's going on. People keep walking off the set to go to the bathroom and returning with the sniffles. No one says we're printing a take or checking the gate or moving on to another scene. Whenever I ask the A.D. a question, he says, "I don't know. I haven't read the script." He seems to take pride in not knowing what he's doing.

It's the stunt coordinator who finally points out that we

can't mount a camera on our second Jeep to save time while we're filming with the first, because the second jeep has been totaled. And since no one bothers to replace the dead battery on the first Jeep, we have to push it to get it started every time we need it.

The stunt guys are great. They sit around all day comparing scars. One of them has a leg that looks like chopped, raw hamburger. The other has developed a fire-retardant gel that enables him to set his whole body on fire and run around in flames for a minute or more. He can't wait to do it.

This is the first movie where I've had to do any serious stunts. All Maggie did in *Escape* was shoot Isaac Hayes, and in *The Cannonball Run,* I was too short to even reach the pedals on the Lamborghini. It's never crossed my mind that I could get hurt. It's the movies, for God's sake, it's not real. What can happen?

I don't get nervous until the stunt coordinator tells me that if I fall while the truck is chasing me through the swamps, I should just stay where I am and they'll try not to run over me.

There are snakes in the water and gators, I suppose. The only things that bother me are the parasites and leeches. We have to stuff our ears with cotton and wash with antibacterial soap as soon as we get out. It doesn't help that the actor playing the bad guy is a macho stuntman wannabe who throws me around like I'm an ex-girlfriend he's got a grudge against. I haven't been hit like that since Gorgeous George threw a chair at me in the ring when I was Miss Wrestling for

Channel 18 in San Francisco. (It was a job my mother arranged. I walked around the ring in a bathing suit, holding up a card to announce which round was starting.) My whole body is bruised and aching.

And itchy. I never sleep through the night the entire time we're in Charleston. I'm sure I've got ticks and chiggers burrowing into my back.

Dick Durock, who plays Swamp Thing, suffers more than any of us. He's a sweetheart of a man who's been hired to spend twelve hours a day, five days a week, in a cheap, rubber creature suit. Without a zipper. It's 97 degrees outside, 100 percent humidity, and this guy can't even go to the bathroom. He's constantly in danger of heatstroke. Every time he does a stunt, the rubber tears and of course, there's no double for the costume. We've got to wait while they glue patches on him, wait for the glue to dry, and then hope to hell the whole thing doesn't come apart.

My costume situation isn't much better. There are days when I show up to work and no one's even brought a costume for that day's scenes. And the ones I have don't fit. I'm not seeing dailies because we're working such long hours it's all I can do to take off my makeup before I fall asleep. By the time I see a video of some edited footage, it's too late. I hate the way I look and I hate what I'm wearing and I really have no one to blame but myself. Budget or no budget, I should have made sure I was happy with the wardrobe before I set foot on the set.

The one man who's always on the set is the completion guarantor. He controls the money. He's also acting in the movie. As we start falling behind schedule, he insists that Wes cut entire scenes—none of his, of course—and make major changes in the script to cheapen the production. The crew, a lot of whom are union members working under false names on a nonunion contract, isn't getting overtime. We're working fourteen-hour days. After two weeks they threaten to walk unless their contracts are renegotiated or we cut back to twelve hours. The makeup artist—the only one for the entire cast because the producers won't pay for two—arrives at work one morning to find all her equipment on the ground at the set because the producers didn't pay the rent on the makeup trailer and the owner drove it away.

Louis Jourdan is the other star in the film. He's playing Arcane, the master villain. I'm honored to be in a film with the suave Frenchman who starred in *Can-Can* and *Gigi* and *Three Coins in a Fountain.* I'm hoping I can practice my French but he barely speaks to me. He barely speaks his lines, for that matter. We set up a scene where he has his men capture Swamp Thing in a net and string him up a tree. Mr. Jourdan tells Wes where he wants the camera placed and then announces that he will raise his hand and point it to the sky and mouth the word "now" and Wes can put the dialogue in later.

Mr. Jourdan's son dies of a drug overdose while we are filming. I don't know how he manages to continue.

It takes me four weeks to realize that the hay fever that seems so rampant around me is actually cocaine use. Two of the local crew members are busted for drugs and we fall even further behind schedule. Someone accidentally sets fire to the church set and mistakenly tries to use a fake, foam rubber prop extinguisher to put it out. The director of photography is fired on a Saturday and rehired on Sunday when half the crew threatens again to walk. Wes is forced to cut more scenes.

On a day off I go to see an advance screening of *Raiders of the Lost Ark*. There's Karen Allen doing a fantastic job playing a strong woman. She lights up the screen. All I can think about is how shitty I look in this movie—old and ugly.

In the midst of all this negativity, Wes and the crew present me with a bouquet of roses with a card signed, "From Wes and all the gang, with respect." It's the nicest thing that's happened to me since we started filming. In June they have a birthday party for me and give me a beautiful, antique kimono. This is the worst work experience I've had since I was go-go dancing under black lights at Uncle Joe's Tavern by the Newark bus stop, but the one good thing about it is that, basically, everyone is very nice.

Which makes it all the harder when I see the finished product. I can't even judge the movie fairly because I hate the way I look, the way I'm dressed, and the way I'm lit. I should have gone to dailies, I should have refused to wear the wardrobe I hated, I should have come up with a hairstyle that looked good in the humidity. The people I trusted to make me look good, didn't, and I was worried I'd be labeled a prima donna if I demanded more time to make things right. I was so concerned with getting the movie made on schedule and on budget that I didn't look out for myself on screen. Now all I can do is hope no one sees the film.

The critics love it, though, which is a happy surprise for me, and I do, in the end, promote the film. Not extensively, but enough, I hope. It doesn't really matter because the audiences love it without any encouragement from me. No one complains about my curly hair. No one complains about my cheesy evening gown. They love the movie. Wes did a great job and that's what they respond to—a love story between a girl and a green monster. I've made more than thirty movies since *Swamp Thing* but it's one of the films people always remember.

I just wish I looked better than the monster.

# *Creepshow*

**"OH, JUST CALL ME 'BILLIE,' EVERYONE DOES."**

Every horror fan loves that line. It's the first thing I hear if I'm signing autographs for fans. They love the movie it comes from, too: *Creepshow.*

Of all the films I've done, Billie is my favorite character. I love Stevie Wayne in *The Fog* because she's a hero and she's got a great voice, I love Maggie in *Escape from New York* because she looks so great, she's so deadpan in her delivery, and she's such a fighter, but I love Billie most of all because she's such an unmitigated bitch. She's so much fun.

I almost turned down the role.

My agents sent me the script. I was being offered the part of Hal Holbrook's wife in a George Romero film of a Stephen King script. Fritz Weaver, Leslie Nielsen, Ted Danson, Viveca Lindfors, E. G. Marshall, and Stephen King himself were all cast. Very classy, I thought.

Until I read the script. And then I thought, *Oh, I can't do this. This is too gruesome, too gross, too vile.*

I hadn't met George. I didn't know anything about him. John went nuts when I told him I didn't think I wanted to do it. He's a huge fan of George's. He went on and on about *Night of the Living Dead* and what a master of the horror genre George Romero is and how I'd be crazy to pass up the opportunity to work with him.

I called Tommy Atkins. Tom and I met when he married one of my best friends; we went on to become best friends ourselves and had already worked together in *The Fog* and *Escape from New York.* He's a brilliant actor. He and George are both from Pittsburgh and they're good friends, too. He was already cast in *Creepshow.*

"Adie," he said, "you're reading it all wrong. You need to talk to George, get an understanding of how he intends to make the movie. It's a comic book, a cartoon. It's not going to be real; it's funny. Go back and read it again with that in mind and you'll see what I mean."

I read it again. I still wasn't sure about it but I figured I just didn't know the genre and so I'd better take a chance.

I'd never done a role like Wilma ("Oh, just call me 'Billie'"). This was not my normal, run-of-the-mill character. She was a drunk, loud and vicious and nasty. And she was big. Over the top. I'd just learned how to keep everything small for the camera and now here I was being asked to overact up a storm. And I've never been drunk in my life. Not even tipsy.

The first thing I said to George when I got to Pittsburgh was, "Look, I'm going to do what I think I should do with this role and if it's not right, you'd better send me home because I really don't know what else to do."

George had his hands full. This was his first feature using "name" actors—he'd used only local talent before—and Viveca Lindfors and Carrie Nye were already a handful. Hal Holbrook showed up looking great, very sexy in cowboy boots, a work shirt, jeans, a turquoise belt, and a leather vest, a far cry from the buttoned-up university professor he was going to play. Fritz Weaver was an absolute sweetheart. The three of us were working together in the longest of the five separate episodes that made up the film: "The Crate." It's the story of a university professor who receives delivery of a crate filled with some unknown monster that kills anything that gets near it. The professor's wife is so horrid he lures her into the basement where the crate is stored and begs the monster to eat her.

The audience has to think the professor's wife, Wilma, is just the bitch of all time. They're rooting for her to bite the bullet. But Wilma doesn't see herself that way. She thinks she's justified in her behavior. I had to understand why she acted the way she did, to love her and accept her. Otherwise I'd just be an actress acting nasty, a one-dimensional character with no humanity. Ultimately, I think that's why she works so well. Everyone remembers "Billie."

Making the movie was a lesson in trust. Every day George asked me to go all out, be a little bigger, take chances. I felt like I was huge, like I was "chewing the scenery," overacting up a storm, but I figured it was George's movie and he knew what he wanted, and I just had to trust that what he wanted was what would work.

I had a ball. Once I settled into the style George wanted, I just became more and more outrageous. It was great fun. The whole experience was one of the best I've ever had. I loved Pittsburgh. I spent my off days antiquing, stocking up on Fiestaware and antique quilts. I loved meeting Stephen King, whose career as a horror novelist was just taking off and who was wondering whether he should build a fence around his house because biker gangs kept stopping by. Most of all, I fell in love with George and his wife, Chris. We became lifelong friends and I jumped at the chance to work with George eight years later when he asked me to do *Two Evil Eyes.* I would go anywhere, anytime, to work with George again.

After all, he gave me the opportunity to immortalize the line, "Get out of the way, Henry, or I swear to God you'll be wearing your balls for earrings."

# John Cody Carpenter

"**I'm dying! I'm dying! Give me something, please.** I'm dying."

"You're not dying. You're in labor. How do you think your mother had you? How do you think your grandmother had her? You're not dying. Now breathe!"

It wasn't me that was screaming. It was the woman in the room next door to mine. I'd been in labor twenty-four hours already and I was trying to sleep through the racket but it wasn't easy. I didn't want any pain medication and my own contractions were violent, but they must have been nothing compared to what I was hearing.

The next morning, when my nurse came in, I asked her how the woman next door was doing.

"Oh, she's Armenian," she said. "They all think they're dying."

Well, that was enough for me. No one was going to hear

a sound. I had the reputation of the entire Armenian woman-hood to rectify. I sang, I hummed, I counted, but I never let out a scream.

It wasn't easy. My contractions had started two nights before, as I was going to bed. John was in Nashville, directing *Starman* with Jeff Bridges and Karen Allen. I was home alone. I tossed and turned throughout the night and called the doctor in the morning. Nancy Loomis and I were giving a wedding shower for a friend. I had twenty strangers coming to my house to celebrate and I damn well didn't want to leave for the hospital any sooner than I had to.

The last guest left about four o'clock and there I was, squatting in the kitchen doing my breathing exercises. Nancy drove me to the hospital.

They didn't want to admit me because I wasn't very dilated but the pains were intense and I had no one at home to drive me back again if they got any worse, so I asked to check in. I called John. I knew the baby was on the way and I was hoping John could make it to L.A. in time. He didn't want to take the chance he'd miss work on Monday so he decided to stay in Nashville. I hung up the phone, wept for a few minutes with disappointment that he couldn't be there, and got down to work.

I'd always known I wanted children and, after fifteen years of working nonstop as an actress, I was ready. It hadn't happened right away. I became pregnant with Cody on the last day of my six-month run in Tom Eyen's play *Women Behind Bars* at the Roxy on the Sunset Strip. John was happy, and my life was complete.

Having the baby was hard work and it was great fun. Nancy stayed with me, and her husband, Tommy Wallace, joined us. My friend and Spanish teacher, Sylvia Ossorio, coached my breathing and her husband stopped by. Tom Atkins and Garn Stephens spent the evening. Friends came to visit throughout Sunday night and all day Monday. There were so many people in the room, my doctor had to ask some of them to party in the hall.

I didn't want any drugs and I didn't want a C-section. After thirty-six hours of intense labor, Dr. Aronberg told me I was going to need one; the contractions weren't doing their job. I fell apart. I wanted a vaginal delivery without drugs. She agreed to give me Pitocin to induce labor but if nothing had changed in two hours, she was going to have to operate.

I went from three centimeters to ten in less than an hour and a half. Cody was born at 6:57 P.M. on Monday, May 7, 1984. It was almost 9:00 P.M. in Nashville. I called John. "He looks like an angel," I said.

John came home a week later. I met him at the airport in a limousine so we could cuddle with our new son in the back-seat during the ride back. When we got home, I took Cody upstairs to change his diaper. John was sitting on the sofa when I came back down. He was upset.

I thought he'd be overjoyed at being home with his new son. I was wrong. He *was* joyful about Cody, but he was feeling alone and unappreciated. I'd had the house painted while he was gone and I hadn't yet rehung all his movie posters in the living room. He took that as a sign that he wasn't important enough to me.

A month later he told me he couldn't stay in our marriage.

I was broadsided. I really never saw it coming. Or maybe I did and I was in denial. My girlfriend Eve once said to me about my mother, "She always made it sound like everything was great in her marriage and then one day your father just walked in and asked for a divorce." I knew it couldn't happen that way, and yet that's how it felt with John. We'd had our problems, but I never thought they were insurmountable. I believed love overcame everything.

We spent the next four months seeing a therapist. Two hours a day, three days a week. I still can't remember her name. After every session we sat in the Old World Restaurant in Westwood, eating lunch and crying. In addition to that, I was seeing my own therapist. It was a different kind of therapy for me because she never spoke about herself unless I asked. It took a long time for me to ask her anything—the lesson I'd learned early on when my father left: if you ask for something, you run the risk of rejection.

But here I was with John, asking him to stay. The counselor

wanted to know why I wanted to be with someone who didn't want to be with me. After four months, she said it was time to make a decision. I'd been going to counseling to save my marriage. I thought we could change, fix things. John was going so he could leave. From early on in our marriage, he'd felt he was disappointing me; Cody's birth changed that. He'd finally made me happy and that released him from a huge burden. He was too responsible to just walk out on me; he wanted me to say I understood. We were two people who loved each other but who really didn't belong together. He'd met someone with whom he had much more in common, he said. They were just friends but their friendship had made him realize what he was missing. Living with me required too great a compromise.

I've suffered great pain only four times in my life: when my father left; when my best friend succumbed to cancer; when Leticia, my dearest friend and housekeeper, lost her three-year-old daughter in an auto accident; and when my marriage ended. John and I worked hard to separate with grace—without anger or guilt—but the sense of failure was overwhelming. It took months for us to admit that we'd separated. I lost that whole year, the first year of Cody's life, to a haze of depression and humiliation. I hardly remember a thing.

John moved out on Easter Sunday, 1985.

# The Healer

**"THE MARRIAGE FAILED," I SAY. THE MAN I'M TALKING** to is six-five and weighs about 200 pounds.

"It didn't fail. It worked for six years and then it ended. You learned from it." He has black shoulder-length hair, a black beard, green eyes, and high cheekbones. He looks like every man I've ever dated.

"What did I learn? How to make a marriage fail?" Actually he looks like my mother. Except for the beard.

"You learned from it, you just don't know it yet."

"Yeah, well, whatever I learned, the price was too high."

"Look, the only thing that exists is this moment."

"No, that doesn't work for me. 'Cause this moment is too painful and I have to believe it's gonna get better in the future or I'll never be able to get through it."

"It will. Some time in the next seventy-two hours you will feel a shift to a greater clarity. And the parts of yourself that no longer work for you, parts of your thinking process you want to eliminate, will be gone."

He is a healer. That's what he does for a living. Travels the world teaching seminars on metaphysics and self-healing. He's been written about in *Omni* magazine as having the ability to alter bacteria with his hands.

He is my introduction to the philosophy of metaphysics.

I first hear about him from Douglas, the masseur who is working on my back. As he works, I wonder if I'll ever feel another man's hands on my body except during a massage. It's the spring of 1986, two years since my marriage came apart.

"I went to a weekend seminar up in Mount Shasta," Douglas says. "It was fantastic."

"A seminar about what?"

"Healing. Learning how to heal yourself. Led by this guy, Dennis Adams."

"You mean, like physical healing?" I'm as healthy as the proverbial ox and Douglas doesn't seem to be suffering, either.

"Well . . . physical, emotional, spiritual, psychic. We actually formed a body and did healing work on each part."

He's lost me. Too much Southern California woo-woo esoterica. The more he talks, though, the more I can tell that the experience has had a strong impact on him. I wonder if this kind of healing could help me get out of the emotional pit I've been in since John left. Douglas hits one of those spots on my back that just radiates pain and the conversation ends.

A month later he brings me a brochure announcing a similar workshop to be held in L.A. Dennis Adams's picture is on the cover.

"I know this man," I say.

"You do?"

"Well, I feel as though I do. I've seen him before or he looks like someone I know." I'm immediately drawn to him. I feel I have to go to his introductory lecture; he has something to say that I need to hear. And besides, I like his face. I want to see what the rest of him looks like.

Well, he's funny, humble, down to earth, and sexy. I'm not sure what to make of his metaphysical philosophy but I'm fascinated by the man himself. I wonder who gave him the huge pearl ring he's wearing. I wonder why the nails on his pinkie fingers are so long. I wonder what it's like having people believe you can heal their ills. I wonder what kind of a lover he is.

We do a meditation at the end of the lecture—sort of a state of self-hypnosis and deep relaxation. I end up weeping. I'm feeling sorry for myself, I think, or lonely. Something he says during the meditation seems to ease my sadness a bit.

I'm still nursing Cody, and can't be away from him for an entire weekend, so I can't attend the workshop. I thank Dennis and leave. When I get home it's late but I can't get to sleep. It's three in the morning before I close my eyes and then I dream that Dennis is in the room with me.

I awaken early and call Douglas. Can I arrange for an

individual workshop with Dennis? He explains the workshop works because of the group consciousness but if I'd like, Dennis is willing to do a private healing on me when Douglas comes to give me a massage.

The healing is not what I expect. There's no hands-on touching or anything. He asks me some questions, moves his hands a few inches over my body, and then tells me I will begin to feel changes within the next three days. Afterward, the three of us sit in the living room drinking coffee and laughing.

The next day, well within the predicted seventy-two hours, Dennis comes over to spend the afternoon and evening. We drive Mulholland in the light rain, stop at one of the outlooks to talk, go to Santino's for dinner. Cody is at his dad's. We go back to my house. I light a fire and a joint.

"You're telling me I created this marriage because I knew it was going to fail? Why would I do that? What am I supposed to learn from that?"

As I ask that question an answer flashes through my mind but I'm too stoned to hold on to it. At the same time, I feel a weight lift off my shoulders. I have a physical sensation of something rising from me, leaving me. *I'm stoned,* I think. *This only seems important because I've been smoking. I'll try to figure it out tomorrow. See if I can remember what the thought was.*

When tomorrow comes, that moment is the first thing I remember. I feel lighter, less burdened. My depression has lifted. Is this what he meant by healing?

And suddenly the thought comes to me. I know clearly what lesson it is I was supposed to learn.

All my life I believed that if my marriage failed, I would not survive. I would collapse. I would not be able to function. This had happened to my mother when her parents opposed her marriage to my father and to my twenty-year-old sister when her boyfriend left her. My mother had a breakdown. My sister wept for weeks. I was sure if my marriage ended, I would fall apart. I wouldn't be able to survive.

Well, my marriage ended and I survived. Not only have I survived, I survived intact. I still have my child and my friends and my home and my career. My estranged husband is still my friend. I'm not in a hospital. I'm not on heavy meds. I'm doing just fine. I'm okay. My marriage ended and I didn't die. And knowing that, I know that no broken love affair will ever be that painful again. If I can survive that, I can survive almost anything.

Dennis was right.

*That* is the lesson I needed to learn.

# More Healing

I SPENT THE NEXT SEVERAL MONTHS WITH DENNIS, seducing him into a full-blown romance. It wasn't easy because my competition for his attention was the "different state of consciousness" that he wanted to achieve; one he didn't believe should include a sexual relationship. When we got too close, he'd invoke his service to "the universe" and pull away. He didn't think he could have attachments and serve the universe at the same time. It took a while for him to trust that I wasn't going to make any major demands on him.

I'd had two dates during the year since John left; both of them with an agent at CAA who'd screwed my brains out and then put me on his "phone list" as in "Oh, I've got you on my list to call next week, I've just been so busy." That was traumatic enough, given my fragile emotional state after the separation from John.

Now I was attracted to a man who was sure we were connected in a past life, during the time of Christ. A man who believed he could heal people with his hands. I actually found myself believing he might be an "ascended master," the next Christ figure, the next true healer who changes mankind for all time.

I was smoking a lot of grass.

And if Dennis was that master, then why me? Why was I the one chosen to be close to him? I hadn't been to church since I was twelve, when my mother stopped taking us because it made her cry. I had no interest in organized religion. I lived by the Golden Rule and that was about it.

Dennis called me "a higher being of light." My soul was a high soul, he said.

I don't know about my soul, but I was high all right. A *lot* of grass.

Dennis liked to shop. He liked to eat in nice restaurants. He liked to walk, to swim, to travel, to party. All the things I'd given up doing when I married John. And in spite of his commitment to the universe, he did like making love.

He traveled a lot with his work so we only saw each other every few weeks. We spent weekends in San Francisco and Mount Shasta and Santa Cruz. I took him to the Kentucky Derby in Louisville. I wrote him long letters and we spent hours talking on the phone. I was terrified of being hurt again but I didn't want to hold anything back. I wanted to let go of all restrictions, all caution, all good sense.

When I could, I attended his workshops. I came to realize

that a lot of what he taught was the way I already lived my life. I'd just never put words to it. "When you judge someone," he said, "you eliminate fifty percent of your ability to understand them." I didn't judge John; I understood why he had to leave. I didn't judge the agent; I understood that he didn't call because he was afraid of getting close. I'd never been very judgmental, but after listening to Dennis speak, I made a conscious effort to stop.

Dennis helped me put my belief system into words. I read Terry Cole Whitaker, motivational speaker and hostess of an Emmy-winning television ministry, and took her advice to worry less about what other people thought of me. I read Shakti Gawain, a leading teacher in the field of metaphysics, and accepted her theory that we create much of what happens in our lives ourselves in order to learn from it. Dennis talked about the power of affirmations: the ability to bring into being what you envision. I wasn't quite ready to tackle the big things like love and career but I started imagining available parking spots when I needed them and, lo and behold, they were there. He also talked about the downside of taking responsibility for other people and how that robs them of the ability to grow. I stopped trying to control things quite so much. And he talked about the power of words and language. I stopped using negative phrases like, "I always get nervous when . . ." or "I've never been able to . . ."

But the major lesson I learned was to ask for what I want.

When I was twelve and my parents were fighting, I begged my father not to leave. That didn't work. He left. No one ever explained that he wasn't leaving *me.* I was the one who had asked. I must not have been lovable enough for him to stay. But if I hadn't asked, maybe he wouldn't have gone.

I stopped asking. For anything. Unless I knew for certain I could get it. I was never again going to run the risk of being denied or rejected. It was too painful. Too humiliating.

Years later, in a Bio-Energetics workshop, the therapist asked each of us to reach out our hands and say "I want—" and fill in the blank. I couldn't do it. I couldn't even say I wanted to be a successful actress. "How do you expect to be a star, Adrienne," she asked, "if you can't even say what it is you want?" But what if I said it? What if people knew that's what I wanted and then I didn't succeed? I'd never be able to live with the shame.

Dennis helped me change all that.

The time came in our relationship when I wanted to know if we had a future together as more than friends and occasional lovers. I learned from Dennis that I could ask for that and not be rejected simply because I had asked. He continued to care for me. His reasons for saying no had nothing to do with me; they had only to do with him. He taught that the importance is in the asking, regardless of the answer. I learned not to take refusal personally; I was still a valuable person with no need to feel ashamed for making a request that had been denied.

I learned to ask without regard for the outcome. To stand up and say, "This is what I want," and to know I wouldn't be any less valuable if I didn't get it. That was a major lesson in my life.

Dennis and I remained friends after our affair ended. I still don't know what to believe about his powers to heal. I've seen him do things for which I had no explanation other than mysticism. He worked on my mother-in-law's knee and she swears he helped her. Eight years ago, he worked on a woman I know who was close to death with multiple sclerosis. She's still alive. He continues to travel the world, teaching people to heal themselves.

I know he helped heal me.

# The Lawyer

IT'S 1988. JOHN AND I HAVE BEEN SEPARATED FOR THREE years. Cody lives with me and sees his daddy once or twice a week, whenever John isn't working. John and I have remained friends.

My therapist has closed her practice and moved back East. I was sad to lose her but the time was right. She spent a lot of time helping me see that I had been unhappy in my marriage to John but unwilling to acknowledge it, and that eventually I would have agreed we shouldn't be together. She listened to my experiences with Dennis and helped me incorporate metaphysics into therapy. I learned so much from her, the tools I need to live a happy life: to understand myself and others, to communicate and to listen, to ask for what I want without fear, and to deal with rejection objectively. I know so much more who I am.

This morning I talk to John about my will and what

might happen to Cody if I die. I want to make sure Cody continues to see Leticia. She's been our housekeeper-nanny since he was born; except for me, he spends more time with her than any other person in his life and it would be devastating for him to lose her. I'm putting a clause in my will that specifies my wishes.

John is hesitant to agree. I'm not asking him to hire her, I just want to know that he'll make sure Cody and Letty can spend time together if I'm not around. He doesn't say no, exactly, but he doesn't rush to reassure me, either. He doesn't sound like himself. Something has changed.

For the first time since he left, I consider asking for sole custody. I don't believe in it. More important to me than anything is that Cody grow up knowing his father and loving him. I didn't know mine. My mother's bitterness toward my father colored my feelings to the extent that he was a stranger to me—a nice man, I'm sure, but not someone I loved as a father. I am not going to repeat that pattern. John is Cody's dad. He is loving and supportive. He has as much right as I do to be in his life.

We've gone three years without any conflicts or confrontations. If we ever do get divorced, we want to do it ourselves. Nonetheless, I think it's time I see a lawyer.

I phone a "divorce expert." When I explain what I'm thinking he laughs in my face. He gives me the names of five lawyers and predicts not one of them will even talk to me.

"Nobody can do what you want to do. You guys can't do it together. You've got to think of it as adversarial." He also implies our business manager can't possibly remain neutral. His voice is aggressive as he attempts to advise me. I hang up thinking, *Christ, are they all going to be like this? How will we ever get through it?*

I call the first lawyer on the list because he has offices in the Valley. He returns my call immediately. Sounds very nice on the phone. We make an appointment for today. Maybe he recognizes my name, I think, maybe that's why he's willing to see me even though I explain that all I want is an understanding of the law.

When I enter his office, the last thing in the world I want is to be recognized. My head is down and I'm not making eye contact. I feel as though there is a brand on my head: THIS WOMAN IS GETTING DIVORCED. I am sick to my stomach.

He is very gentle. I think about the word "grace" when I think about what John and I want to do. To separate with grace. This lawyer seems gracious. As it turns out, he happens to be one of the original authors of the definition of joint custody in the state of California. He explains to me the whys and wherefores, the drawbacks in sole custody, the details that would have to be addressed in any decision. He suggests I might want joint custody with primary physical custody being mine. Since that's basically what John and I have been doing during the past three years, I'm hoping John will agree.

We finish talking about custody and I ask him to explain to me exactly what he does. Criminal law and family law. Would he be willing to help me if necessary? Gradually we get into a discussion of my divorce. The more questions he asks and the more he talks, the more I realize I am going to have to have a lawyer who is dealing only with me. It's hard for me to even use the term "represent." He tells me his fees. He says if I decide to hire him, he and I may have some "I.C.Y." conversations in the future: ones in which he says, "I called you," meaning he gave me advice, warned me I was not making the right decision for myself, and I went ahead and did it anyway. I'm sure he's right and that's what I'll do. Because keeping John and me from becoming enemies is more important to me than any assets or community property or tax breaks.

The whole consultation takes only an hour. It seems twice that long. I shake his hand and walk out. Go down to my car in the underground garage and weep. I feel so degraded. So humiliated. After three years of separation, I want to call John and have him tell me it will be all right. Have him promise we will get through this without turning against each other. Without hiring one shark to fight another.

I do. And he does.

# Mt. Whitney

ALEX WANTED TO CLIMB MT. WHITNEY: 14,000 FEET. I'd never climbed anything in my life but, what the hell, I could do the stair machine at the gym. Besides, my friend Maggie climbed it and she's not especially athletic. Of course, when she did it there was snow on the ground. She didn't have to take switchbacks all the way down; she just sat on her butt and slid to the bottom. But I didn't know that when I said yes.

Alex had tried to climb it once before. The friend he was with, a 190-pound stuntman, had a medical condition that flared up and he had to be flown out by medivac. Alex spent the night with him on the mountain, praying his friend wouldn't die before the helicopter arrived.

This time he was determined to get to the peak. We had two days off from the play we were doing: a musical version of Nelson Algren's novel *Walk on the Wild Side.* My friend Pat Birch, our choreographer on *Grease,* was directing. At least, she was until the producer replaced her with himself. He was an actor who taught acting but when it came to directing, I didn't understand a word he said. Something about hot tubs, I think.

I played a whore in a bordello who's in love with a legless man. Alex Daniels was the legless man. A handsome, six-foot-two actor, director, and stuntman, with a gorgeous singing voice. We met during the show, dated for three years, and stayed close friends when our lives took us in different directions. He's one of the all-time good people in the world.

He's also the perfect person to climb a mountain with if you want to climb a mountain. And since this was at the beginning of our relationship and he wanted to climb the mountain, I did, too.

I'm not terribly athletic. I love racquetball but rarely play. I like swimming but I have no stamina. Hate to run. Don't like tennis. Can't ski. Think golf is boring and I'm afraid of baseball. Won't even watch football. I was great at tetherball and bongo boards but that was a while back. The last time I rode a bike, I was pregnant with Cody.

So, what does that leave? I lift weights and walk on a treadmill. In 1986, when Mt. Whitney loomed before me, Gold's Gym didn't have treadmills. I did the stationary bike an hour a day and figured that was enough. How hard could it be to walk up a mountain? There were paths, weren't there?

We started out at 6:00 A.M. I was carrying a seventy-pound pack and Alex had one hundred. We hiked for two hours and then stopped so I could vomit. I never ate again that day. After four hours, Alex went ahead to set up camp and two German hikers saw me limping along alone. They corrected my walking technique to help ease the pain. Who knew there was a right way to walk? I caught up with Alex and we stopped for the night at 6:30. It was so cold outside I couldn't face leaving the tent to go to the bathroom. Besides, we were sure we heard bears out there. We tossed and turned for five hours and started climbing again.

By then I hadn't eaten for a full day and night. I was nauseous and shaking. My heart was pounding at two hundred beats a minute. Altitude sickness and a thyroid gone haywire. I couldn't get enough oxygen. I was hiking for forty-five seconds and then bending over to breathe for thirty.

There were paths, all right, covered with ice, and sometimes the trail was only a foot wide with the mountain straight up on the left and an abyss on the right. Alex was breaking the ice with his ax. I was hanging on to a guide wire, praying. A mile from the summit I tried to convince Alex to go on without me, but he wouldn't let me stay behind. I'd come that far, he said, I had to do the rest.

I did. I was amazed to find there were birds up there. At 14,000 feet. Tiny little birds flying everywhere.

I'd slowed us down so much getting there that we couldn't stay more than twenty minutes. We'd taken a day and a half to get to the summit and we only had half a day to get back down. That would have worked if it had been anyone but me doing the descent. I'm terrified of going downhill. It hadn't crossed my mind to mention this to Alex when we were making our plans. Forget about running, I walk slower downhill than I do going up.

We started down at 3:00 P.M. I was in such pain, I could

barely bend my knees to walk. Two hours after it got dark, Alex's flashlight gave out. We didn't have backup batteries. He lit the lantern and led the way but he was walking so fast—well, a tortoise would have seemed fast compared to me—that I continually lost sight of him. I kept calling out and trying to judge where he was from his response. He tried carrying both our packs to see if I could walk any faster, but he had to give that up after an hour. Finally, at 10:00 P.M., he gave me the lantern, took my flashlight, and headed off alone. His plan was to run down the mountain, drop his pack at base camp, and come back and get me. I kept walking stiff-legged at my snail's pace.

Ten minutes later, my lantern burned out. I had matches in my pack but knew if I knelt down to take it off, I wouldn't be able to get it back on and stand up. I couldn't bend my knees. I couldn't leave the pack behind because I'd borrowed it from Maggie. I seriously considered just buying her a new one when I returned. If I returned. Finally, I found a waist-high boulder on which to unload it. Relit the lantern and saddled up again.

I got to base camp and Alex's motor home at midnight. I'd been hiking since 6:00 A.M. Alex wasn't there. He'd borrowed a mountain bike and was out looking for me. I was frozen to the bone, couldn't bend my right leg at all, and eight pounds thinner than when I'd started the day before.

I was making soup when Alex came in. He went nuts because I'd used the nonpotable water. I nearly hit him in the head with a frying pan.

But . . . I climbed Mt. Whitney.

# Meeting Billy

BILLY SAYS THAT HE KNEW HE WAS GOING TO MARRY ME three days after we met.

I sure didn't.

I didn't even know we were going to date.

It was August 1991. I was forty-six years old. I'd just ended a seven-month relationship with a man my psychic friends were sure was my soul mate. I'd believed them for a while. He had a lot of soul. The mating was the hard part. It was an obsessive relationship on both our parts and the closer we became, the more frightened he got.

My tarot cards said the man was in my life to mirror the final problems that needed attention. I knew it was true. I was reading *A Course in Miracles* and Gerald Jampolsky's books on attitudinal healing and I felt like I was on the brink of a new realm of happiness. Closing the door on that relationship, as hard as it was to do, told me I had achieved what I'd set out to do. I knew who I was and what I wanted in life: growth and love.

And that's when I met Billy.

My manager sent me a script for a new play that was being produced by two "hot, young television writers," Billy Van Zandt and Jane Milmore. It was called *Drop Dead* and it was the funniest thing I'd ever read. I agreed to meet them for tea at the Peninsula Hotel.

While I was driving to the meeting with the playwrights, my lawyers were representing me in a court proceeding against a stalker. The man was obviously schizophrenic; he told the police I was his psychiatrist and I had instructed him to leave his wife so he could marry me after he killed my ex-husband, John. He was convinced he'd seen me gang raped when I was thirteen and that I had a cross carved on my breast. He'd been writing letters like that to me for years and I hadn't taken any action, but once he arrived in California and called my mother, I got nervous. When he went to my manager's home, saw the neighbor children's toys on his porch (they belonged to Chris Albrecht's kids—the head of HBO), and threatened my manager for my address, I hired private detectives to track him down.

They got him into court where he waived his rights and agreed to a seventy-two-hour psychiatric commitment. He'd been drinking heavily and was on Prozac, which probably contributed to his bizarre behavior. After the seventy-two hours, he agreed to remain hospitalized for several weeks and then left the state.

It made me terribly sad for him. I never did feel I was in

serious danger. I kept thinking the entire court proceeding could have been avoided if I had seen him and talked to him, but the detectives were adamantly against that. They wouldn't even let me stay in my own house the night before they brought him to town for the hearing. I spent the night with Nancy Loomis and Tommy Wallace.

Anyway, that's what I was dealing with as I drove to meet Billy and Jane. That and the breakup of the neurotic relationship.

I made a conscious decision to be optimistic. *Wouldn't it be nice,* I thought, *if this guy Billy Van Zandt turned out to be interesting?*

Well, he was interesting, all right, but definitely not for me. Way too young. Early thirties, probably. And he and Jane looked like they were a couple. Oh well.

It turned out that they had been a couple off and on for fourteen years, but the romantic part of their relationship had ended two years earlier. Billy says that when I found that out, I turned my back on Jane and addressed all my questions to him, but I swear that isn't true. I wasn't thinking of him in a romantic way at all.

What I *was* thinking was that I very much wanted to do their play. I was fascinated with them as a writing team. Billy had started his professional career as a film actor in New York but began writing for television when he and Jane moved to L.A. They were Emmy nominees for their *I Love Lucy* special: *I Love Lucy—The Very First Show.* They'd been writing and acting in sitcoms for four years, but their first love was theater. During their television hiatuses, they wrote a new farce every year, which they produced and starred in, working with a repertory company in their hometown in New Jersey. Thirteen of their plays had been published and were performed all over the world (imagine *Love, Sex, and the I.R.S.* being done in Brazil). They'd been boyfriend and girlfriend since they met in 1975 and had managed to stay friends and writing partners when they broke up in 1979 and again in 1981, and '82, '83, '85 (twice), '87, and finally, for good, in '89.

I agreed to do the play and Billy said he'd call to set up another meeting to discuss the script.

The two of us met for breakfast at Jerry's Deli. When we said good-bye, he gave me a hug. Billy's a tall, strong man. His hug felt good: safe and comforting.

Rehearsals were great fun. Billy is a brilliant physical comedian and he and Jane are both expert farceurs. We had Rose Marie, Barney Martin, Donny Most, and Craig Bierko in the cast. I was playing a washed-up TV star who used to have her own show called *My Little Mona*. (Billy had offered the role to Tina Louise—Ginger from *Gilligan's Island*—but she turned him down. At our wedding, one of Billy's friends got up to make a toast: "All I can say is, it's a good thing you didn't cast Tina Louise.")

We started going out for dinner after the performances— the cast and any friends who'd come to see the show that evening. There were usually ten or fifteen of us at the table.

Gradually I became aware that Billy and I always ended up sitting next to each other. I wasn't sure if I was making it happen or if he was, but I knew I liked it. I liked feeling his leg bump up next to mine. He made me laugh and that's always a primary aphrodisiac for me. Behind our backs, Barney and Craig made a bet on our pending romance. Barney told Craig he'd been in show business a long time and he could smell it a mile away. They knew a lot sooner than I did.

And then one night, three weeks into the run, Billy got a bit plotzed on White Russians after the show. When I got home at 1:15, my phone was ringing.

"I wanted to ask you to go home with me," he said.

"Oh, I never go to a man's house, they always come here," I replied. "Besides, I don't think our getting together is the wisest thing in the world."

I told him about the relationship I'd just ended. I knew I was lonely—I was still missing the neurotic former soul mate—and my motives weren't clean. I wasn't interested in getting married again but I liked sharing my life with someone. Besides, I didn't know if he realized I was twelve and a half years older than him. (He told me later he had looked my age up in the World Almanac but by then it was too late, he was too much in love with me to care.)

"I'm afraid I'd be taking advantage of you," I said.

"Okay. Take advantage of me," he said.

We've been together ever since.

# Marrying Billy

IT'S JULY 3, 1992, AND BILLY AND I ARE ON THE BEACH at Malibu. He's giggling. This is not a man who giggles.

"What?" I ask.

"Nothing," he replies, "I was just going to push you in the water."

This is not a man who would push me in the water.

He takes me in his arms and I can feel his heart pounding like a piston. He's got a big, shit-eating grin on his face. Suddenly, I know. He's going to ask me to marry him.

This is the day before the Fourth of July. I tell him, if he sees fireworks in the sky the next evening at nine, my answer is yes.

We decide to get married on New Year's Eve. Two hundred people in our backyard, with our friend Douglas officiating, my sister Jocelyn as my maid of honor, my nieces Jaime and Jennifer as flower girls, and Cody giving me away.

Two weeks after his proposal we're hiking in the Idyllwild Mountains. He's calling back to me from ten feet ahead.

"The wedding should definitely be black-tie." Billy's a WASP from northern New Jersey.

"Black tie?" I say. "I can't ask my family to wear black-tie. It's expensive and it's uncomfortable." I'm a sixties hippie from Northern California.

"My New Year's Eve parties are always black-tie. If they don't want to wear a tuxedo, they don't have to come."

I call my sister. She's from Northern California, too.

"What would you say if you received an invitation that said black-tie?"

"I'd say I wasn't coming."

We settle on BLACK TIE OPTIONAL and I start preparing.

I read *A Bride's Shortcuts and Strategies for a Beautiful Wedding.*

A friend asks Billy to describe the perfect wedding. "Formal, loud music, dancing, lots of food, flowers, candles, black-tie, and don't worry about the cost." My description? "A bunch of our best friends standing around the house having a good time when someone finally says, 'Okay, it's time,' and everyone moves into the living room and we exchange our vows. Then everyone whoops and hollers and has a party. No loud music 'cause then no one can really talk. Casual. I'd make all the food. I'd rather spend all that money on a honeymoon."

The man from the first tent-rental company I call says we can put up a tent in the front yard and invite 160 people.

I read *Wedding Hints & Reminders.*

The man from the second tent-rental company I call says the front yard is definitely a mistake. We should tent the backyard instead. Then we can invite 200.

I call a wedding planner. The wedding planner wants to level the floor of our tennis court, build a stage, move all our living room furniture into storage, put several more ovens in my kitchen, and decorate the house with sunflowers. In December.

I read *The L.A. Wedding* and call a caterer.

Billy and I rearrange the bookshelves to accommodate his things and mine. Billy wants me to throw out all the books with pictures of cats on them.

"I skeeve cats," he says.

"There's no such word," I say, even though his meaning is clear.

"There is in my family. My mother's Italian."

I throw out three books with pictures of cats on them.

We combine our music albums. Out of 500, we have only nine duplicates and four of those we gave each other. Picking out a wedding song we both agree on could be a problem.

I stop by the two nice hotels that are closest to our house. They will each hold twenty rooms for our out-of-town guests.

Billy wants everyone in his family at the wedding. His eighty-five-year-old grandmother hasn't spoken to her daughter Angie since they had a falling out fifteen years ago.

Nana won't come to the wedding if Angie is there. Billy convinces Angie to call Nana to apologize.

"Hi, Ma. This is Angie."

"Angie who?" Click.

Angie won't be coming to the wedding. Nana will.

One of my relatives sends a huge sample book of wedding invitations for us to peruse. She sells them.

I hate them.

The caterer presents her suggested menu: tuna tartar with daikon sprouts in porcini mushrooms vinaigrette on fried wonton, soft duck tacos with ancho chile sauce and Cantonese slaw, jerk chicken with mango chutney and asparagus fritters.

My sister asks if McDonald's is open on New Year's Eve.

I read *It's Your Wedding; Enjoy It* and call another caterer.

I go to my favorite stationery store. I'd like invitations printed on recycled paper. They have three to choose from. Billy hates them.

I read *Message of Marriage*. This isn't a spiritual book. No. It's an entire book devoted solely to the wording of the wedding "ensemble": the envelope filled with the wedding invitation, the R.S.V.P. card, the invitation to the reception, the hotel and parking information, and the directions. A hundred pages to tell you how to phrase whomever is requesting the honor of your presence.

We visit our first jeweler. Billy has his heart set on a five-carat blue diamond for me. I don't like diamonds. There's a gold-and-enamel antique art deco frog ring I'm angling for. I tell him he's the prince the frog turned into. "Nice try," he says. No frog ring.

We return to the stationers. Billy picks the most expensive invitation they have. He looks at me with those liquid brown eyes and says, "It's my only wedding and it's important to me and I don't mind spending the money."

I read a book on calligraphy. Maybe I can learn fast enough to address my own invitations.

The second caterer wants to use an ice sculpture to keep the seafood cold. He says it can be anything that has meaning to us. I suggest the word "BANG."

"Why 'BANG?'" asks Billy.

"Well, that's how we'll be starting off the New Year . . . with a bang. Or two."

No frog ring, no recycled invitations, no BANG. I'm 0 for 3.

Billy calls his brother, Steven, and asks him for me if he'll sing Marc Cohn's "True Companion" at the wedding. Steven is Little Steven of the E Street Band. He says no, he'll be too nervous. He offers to get Marc Cohn to sing it. Billy says he'd rather have Peggy Lee or Tony Bennett.

We talk to the valet service. The church down the hill where they want to park the cars is having New Year's Eve services. If we double our donation we can use their parking lot. Does that make it tax deductible?

The third caterer wants to charge double time to work on New Year's Eve.

I read *Coopwood & Field's Guide to Planning a Wedding in Dallas.* Maybe we can move.

Billy and I find a ring we both like at a gallery in Capitola. The artist says it can't be sized down for my hand; the leopard agate is too large. Billy returns to L.A. and I find another one I like and photograph it to show him.

We hire the fourth caterer. He's Italian from New Jersey.

Billy's mother refuses to wear a corsage because the "jackasses in the Veterans' Day parades always wear them."

The photos of the ring don't come out. We spend three hours looking at gemstones and when I fall in love with an apricot-and-cream-colored opal, the jeweler warns me it's very fragile—I'll have to remove it every time I work out.

My mother wants to wear a corsage because she "wants everyone to know who I am!"

In the middle of all this, Cody has Back to School night for his third-grade class. Billy ducks out on the *Martin* writing staff (he's co-executive producer of the Martin Lawrence TV series) to attend the entire evening's event and then returns to work until two in the morning. "I needed to be at Cody's school," he says. "I need to know what's going on with him." It's the first time in my life I can remember the man I'm with putting me ahead of his work. Not even my father. My friend Suzanne says seeing Billy there really brought home to her the knowledge that he's here to stay. "He's part of the equation." No wonder I'm marrying him.

I read *I Need to Do What?!: A Wedding Guide for the Groom.*

I call my brother-in-law, Bill, to ask if he'll sing Marc Cohn's "True Companion" at the wedding. Bill has a beautiful voice; he jams with a band on weekends. He says no, he'll be too nervous.

We drive downtown to the Jewelry Mart to look at a ring we've seen in *Town and Country* magazine. Instead we find a designer whose work we like and she does some sketches for us.

The Italian-from-New-Jersey caterer brings over five bottles of champagne for us to try. Billy takes them to work for his writing staff. One of them explodes all over the interior of his brand-new convertible.

Billy throws out *I Need to Do What?!: A Wedding Guide for the Groom.*

I drive back downtown to find a stone to go on the ring. Billy wants me to wear a sapphire. I don't like sapphires.

I finish addressing two hundred envelopes and then realize I've written on fifty of the wrong ones. I've addressed the decorative enclosures, not the mailing envelopes. Call the stationers to order more. Billy's sister Kathi won't give us an address for her best friend because if her best friend is invited, Kathi won't have anyone to dog-sit.

I tell Billy I'm going to call my ex-boyfriend Alex and ask

him if he'll sing Marc Cohn's "True Companion" at the wedding. Billy unplugs the phone.

Maybe I'll sing the damn song myself.

I read *The Bride's Consumer Guide*. I'll be damned if I'm going to spend money on a wedding gown when I've got a designer dress I love hanging in the closet. I spent more money on it than I've ever spent on a dress in my life and I've only worn it once. It's not white but then I'm not a virgin so . . . what the hell.

We both go downtown again. Billy wants me to get an emerald. I don't like emeralds. We settle on a green tourmaline.

We start construction on the backyard. We have to increase the gardener's visits, move the septic tank, replace the sandstone with used brick, and resurface the tennis court. In four weeks.

I spend three hours recording Armenian dance songs for the DJ. Billy makes a list of everything he wants played. Dean Martin sends us a CD of his recording of "In the Chapel in the Moonlight" because we can't find it anywhere. Billy makes an even longer list of everything he *doesn't* want played. I sneak in the "Chicken Dance" but I can't get the "Hokey Pokey" past him.

My mother calls to tell us that the hotel we arranged for took her reservation but wouldn't accept her credit card to guarantee it. I call them to inquire. Not only do they have no record of her reservation, they don't have any Van Zandts, Barbeaus, Lentos, Bartons, Nalbandians, or Shamshoians reserved, and I know all our relatives have booked rooms. They're not holding the twenty rooms they promised me at a discounted rate, either. It's New Year's Eve and they're not holding any rooms at any rate—they're totally booked. I have to wait until the next day to talk to the manager.

I call the second hotel. They have no record of the form I filled out, guaranteeing they would hold twenty rooms for the night. The woman who signed it is on a six-month leave of absence. And yes, they're totally booked for New Year's Eve, too.

Billy has twelve more people he'd like to invite, including an ex-girlfriend who just called him for the first time in four years. I suggest inviting my ex-husband, John. Billy doesn't think I'm funny. I call the stationers to order more invitations.

Billy brings the rings home. Mine doesn't fit. Cody's friend Rhett tells his mom he wants to be the "ring bury-er" in the wedding. We may need him.

I clean out the downstairs freezer to store any leftovers from the party so the Valley Shelter can pick them up the next day. The electricians arrive to upgrade the wiring to handle the catering equipment. We've got to replace a toilet, repair the fireplace, and paint the living room. In three weeks.

Billy's sister calls off her engagement. Her fiancé was going to be our wedding photographer. I'm hoping they'll stay together 'til New Year's.

I read *Words for a Wedding.*

I read Kahlil Gibran, Elizabeth Barrett Browning, and

Rainier Maria Rilke. I'm trying to write my vows. The only thing I like so far is by Dorothy Parker:

> Oh, life is a glorious cycle of song,
> a medley of extemporanea
> and love is a thing that can never go wrong
> and I am Marie of Roumania

Our caterer has a seizure while he's buying groceries to make our cake samples. It's a viral infection of the brain. Or stress.

We settle on two simple Mokume Gane wedding bands. Mokume Gane is an ancient Japanese sword-making technique in which white gold, pink gold, sterling silver, and copper are folded over and over on themselves, then layed out in a sheet and cut and etched to form the metal the piece is made from. No diamonds, no sapphires, no emeralds, no opals, no tourmalines.

If the marriage doesn't work, we can melt them down and make miniature sword-shaped letter openers.

We spend Christmas vacation in New Jersey with Billy's family. He's worried that his mother is going to have a heart attack at the airport on her way to the wedding and his grandmother is going to fall and break her hip on our hardwood floors.

On December 27, Billy turns on the Weather Channel. It's

raining in L.A. It's going to rain all week in L.A. It's raining so hard, the landscapers may not be able to get the new lawn planted before the ceremony.

With two days to go, I get a call from a tent-rental company. They want to confirm a next-day delivery.

"What are you talking about?" I ask. "My caterer has already had everything delivered."

"Well, we have an order here for one hundred sixty chairs and a thirty-by-ninety-foot tent for your front yard. You placed it when you met with our representative last July."

The day before the wedding, the caterer has all his equipment stolen. Stoves, cappuccino maker, chafing dishes. All of it has disappeared from his warehouse. He's calling rental companies. Maybe I should tell him about the guy with the tent for the front yard.

Finally, it's time. The house looks incredible. The rain has stopped and the sun is shining. The last of the sod goes in at 3:00. I buy welcome mats, get my hair done, and take a nap. The guests arrive at 6:30 and I'm banished to my bedroom until the ceremony. All my girlfriends stop in to keep me company. One of them is distraught; she spends half an hour talking about her divorce. Cody comes in, looking so handsome in his double-breasted tuxedo, and when we see the harpist moving his harp out to the backyard, we know it's time to begin. We shut off all the lights in the bedroom and watch our guests in their black-tie-optional finery file out the living room door, through the garden, onto the new lawn and new bricks, and past the pool to the newly surfaced tennis court. My uncle Ralph has on his cowboy hat and snakeskin boots. I love it.

Cody practices how he wants to hold my arm. "I feel like I'm going to throw up," he says. He's eight years old and I think it's the first time he's ever been nervous in his life.

We wait for my sister and my nieces to walk down the aisle, all three of them beautiful in their black and white velvet dresses. The "Wedding March" starts and Cody gives me his arm and the doors to the tent open and everyone stands up as we walk in. I never expected them to stand up. I start crying. My cousin Erwin says, "Oh, she looks beautiful," and I cry even harder. Billy is waiting at the altar. He looks incredibly handsome. He's crying, too.

In the middle of the ceremony, Billy turns to all our friends and says, "Not only am I marrying the woman I love, I'm marrying a woman with a child that I love." Then he bends down to Cody's eye level, takes Cody's hands, and thanks him for letting Billy be a part of our family. "I will always love your mom, Cody, and I will always love you and I will always take care of you."

And I know saying yes was the right thing to do.

# The Rat Movie

**WHENEVER I HEAR A PRODUCER SAY ABOUT AN ACTOR,** "Oh, we can't get him for this role. We don't have enough money," I think, *Make the offer. You never know why an actor wants to work.*

I've taken roles because I loved the character. I've taken roles because there was another actor in the cast with whom I wanted to work. I've taken roles because the director was great. I've taken roles because termites were eating my roof and Cody's tuition was due. I've taken roles because I just didn't want to sit home, and I've taken roles because I love to travel.

It's fall of 1994 and I have accepted a job that takes place in Russia. The money is good, the time commitment is short, the character is fun. Everything else is drek. But we are filming in Moscow and I've always wanted to go to Moscow, so I say yes. With any luck at all, the film will never be seen.

Lufthansa first class gets me there in fifteen hours, three

movies, and a full night's sleep. I've never been away from Cody for more than a week and even though he's now almost eleven and could care less when he sees me, I have insisted on a contractual stop date in eighteen days. Russia seems like another planet to me. All those Robert Ludlum and Helen MacInnes books I read in my twenties come back to haunt me. What if I get caught "behind the Iron Curtain" and I'm never allowed out? I've left notes for Billy and Cody hidden under their pillows, describing my limitless love for them and assuring them I will watch over them from wherever I am— just in case I'm dead.

There's a news program on the plane, broadcast by CNN. A rebel faction of the Russian government has opened fire on the Parliament buildings. In Moscow. Where I'm landing. Any minute.

Our Russian producer is waiting for me at Sheremetyevo Airport. His English is minimal and my Russian is nonexistent so I try for French. We get by well enough for me to understand they have rented an apartment for me and he is leaving me there and doesn't know when he will return. "Don't leave," he says. "We have martial law now. Maybe civil war. *Dasvidanya.*"

The flat belongs to a diplomat's ex-wife. The halls smell like urine and rotting pork but the apartment is clean and, wonder of wonders, there is a small black-and-white television. I can get two channels, a local Russian station and CNN. Most of the CNN broadcasts are in Russian but occasionally there is English translation. From my window I can see the smoke from the same machine guns I can see being fired on television. I am sure the airports will close and I will never see my family again.

I thank God I had the sense to learn every possible way to place a long-distance call from Moscow before I left L.A. And thank God there's a phone in the apartment. I get through to Billy who has already been screaming at my agent that he's got to get me out of here before I get killed. "I'm fine," I say, downplaying my anxiety. "Whatever is going on is miles away. You wouldn't even know there was a problem where I am. Mothers are walking children home from school and everything is calm." Of course, they're walking them home from school. The police just told everyone to get off the streets! I don't tell him that.

Well, there's nothing I can do about any of this except reassure Billy and make the most of the experience. I explore the apartment, watch TV, cook some spaghetti, and fall asleep reading Martin Cruz Smith's *Red Square.*

Filming is postponed for a day while the city adjusts to the state of martial law. The Kremlin closes to visitors. A curfew is enforced. To get to Mosfilms, the studio where we will be shooting interiors, we have to circumnavigate the downtown area. We are not allowed on certain streets. My driver compensates for his lack of English and my lack of Russian by speaking very loudly. It doesn't help but at least the police don't think we're sneaking up on them. We start work with a night shoot. My call is for 3:30 P.M. at Mosfilms, where I get into makeup, wardrobe, and wig. The wig is two feet high, light blue, festooned with jewels. It takes an hour to get it on my head.

From Mosfilms, we drive 30 kilometers out of town to the location. Because of the curfew, we are each given a special pass to be on the streets after dark. Felix, the Russian producer, warns us to leave money and jewelry in the studio safe. The military has the right to confiscate anything they want. Amy, the American producer, warns us that if stopped, we should put our hands behind our heads and do anything they demand. I am wearing pink silk long johns, jeans, cowboy boots, a 300-year-old Marie Antoinette gown, a pink chenille robe, purple eyebrows designed to look like rats' tails, and the two-foot-tall blue wig. It seems unlikely they will mistake me for an enemy of the state. I keep my pass inside my boot, just in case.

By the time we get to the location, it is 10:30 at night. We are herded into the actors' room, which is nothing more than an empty space in a cinder block building three miles from the actual set. It has two light bulbs. I sit as close to one as I can and read my book. The toilet paper in the bathroom is a 1991 calendar. The toilet seat is made of pressed hay. I can feel my quads growing stronger as I squat to avoid touching anything.

At 2:30 in the morning, I have been on call eleven hours and have just been driven to the set for the first time. It is a palace built for Catherine the Great. Since it was prophesied she would die there, she never completed it. There is no floor and no ceiling, only brick walls three feet thick and thirty feet high. I understand now why Amy asked if I were afraid of heights. My throne has been placed on a four-foot-wide platform in an arched opening high in the walls. Fear doesn't set in until I see the makeshift lean-to that passes for a wooden ladder. I must climb it in my gown, my crinolines, my boots, my wig, and a floor-length ermine stole. I imagine the ladder tipping over backward, my body crumpled on the stones below.

Once I do get up, it's too scary to climb down. It's 30 degrees inside. I am sitting in a wind tunnel with an increasingly full bladder. The only bathroom is back at the actors' room three miles away. People keep offering to send up coffee or tea or vodka. I keep refusing.

My plight pales when I see one of the extras climbing the ladder to share the platform with me. She is wearing sandals, a bikini bottom, and halter top, all made out of possum fur. I am the Queen of the Rats; she is my handmaiden, a rat woman. A rat woman with goose bumps the size of warts.

At 4:30 A.M. we shoot the master. Only it isn't really a master because it must be shot in segments. The prop department has designed a pendulum that only swings one way and must be reset halfway through any take. The camera department has only one magazine and so we must wait while they unload it and load it again. By the time we finish the master my bladder is so full and I am so cold, I can't control my shaking. I shed the ermine stole, climb down the two-story ladder, and head out to the artificially lit bushes with several pieces of borrowed notepaper in hand—keeping an eye out for frogs. As I squat behind the palace of Catherine the Great, it crosses my mind that I am the star of the film.

Back up the ladder to my throne. From where I sit, I command the entire room. There is a pit dug in the floor in front of me with the pendulum suspended over it. The audience will believe it is filled with rats. On the far right of the room is a rack designed to separate a man's arms and legs from his body. It doesn't work. So far, the only things that do work are the huge flares suspended from the walls on either side of my throne. Well, they work in terms of being lit and burning. As for suspended . . . the one to my right breaks and falls on the platform behind me. Immediately the straw on the floor around the throne catches fire. The director picks this moment to throw a fit. He starts screaming, "I quit! I quit!" I start screaming, "Fire! Fire!" No one speaks English so it doesn't matter what we're screaming. I'm sure the poor hand-maiden's pseudo-rat sandals are flammable and I have visions of my blue synthetic wig going up in a blaze and melting down my forehead. Fortunately, I have returned from my bathroom foray with a full cup of tea. I pour that on the burning hay and Amy comes running up the stairs to stamp out the flames with her boots.

We scrap the entire night's work and start over again the next night with the flares in a safer place and the movie section of *Pravda* for toilet paper.

The set has been redesigned. Not well enough, obviously, because halfway through our second take, another fire breaks out. This time it is on a platform opposite me, again peopled with rat women. Dan, the director, is no longer yelling. He just stares in amazement as the grass goes up in flames around the girls' feet. The Russians make no attempt to put it out. "It will go out by itself," they say.

So will this film.

Tonight is the rat women's ballet sequence. Don't ask. The dead-possum halter tops come off and the women pirouette topless around the banquet tables. The Russian crew gets paid by the hour. On a good day, they're slow. Tonight they're catatonic. We have no script supervisor, no assistant director, no walkie-talkies, a director and three actors who don't speak Russian, an entire crew that doesn't speak English, and one and a half translators. In five hours, we get two three-minute takes. Not two takes that are good enough to be printed, just two takes. Dan starts throwing out entire scenes. It's just as well because some of them call for an army of men. We have ten.

The other two lead actors are from the States. They were hired together because they are boyfriend and girlfriend off screen. She is incredibly neurotic, insecure, needy, temperamental, and unprofessional. The crew hates her. Perhaps her boyfriend does, too. He has moved out of their Moscow apartment.

The fourth lead is a well-respected Russian actress. She has a beautiful face and figure and she can act. In Russian. Unfortunately she barely speaks English and although she doesn't know it, her entire performance will be dubbed.

We break for dinner. It is the same every night: kasha, unidentifiable meat, a broth with undercooked chickpeas. I eat bread and drink tea with sugar. There is no milk.

Dan has requested a "ratapult," a fantasy weapon that will fly ten rats through the air at one time. After dinner, he tries it out. On the fourth attempt, it shoots one beer can three feet.

The rats, I am told, are circus rats. Whether that means they were whisked off the floor of some elephant's cage or they have been trained to do amazing feats with high wires and nets, I do not know. For my peace of mind, I choose to believe the latter. Their trainer, Natasha, tells my interpreter that they have been born and raised in sanitary conditions. "These are not gutter rats, *da*?"

The director is expecting fifty rats. Natasha arrives with sixteen. The prop man is sent to find more. He returns with another sixteen. His are dead. They are so old it is hard to tell whether they are the work of a taxidermist or a toy manufacturer. Whatever, they do not move. It will be the director's job to make us believe they are real. I will do my best to help.

Our leading man decides that the best way to work with

the sixteen live rats is to get to know them. He puts his hand into the cage and they bite him. Natasha assures me that it is the actor's fault and not the rats' and that they will not treat me in like manner. She also reiterates they do not have rabies. At least, I think this is what she is saying. Sveta, my translator, has had to leave for the day. The film company cannot afford more than two translators and she is needed elsewhere.

It is eleven in the morning and the crew breaks for tea and vodka. One of the grips grabs for my breast as I walk past. He is grinning and saying something I'm glad I can't understand. He collides with the wall. We've got ten more hours of filming and he can barely stand up.

The translator calls places. I settle into my red velvet throne while the prop man arranges the dead rats at my feet. Periodically he will rearrange them in an effort to make us think they're alive. Natasha approaches me with a fish head in her hand. She rubs my hands and arms and chest with the cut end of the trout and then squeezes fish juice on the folds of my gown. The gown is 300 years old and smells it. Each morning the costume mistress sprays it with a pine deodorizer. Now it smells like dead fish in a very old forest.

The scene takes place in a cavernous banquet room in the queen's castle. I am the queen. My throne is at one end. Lining all the walls are candles and flares. One hundred sixty-three candles, twenty flares. I know this because the prop man waits until I am seated and covered with fish juice before he lights each one. By hand. By himself. I have fifteen minutes to count them all from the time the director yells, "Let's shoot it" until they are lit.

Finally, we are ready to shoot. Natasha releases the trained rats. All they've been trained to do is eat fish. They swarm over me, nibbling at my velvet gown, sticking their noses in my hair, running up one arm, across my neck and down the other, looking for the fish. In the absence of fish, they get more and more frantic.

The movie is based on a novella by Bram Stoker. In this scene, the rats are the queen's companions. As long as I play my flute for them, they dance joyfully around me. When I break the flute in a fit of rage, they attack me and devour me. That's the scene. I didn't write it, Bram Stoker did. He may not have had this film version in mind.

# The Twins

I WAS FIFTY-ONE YEARS OLD WHEN I HAD THE TWINS—
the only woman on the maternity ward who was a member of
AARP.

I didn't think of it that way, of course. I didn't think about
it at all. It didn't seem out of the ordinary to me. It still doesn't.
It's just what you do when you love having kids and you're
married to a man who's twelve years younger than you are who
has never had kids and really wants them, too.

I was forty-seven when Billy and I got married. He had just
turned thirty-six. I started taking fertility pills almost immediately. It had taken me a long while to get pregnant with
Cody and that had been nine years earlier. My doctor felt I
could use a little help.

Days after I started the pills I knew I was in trouble. We
went to see *Lethal Weapon 3* and I burst into tears when Joe
Pesci's character told the story about running over his pet frog.

I was crying over television commercials. Everything was turning gray. I felt like I'd entered a long black tunnel with no exit in sight.

What I didn't know, and my first two fertility specialists hadn't bothered to tell me, was that the medication I was taking can have major side effects, including emotional instability and depression. I had chosen it because it was just a pill, and in my mind, I could rationalize that I didn't really have fertility problems; I just needed a little pill to help me get pregnant. The alternative was taking shots and I didn't want to do that. It would have been an acknowledgment that I really did need medical intervention. I wasn't ready to admit that.

I am amazed to this day that Billy didn't leave me that first year. All I did was cry. Finally, after ten months of driving for an hour to Santa Monica to sit in a doctor's office for two hours before I had a ten-minute examination, and then driving another hour home, one of the lab technicians asked me why I didn't take the shots instead. That medication, he explained, works directly on the ovaries and has no effect on brain chemistry—hence, no emotional upheavals.

I taught myself how to administer the shots—Billy was too squeamish to do it and I wasn't about to make that hour-long drive every day for a five-second injection—and we continued trying for another year and a half. I also worked with an acupuncturist and herbalist who specialized in infertility.

During all this time I was very aware of how lucky we were to be able to afford the time and the treatments involved. If I'd had a full-time job, I wouldn't have been able to get to the doctor, let alone sit in a waiting room for hours on end. And if we hadn't had the insurance coverage we had, we wouldn't have been able to do any of it.

After two and a half years of trying, I took a break. It wasn't a conscious decision; I went to Australia to film a television show and then to Florida to do my concert act. Several months slipped by.

When I returned, I called the doctor and asked if there were any new techniques that we should consider. He said yes, he'd been having success with washing the eggs, which thinned their lining and made implantation possible. My problem wasn't that I wasn't making eggs, it was that the eggs I was making were old and their lining was too thick to successfully attach to the walls of my uterus. I made an appointment to go in and discuss the new technique.

On my way home from the doctor's office, I fell apart. I couldn't do it. It was one thing to mess with my body by taking fertility drugs but the thought of altering my eggs was too frightening to me. The impact of such a technique wouldn't affect only me, it might affect the baby. Who knew what might happen? I drove home crying.

That very same day, Billy had lunch with a friend who told him about a mutual friend who had used a surrogate to carry her child. He was excited about the possibility that we could do that.

"You don't understand, honey," I said, "I can carry the baby, I don't have any concerns about that, I just can't produce an egg that is viable."

I would have adopted a child in a minute but Billy wasn't comfortable with that. Since I didn't care if the baby was mine biologically, we started talking about using an egg donor. I called my friend, Meg, whose best friend, Shelley Smith, had a business matching egg donors with prospective parents. She was willing to see us immediately.

Choosing an egg donor is like attending a casting call, only you're the producer. We sat in an office and read through a binder of photos and bios, deciding what traits were important to us in the histories of the young women who were willing to donate their eggs. Did it matter that she looked like me? Did she need to be smart or artistic or athletic or religious? What about her SAT scores or how much college she'd had or what her nationality was? Shelley gave us detailed information about the girls and their parents and grandparents. She'd screened them very carefully: their motives, their psychology, their personalities, their histories, their lifestyles.

We never met the woman who gave us her eggs. We knew as soon as we read her file that she was our blessing. Her warmth and intelligence and caring were evident on every page. She even looked a bit like me. And when I spoke to her on the phone, there was no question in my mind. We never knew her last name, nor she ours, but whenever I run into Shelley, I ask about her. I don't think she'll ever really understand the magnitude of her gift: the overwhelming joy we experience every day because she helped bring the boys into our lives.

Four of her eggs were fertilized with Billy's sperm. We got to see them under the microscope before they were transferred directly into my uterus. Then I laid on the couch in our living room and talked to those little buggers, doing my best to convince one of them to stick around and grow.

When the nurse called to say that my blood tests had come back, I asked her to hold on so Billy could pick up the other phone. Not only was I pregnant, she said, but my levels were so high it looked like I might be having triplets. The doctor wanted to see me the following day.

I never slept that entire night. All I kept thinking was, *How do I nurse three babies at one time?*

Well, they weren't triplets, they were twins. Identical twins. Which has nothing to do with fertility treatments or heredity. Identical twins are just a happenstance of nature—one egg that decides to split after conception.

I figure it was Nature's way of saying to Billy, "You've only got one chance for a family, might as well give you two at the same time."

My doctor had a different idea: "If you die early," he said, "they've still got each other."

I went out and bought a special-edition laser disc of the Japanese film *Akira,* and Billy and I presented it to Cody.

"We have something to celebrate," I said, "so we bought you this on one condition: You'll share it with your brothers or sisters."

He was looking down at the disc and it took a second to register. "You're pregnant?" Absolute awe in his voice. "*You're pregnant?*" A huge smile.

"How do you feel?" I asked.

"I don't know." Like he just couldn't believe it but it was great. Then a delayed reaction. Distress. "Where are they gonna sleep?"

And immediate relief when I said, "In the guest room."

One of the first things I did after we passed the three-month mark and felt safe telling people we were pregnant was to call Conrad Bain. Connie is an identical twin and used to regale me with stories about his brother, Bonar.

We took Conrad and his beautiful wife, Monica, out to dinner so we could pick his brain about what it was like being a twin.

Connie's family moved around a lot when he and Bonar were young. They lived in a series of very small, sort of back-woods towns in Canada and they were in grade school during the late twenties and early thirties. Very few people there had even seen a set of twins. They were treated either like movie stars or circus freaks. He told one story I'll never forget. When they were in first grade, Connie didn't do very well on a test. Nor did his brother. The teacher announced to the class that their failure was to be expected because they were twins and, consequently, had only half a brain each.

The one piece of advice he gave us was to always buy two of everything. He told us about the Christmas he and Bonar and their younger brother all asked for bikes. His younger brother was given a bike of his own, but he and Bonar got a bike between them—one bike for two boys. It wasn't a good Christmas.

I had a great pregnancy, annoyed only by the fact that I wasn't allowed to exercise between my tenth and eighteenth weeks. Those weeks are crucial in the development of twins, when there is the risk of one twin drawing nutrients meant for both, leaving the second twin undernourished and underdeveloped. My boys were fine, five pounds nine ounces and five pounds two ounces, and I carried them to term.

I went in for my weekly checkup on a Friday. The doctor was fairly aggressive with my exam and by that night, I started having some discomfort. On Sunday night, around eleven o'clock, I took some Tylenol and told Billy we should head for the hospital.

Again, I wanted a natural birth with no drugs. My doctor had to fight off the anesthesiologists who kept popping in to say, "Let us just put in a shunt so it will be there in case of emergency." I didn't want any needles in my back; I'd rather have excruciating contractions than needles in my back.

The first thing Billy did when we got into the labor room was look for a couch. He was sure he was going to pass out.

The nurse might as well have. I knew I was in trouble when I told her I was having identical twins and she said, "Oh, a boy and a girl?" When our labor coach, Judy Chapman, told her my blood sugar was low and I needed an IV, she left for the bathroom instead. Judy got me a Popsicle. Then when the nurse finally returned, she couldn't get the needle into my vein. After five tries the room looked like a scene from *Dawn of the Dead.*

I was pretty much out of it from the pain. I looked at the clock and it said 6:00 A.M. and then I looked again and it was 9:00 A.M. The problem was I never fully dilated. I never got to the point where I wanted to push. I remembered what that felt like when Cody was born. It was a great feeling and I sure wasn't having it with the boys. The doctor kept saying, "Push," and I kept saying, "You don't understand. I can't. It's too painful." I knew what he wanted me to do, I knew what it looked like, I could even act it out like an actress doing a scene, but boy, I couldn't do it. I believe it was because the babies weren't ready to be born and the doctor had hastened the process by stripping my membranes. Whatever the reason, he finally decided he needed to use the vacuum forceps and Walker came out screaming. He stopped a year later.

"Okay," I said, "give me a few minutes to relax and then I can try again." I still didn't feel the need to push.

"You don't have a few minutes," he said. "Here comes number two."

And William arrived.

In spite of his anxiety, Billy was a champ through the whole process. He practically pushed the doctor out of the way to get to his sons. As soon as Walker was born, Billy went with the nurse to one side of the room to watch him get weighed. When William came out, Judy went with him. There were ten people in the room, all paying attention to the babies.

That's when my back went into spasms. I couldn't move from my neck to my knees. That's the only time I ever really thought about my age. I thought I was having a stroke.

Walker was screaming so loudly that no one heard me calling for help. Finally, Judy turned around and saw the panic in my eyes. I kept telling myself to stay calm but I was terrified. She did her best to help me relax and the paralysis passed about five minutes later. One of the longer five minutes of my life.

The boys were born on St. Patrick's Day, March 17, 1997. Walker Steven Van Zandt and William Dalton Van Zandt. Our Dutch-Italian-Armenian-French-Canadian leprechauns.

We didn't publicize the fact that we'd used an egg donor as part of our fertility treatments. We told our family and friends but Billy wasn't comfortable making public so personal a choice. As far as the media was concerned, I said simply that we underwent fertility treatments for five years and one of them finally worked. But on a one-to-one basis, whenever I feel someone will benefit from knowing how I got pregnant, I am happy to tell our story.

What I wasn't expecting, and have never really understood, is that women looked to me as some kind of hero; they find hope and comfort in my achieving something they have yet to do. I don't think having children at age fifty-one is heroic. It's unusual, yes, and for some people probably even controversial, but there's nothing heroic about it. It's hard—emotionally, physically, and financially—and there's no guarantee that it's possible for every woman.

Whenever someone says to me, "Oh, I really want to have children and I'm so glad to know I can wait a little longer because you did," I set them straight. Even with a donor's egg, I am the exception, not the rule. Don't wait because you think you have all the time in the world. You may not.

Billy is still not comfortable broadcasting our story although he was the one who said I needed to write this. He worries about the children and their reaction. As soon as I felt they were old enough to understand, I started explaining how sometimes a mom has to borrow an egg because hers don't work as well and how there was a lady who was so loving and wonderful she gave us one of hers. What's important is that they know they are the most loved, cherished children in the world. To us, they definitely are.

People come up to me and ask, "How do you do it? Aren't you tired all the time? Isn't it hard having twins when you're older?"

It's hard having twins at any time but that doesn't have to do with being older. In my mind, I'm about thirty-five. My Armenian relatives are my role models. My mother was working two jobs until three months before she died, at age eighty-one. My uncle Ralph is seventy-eight and his brother Ken is seventy, and they spend their evenings out dancing. My aunt Anna, seventy-six, single-handedly takes care of my uncle George, who has Parkinson's disease. My aunt Ruby takes care of our entire family. After we celebrated her ninetieth birthday with a luncheon for a hundred people, she went back to her house and cooked dinner for forty-five of us, stayed up entertaining until midnight, and then had breakfast ready for thirty-five of us at nine the next morning. She served lunch at two o'clock. She does that every holiday, most weekends, and at least one night a week. She just had her driver's license renewed for five years. When she's not cooking or cleaning or gardening, she's convincing us to go play the slot machines at the casino nearby. So . . . starting again at fifty-one? That's nothing.

The hard part just has to do with having two kids at one time. I worried about that before they were born:

*August 19, 1996 (Four months pregnant)*
*I'm frightened I'm going to be too tired. Too weary. I won't have*
*enough energy. What do I worry about? I worry I won't be able to*
*tell them apart. I'll be too jaded to approach everything with the*
*wonder and enthusiasm I had with Cody. Will I ever sleep? Will I*
*turn into a shrew? Already I'm too tired to play Star Wars cards with*
*Cody at 5 in the afternoon, it requires too much concentration.*

*Cody says, "Mom, don't forget, you'll have three people*
*helping you."*

Thank God. Our boys didn't turn out to be mild-
mannered, easygoing babies like Cody. These guys would be a
challenge to anyone at any age. William had a temper and
never stopped moving long enough to nurse; Walker cried if I
put him down and never slept through the night until he was
a year old. All I did was nurse: Nurse one, he falls asleep; nurse
the other one, he falls asleep just as the first one wakes up to
nurse again.

*May 30, 1997*
*Yesterday I had a voiceover job at 9; at 8:25 Leticia hadn't*
*arrived. I was getting ready to take them with me to the studio*
*when she walked in. Then I raced home to nurse, met the musical*
*director for an hour, nursed and pumped, had a 2:30, 3:00,*
*4:00, and a 5:10 audition at four different places. In between the*
*4 and 5 I came home to nurse and Walker was so upset, I*

*cancelled the 5:10 and made a doctor's appointment for him
instead. He finally calmed down and I cancelled the doctor.
Can't stay awake.*

Okay, so maybe it was harder than I remember. And I
know I wouldn't have been able to get through the first year
without Billy and Cody and Leticia. But the truth is, when
you're doing it, when you're inside your life and just living it,
you don't think of it as anything unusual or different or special. I was fifty-one. I had twins. That's just my life.

Besides, I didn't have much imagination. It never dawned
on me that at a time in life when most of my friends would be
vacationing in Europe while their kids were in college, I'd be
standing in a video arcade with Letty looking for lost Yu-Gi-
Oh cards.

Leticia and I have been together for twenty-two years. Five
days a week, eight hours a day. Sometimes more. She's as much
a part of my children's lives as I am. She's fixed my car, repaired
my plumbing, moved my furniture. She's taken care of me
when I couldn't walk with a torn disc. She's seen me through
a divorce. She's slept at my house to baby-sit when I had to
work nights. She's taken my kids to her house when I had to
go out of town. She celebrated my fortieth birthday with me,
driving home from a film shoot in Lake Havasu, Arizona,
while we stopped along the road to let the kids throw up. Her
children are my children's best friends.

When Cody was four, I went to Australia for a week to co-host a Los Angeles morning talk show on location. This time Letty left her family and traveled with us. We stayed in a lovely, upscale hotel where I had to convince her it was okay if she didn't make the bed. A year later, when George Romero asked me to return to Pittsburgh for three weeks to make *Two Evil Eyes,* Letty brought her son Kevin with her so she could help me with Cody during the first week. After she left, I was on my own. We shot the entire movie in a huge house and I had one of the bedrooms there all to myself. Cody and I went to the set every evening and he'd play video games or watch TV and color or play with LEGOS in my bedroom until we broke for "lunch" at midnight. One of the production assistants stayed with him while I was on the set. Sometimes they took him swimming in the backyard pool. Then I'd put him to bed at 1:00 A.M. and when I wrapped at 6:00 A.M., carry him sleeping into the van to go home. I'd sleep with him for five hours, have breakfast, take a walk, play games, and sometime around 3:00 P.M. put him in front of the TV to watch cartoons while I took a nap. I realize now that starring in a film and taking care of a five-year-old by myself was insane but Letty was so important to me, it never crossed my mind to hire anyone else. We've been through a lot together—her seven boys and my three, my divorce, the death of her daughter. She's my sister, my mother, my caretaker, and my friend.

The only thing I really didn't like about having children at a late age is filling party bags for their birthdays. It made me crazy when Cody was young; it makes me crazy now. I never know what to put in those bags. What are the boys going to like? What are the girls going to like? Will the parents get mad because there's candy in there? If I buy the boys baseball cards, what do I buy the girls? How many kids are actually coming and how many bags do I need? What if someone brings his or her brother or sister? These bags are too short for comic books. They're not wide enough for Magic Tree House books. Did I put a bracelet in that bag or is one of the boys going to pick it up? If six water pistols come in one package and four yo-yos come in another, how many packages of each do I need? Now that I've got all the bags opened up on the kitchen table, did I put the same number of KitKat bars in each one? I know one mom who goes downtown to the merchandise mart and buys real watches for all the kids. Am I going to hear, "Jeez, Andrew gave us soccer balls at his party, there's nothing in here but junk?"

Makes me crazy.

That and Halloween costumes. When Cody was four years old, John's girlfriend made him a dragon costume. I think it was a dragon. Maybe a dinosaur, I'm not sure. She'd sewn it by hand and it had hundreds of individual green wool scales on it. It was very impressive. All I'd ever been able to come up with were the Chinese pajamas someone had given him when he was two. I drew a Fu Manchu mustache on him and tried to get him to let me spray his curly blond hair black. Costumes are not my forte. I never liked sewing in Home Economics class because none of the patterns fit my bustline and I had to do major mathematical calculations to alter them. I have to wear costumes when I go to work so for me putting on something different is not a fun, once-a-year event. I hate it, actually. I was overjoyed when Cody outgrew the desire to dress up for Halloween. And now here I am again, having to face October 31 with not only one reveler who needs dressing, but two.

But other than that, no, it's not hard at all.

# Kander and Ebb

**THE BABIES ARE TWO MONTHS OLD AND I'VE AGREED TO** do a musical my friend Glenn Casale is directing. It seems like a fun idea.

I first worked with Glenn in 1986 when he directed me in a stage production of *Strange Snow.* We've done six shows together and become very close. I trust him completely.

"It'll be easy, Adrienne," he says. "It's a three-week rehearsal and a three-week run and we're only performing six shows a week: four nights and two matinees. We can do the early music rehearsals in your game room and we can even start learning the choreography on your tennis court so you can take a break whenever you need to nurse the babies. You'll have them right there with you. And when we move down to the theater, you can bring Letty and the babies with you." This is an actress's dream, to be with her children and work at the same time.

The show is *And the World Goes Round* by the legendary John Kander and Fred Ebb (of *Chicago* and *Cabaret* fame). There's no book, really, it's more of a musical revue. There are five of us in the cast, two guys and three girls.

We start the rehearsals around the piano in my game room. An hour into the first day, my friend Suzanne's husband brings Cody home from school and pulls me aside to tell me Suzanne's cancer has spread to her lymph nodes. She's going to have to undergo stem cell replacement, which is almost as life-threatening as the cancer.

I'm devastated. I can't concentrate. Everyone around me is learning harmonies and I can't even see the music on the page. I should quit. I want to quit. But I don't want to leave Glenn without an actress at this late date. I call Suzanne and she tells me there's nothing she needs me for now; she's going to be in isolation for the treatment. She'll need me when she comes home and by then the show will have opened.

When I get off the phone the cast is rehearsing "How Lucky Can You Get?" I can't get through the song without weeping.

We're working on the music first. Every two hours we take a ten-minute break. The other four actors go to the bathroom, check their answering machines, return phone calls, have a snack. I feed the kids. I race upstairs to the family room, grab the boppie (a maniacal version of a nursing pillow), attach one baby to my right breast and one baby to my left, and try to nurse. It's not easy because William has decided he'd rather have breast milk in a bottle; it comes out faster and he doesn't have to work as hard. So he screams and kicks and bites my nipple, then gives me a big smile and starts all over again. Walker will nurse all afternoon if I let him. He starts crying when I have to leave.

Back to rehearsal. I have to sing a song in German. I don't speak German. I speak French, a little Spanish, and less Armenian—nothing close to German. I'll need to memorize the damn thing phonetically. I can do it if I have time. It's been years since I've done a musical and I've forgotten how much work we have to do *after* rehearsals. Everyone else goes home at night and studies the material. I change diapers and nurse. The boys are no longer on the same schedule. As soon as William falls asleep, Walker wakes up. Billy's in New Jersey working on his own stage production so I'm alone at night. I'm averaging five hours of sleep in two-hour increments. There's no time to eat. I'm living on Balance Bars and decaf tea with brown sugar and milk. My milk supply is diminishing and the babies are taking longer and longer to nurse.

Next comes the song with the banjos. No, not with the banjos in the orchestra pit—the banjos we all have to play on stage. I don't play the banjo, just like I don't speak German. I need more time at night to practice the banjo and the German. Problem is, every time I play the banjo, Walker gets upset and starts screaming. I don't blame him. I'm pretty god-awful.

Once we get a handle on the vocal material, we head out to my tennis court to learn the choreography. I must have been nursing when Glenn told me the details of the show because I don't remember him saying we'd be doing a tap number. In roller skates.

You guessed it. I don't know how to tap like I don't know how to play the banjo and I don't know how to speak German. I can roller-skate, though. Forward. As long as I don't have to stop.

The number is choreographed with the five of us in a row doing slap, ball change, whatever, as we circle around the stage in our skates. With me there, it's four in a row and one drifting two feet in front, hoping nobody notices. The poor choreographer is having a breakdown.

When it's time to move to the rehearsal studios, I arrange with Leticia to drive there directly from her house and meet me and the babies at 11:00. I take blankets and toys and diapers, an ice chest with extra breast milk, and two vibrating chairs and two baby seats. My neighbor asks if we're moving. At noon, Letty still hasn't arrived. I've got one baby in my arms and the other vibrating away in his chair and I'm fracturing my German solo. Letty finally shows up at 12:30. She had to change a flat tire on the freeway.

Ah, the freeway. Somehow I've ended up with a child who hates sitting in a car seat. In traffic, the drive from my house to the theater takes an hour. Walker screams nonstop through all of it. Every day, both directions. I try everything I can think of to calm him but nothing works. I'd planned on listening to my rehearsal tapes and learning my harmonies while I drive. Instead I play a white noise tape of a hair dryer. He's still screaming. Another tape: a mother's heartbeat as heard from the womb. More screaming. Finally I pull over to the side of the road and nurse him in the hope he'll fall asleep. William starts screaming instead. Walker calms down while he's got something to suck on but as soon as I get back in the front seat, he joins his brother. Thirteen-year-old Cody says he doesn't know how I do it. "Is there a hormone that keeps you from throwing them against the wall?"

I can't keep up with my nursing. Believe me, there's no correlation between breast size and capacity. I rent an industrial-size electric breast pump so I can build up my supply and leave bottles in the freezer. The boys are drinking faster than I'm filling. My neighbor, whose son is two weeks younger than Walker and William, offers to give me some of the breast milk she has stored in her freezer. I consider walking up and down the hill we live on, knocking on doors, asking to check milk supplies in freezers. My pediatrician nixes the idea. I don't want to use formula if I can help it. I take the pump with me to the theater.

We're in the final days of rehearsal. I'm faking my way through the banjo number, the tapping roller-skate number, and the German. My solo songs are beautiful as long as you don't notice the milk stains on my gown. It's a strapless red satin sheath and once I'm zipped into it, I can't get out. I spend intermissions sitting at my dressing table, my breasts popped up over the top of the gown, the electric pump sucking away. The stage manager is afraid to come into my room to call "Places"—God knows what he'll see.

The show is a big success. We sell out. On opening night a fan from the audience comes up to ask for my autograph. I have a baby in each arm. "So what have you been doing lately?" he asks. "I don't hear too much about you."

# Manifesting

**IT'S SUMMER OF 2000 AND I'M VISUALIZING WORK.**

"I want a short-term job in a desirable location that pays a lot of money."

My agent calls to offer me a hundred thousand dollars to go three rounds in the ring with Anna Nicole Smith on *Celebrity Boxing.*

I try again. "I want a GOOD short-term job in a desirable location that pays a lot of money."

I get an offer for a million dollars to do an infomercial promoting antiwrinkle cream. All I have to do is sell my soul on late-night TV letting someone vacuum my pores and spread white glop on my face.

Okay, so I haven't got this visualization thing down exactly right but I'm working on it. I've got to be more specific about what I ask for.

And it's time to ask. The boys are in preschool, the house

we've been remodeling in New Jersey is almost finished, Cody's college applications have been submitted. I've just returned from Pittsburgh where I played Golde, Tevye's wife, in a beautiful production of *Fiddler on the Roof.*

I want to work.

I believe in my power to manifest the things I want in life. All my life I said I wanted twins. Okay, maybe I should have said I want twins while I'm still young enough to walk without a cane but, nevertheless, I have twins. When I was ready for a good man to come into my life, I met Billy. If I imagine money raining down on me, I come home to find residual checks waiting. I can get a parking spot when I need one. I make all this happen.

So I'm going to make work happen. Really good work. Work I care about and love doing.

The first step is to hire a manager. I've been around a long time, working in L.A. nearly thirty years. I have a film awaiting release and I'm playing a recurring role as Oswald's mom on *The Drew Carey Show,* but today's casting directors are either so young they don't know most of my work or so old they have a John Travolta-before-*Pulp Fiction* image of me: I'm a sitcom actress; I'm a scream queen; I'm filling someone else's fairly narrow pigeonhole.

I need to start again. I need a manager who has enough power to convince people to see me with new eyes. Once I'm in the office, I can get the job. I need someone to open the door.

It's not easy. I feel like I'm back in Greenwich Village at age nineteen, writing out my three-by-five cards. Only this time, instead of calling casting directors, I'm calling managers.

I tell my brother-in-law, Steven, what I'm doing. When he's not playing guitar with The E Street Band or producing his popular syndicated radio show, Steven is playing Silvio on *The Sopranos.*

"You can't do that. It's embarrassing. You can't do that. I mean, I don't know what you should do but you've got to initiate some project yourself, you and Billy. That's terrible. Stop."

He's right. It *is* embarrassing. But it's not going to happen if I don't make the calls.

I talk to ten managers. One doesn't think she has enough power to help me. One is pregnant and cutting back on her client list. One is worried about how the pending SAG strike will affect his top clients like Jack Lemmon and Richard Dreyfuss; he's not signing anyone new. One has two women in my category already. He bemoans the industry's attitude toward women in their fifties and is extremely gracious as he apologizes for not being able to meet with me. One promises to call me back and doesn't. One says she's very interested and wants to set up a meeting. I never hear from her again.

The entire process takes almost two months. It's exhausting. I'm setting myself up for rejection on a daily basis.

Eventually, there are five firms that would like to manage me. It's a difficult decision but one I'm happy to make. I go with my instincts and hire a man I met twenty years ago. I remember at the time wishing he represented me. Maybe I should have said I wanted it to happen while I was still young enough to walk without a cane.

Sometimes I'm slow on the manifestation thing but it always works.

Within a year after I sign with him, I am working steadily: two films, a musical, several television shows, and, finally, *Carnivàle:* work I care about and love doing.

In summer of 2001 I start visualizing a book deal.

# My Mother

**MY MOTHER AWAKENS AT 2:30 IN THE MORNING. SHE** needs more pain medication. As the doctor has explained, the swelling in her spleen is pushing against her ribs. I press the call button and then walk into the hallway to find the nurse. I am wearing a long red nightgown, a blue and yellow Lucky Brand T-shirt, and a denim jacket with purple sleeves and hood to fight off the extreme cold in the room. The air conditioner is on high, the windows are open, and a portable fan blows on my mother's face. She is sweating. Her bedsheets are damp, her gown is wet.

An hour later she moans in her sleep. I don't know if the pain has increased or if she is dreaming. If it is pain, I don't want to wake her to have to face it. I lie still on the cot and listen; ready to jump up the second she calls my name. Instead she says, "Ma, Ma." In the next moment, through my half-closed eyes, I see my dead grandmother standing at the foot of

my mother's bed. She's watching my mother. The room grows
warm and I am filled with a sense of peace. It settles on me like
a fleece blanket.

For the rest of the night, whenever my anxiety takes hold,
I push my eyes open. My grandmother is still standing there.
I relax.

I have promised my sister that I will abide by her wishes
and not tell Mom she is dying. Jocelyn is sure she will lose her
optimism and stop fighting the disease.

It's Tuesday. My mother's been in the hospital in San Jose
since Sunday when she left a Rita Moreno concert com-
plaining of severe pains in her stomach. The doctor wants to
send her home. I speak to the hospital representative about
our alternatives. We will not put her in a nursing home and
although I am willing to arrange for a private-care nurse, the
likelihood that we can find anyone on a day's notice is minimal. Jocelyn and I agree that hospice is the best choice for the
time being. They will come to the house and help with whatever needs to be done and we will alternate staying with her
until we can find full-time care.

An attendant comes to take my mom for another X-ray. As
we wait for him to prepare the room, I ask her if she is scared.
She doesn't answer me and I think perhaps she hasn't heard.
Later, when we've returned to her room and I am helping her
get back into bed, she says, "You know when you asked me if

I'm scared? I'm not scared. I just want my family around me." So, I think to myself, she does know what's going on.

Wednesday afternoon the hospice representative comes to speak to us. My sister is sitting on the cot to my left and I am next to my mother's bed. The hospice worker sits facing me, at the foot of the bed. She begins to explain that hospice care is for terminally ill patients for whom no further treatment is prescribed save pain management. My sister is crying but my mother cannot see her. My mother is a bit groggy from the morphine. She seems to be listening but her eyes close occasionally. She nods in agreement and thanks the hospice volunteer for coming. My sister assures me that Mother "didn't miss a trick," and that she understands.

That evening I am explaining to my mother that I will leave for Los Angeles the following day to take the boys to New Jersey so they can stay with Billy and I will be back to take care of her on Tuesday.

"Why?" she asks. "You don't need to do that. Once I'm at home, I don't need any help."

"You do, Mom, hospice insists on it. You're going to be on pain medication and someone has to be with you twenty-four hours a day to make sure you don't get dizzy or fall or something."

"Well," she says, "it's not really hospice, Adrienne, because that's for terminally ill patients."

It takes me a few seconds to respond.

• • •

Early on Thursday morning I find Dr. Brennan at the nurses' station. My mother's white blood count has dropped from 188,000 to 186,000. This seems encouraging to me until he reminds me it is supposed to be around 12,000.

"Listen," he says, "I am afraid I haven't been completely clear with you and your mother. She needs to know she is dying."

"You've been clear, Dr. Brennan. It's just that we've been hesitant to be too explicit with my mom."

"I'd like to talk to her. I'm going to have to talk to your mother now and I'd like to talk to both you and Jocelyn before I leave the hospital. Do you think you can get her here in the next half hour?"

I call Joc and go back to my mom's room. Dr. Brennan follows me in.

"Hi, Armen. How are you feeling?"

"Oh, not too bad. I took a pain pill in the middle of the night and that seemed to help. Am I going home today?"

"Yes. I'm sorry, Armen, but there's not much more I can do for you except make you comfortable. The medication isn't working and your numbers aren't good."

"Well, can I ask you a question? What about a bone marrow transplant?"

The doctor has tears in his eyes. "No, Armen, it's not likely it would work and at your age, we wouldn't attempt it."

My mother turns and looks at me. "I wanted more time," she says.

• • •

I am screaming at my sister in my dream. "You lied to me! You didn't tell me she was dying! You didn't tell me she had so little time."

In truth, none of us knew. My mom worked up until four months ago and then just complained about feeling tired. Her white blood cell count wasn't good but she was waiting for the medication she was taking to work so she could go back to her job as a hostess at an upscale, neighborhood deli. She was eighty-one.

I awaken at 6:00 A.M. at our farmhouse in New Jersey. I'd flown home from San Jose Friday morning in time to attend the Mother's Day Tea at the boys' preschool. It was absolutely surreal, having just left my mother who was dying, and then sitting at a little nursery table being served cupcakes William and Walker had made for me. On Saturday the boys went to a birthday party and that evening I took Cody to see *Mamma Mia!* to celebrate his birthday (which was a big mistake—I doubt he'll ever see another musical as long as he lives). We flew to New Jersey on Sunday, in time to have Mother's Day dinner with Billy's family, and now it's Tuesday and I'm supposed to fly back to San Jose this afternoon. But I know the dream is a message and I know my afternoon flight will get me there too late. Quietly I go downstairs to call the airlines and change my reservation. I can get there two hours earlier. I want to call my mother's house to tell them, but it is the middle of the night there. I hope they are all asleep.

The children are watching the Marx Brothers in *Duck Soup* and Billy has gone to work. I have an hour and a half before my flight. I take my coffee out onto the deck and sit with my face in the sun. I do not read, I do not think, I do not move. Again I know what I need to do. I pick up the phone and I call my mother's doctor. He is at an oncology conference in San Francisco but I know I will reach his voice mail.

"Hi, Dr. Brennan, this is Adrienne Barbeau. It seems likely my mother just has a day or two left but I wanted to ask you a few more questions, just to put my mind at rest. I suppose this is an expected part of the process of letting her go, fighting until the last minute. I just wanted to make sure that there is no course of action we might take that we could pay for ourselves, something that might fall outside the guidelines of her insurance company, Secure Horizons. I know we talked about thalidomide. I also wondered about cytarabine. I know these are things an HMO would not agree to pay for, but that isn't a consideration for me. I guess we all just want to feel we didn't overlook anything. I'm on my way to Los Gatos now and I'll be at my mother's tomorrow when you get this. I believe you have the number there. I think I'll also try to reach Dr. Liu as you suggested. Thank you."

Dr. Liu is his associate. She is on call while he is out of town. I reach her assistant who is very understanding. She knows Secure Horizons won't pay for thalidomide. I assure her money doesn't matter. In the middle of the call, the battery on my phone dies. I reach her a few minutes later. She says she'll have Dr. Liu call as soon as she finishes a consultation.

I am just closing my suitcase when she calls. In spite of her accent, I get a clearer, more specific response to my questions. Perhaps Dr. Brennan was too caring and too close to my mother; his answers seemed less definitive. When we hang up I believe everything that could have been done was done. I will be able to tell my sister we did not wait too long or not fight hard enough.

My sister has also had a consultation. The doctor who oversees the hospice program is a retired hematologist. When I call her from the airport to check on my mother, she relays what he has told her. Most people with a myeloproliferative disease live a year; my mother has lived eight. When the disease progresses to acute leukemia, there is nothing left to do. They could have removed her spleen but she would have died from the operation. Now she has a tumor in her stomach the size of a football. Most likely it will rupture; she will have no more pain but she will go into shock and die within an hour.

My friend Mews gets on the phone. She's been staying with my mother since I left so my sister could go to work, but Jocy hasn't left my mother's side, either. She tells me my mother was doing great on Friday, she actually took her morphine drip and went to the hairdresser's to get her hair done. And on Saturday she was yelling at the Giants' game on TV. She's a big Giants fan.

"She's had quite a downturn since yesterday, though, Adie. I think you'd better get here fast."

"I am. I changed my reservation and I'm getting in tonight at eight."

"Oh, good. I think she'll wait for you but I'm real sorry . . . yesterday I was talking about getting a wheelchair to get her out into the garden. She wanted to go in the garden. She was feisty. But today she's really gone downhill. I think she'll wait for you, though. My mother did. She waited five days for my sister to get back from a camping trip."

"Well, I'll be there soon. Make sure she knows that. I know Jocy already told her but make sure she knows."

My plane sits on the runway for an hour. An hour after we take off I want to call to see how she is. *Wait*, I tell myself, *Bill is probably taking Mews to the airport and Jocy is there all alone and may not be able to handle Mom and the phone at the same time. Wait until halfway through the trip and then call.*

When I do, my sister's voice sounds clear. It's hard to hear over the engine noise so I say I just wanted to check on Mom and I prepare to hang up. Then I realize my sister is very calm. She is telling me my mother is gone. The serenity in her voice doesn't make sense with the words she is saying so I think I must be misunderstanding her. I think she is telling me Mom is fine but I know she is not. Finally I hear her clearly. "What time, Jocy? What time?" I cannot comprehend the difference in time zones even though I am wearing a double-faced watch.

I need to know if it was when I felt I should call. It was. Somehow I sensed something. I knew.

Jocelyn keeps telling me it's okay now because Mom is free of pain. I know. I am worried for Jocelyn. She is worried for me. I tell her I will be all right. I hang up.

I try to reach Cody but he is not at home. I call Leticia and Glenn and Cody's friend Kenny in case he is there, but he is not. I reach Billy. "I should have taken an earlier plane," I cry. "I didn't want to leave the children early in the morning without saying good-bye because I didn't know how long I'd be away. I thought I could see them for a few hours and still get there in time. I thought I had more time." After I get off the phone, I go in the bathroom and weep. "I'm sorry. I'm so sorry I didn't get there. I am so sorry." It is something I will have to forgive myself for and hope that others will forgive, too. I think my mother will understand. She always put her children first.

We scatter my mother's ashes over left field at the Giants' stadium in San Francisco and play "Take Me Out to the Ball Game" at her memorial service.

When we clean out her condominium, I discover something about her I never knew. She has a collection of shoes that rivals my own: close to a hundred shoeboxes filled with shoes in pristine condition.

Weeks later, I go to see a psychic.

"Did your mother just pass over?" he asks. "She says to tell you her hair looks good. She says you'll know what that means."

My mother, who took her morphine drip and got her hair done right before she died, is sending me a message.

"She's with another lady who's wearing strange-looking shoes. They're sitting in rocking chairs on the front porch of a farm and they're very happy to be together. They're very proud of you."

The other lady he's describing is my grandmother.

"And she has a lot of shoes with her. She has over a hundred pairs of shoes."

# Carnivàle

**I** SPENT THE DAY BEFORE YESTERDAY GOING DOWN ON A large, attractive woman with a full beard. At least, I think she was attractive. I couldn't say for sure because I was blind. Which meant I didn't get to see the nude man crawling back and forth across the floor, either.

I didn't think much about it until last night when a friend asked how my week was and I thought, *Well . . . interesting.*

I've been working. On *Carnivàle.* Playing Ruthie, the snake dancer, who turns blind when she channels Lodz, the dead mentalist, and makes love to his lover, Lila, the bearded lady.

It's what I do for a living.

When I first hear about *Carnivàle,* it's a role I think I might be right for: a woman in a coma.

Billy mentions it to his manager, Howard Klein, who is producing the series. "Oh, there are other roles that are more interesting," Howard says. "We'll get her in."

He does. Three weeks later I have an audition for the role of Ruthie. Ruthie isn't in a coma. She's a "wizened, tattooed snake charmer." Sounds okay to me.

There's no script available so they send me the "sides." These are individual audition scenes. All I can tell from them is that a bunch of carnival workers are helping bury the mother of a young boy who's on the lam. Ruthie is one of the carny workers. She makes a speech at the woman's graveside, then goes on to convince the other carny folk to save the boy from the cops. I love the speech:

*Lord, never met this woman. Don't know what kind a life she did. Whether she sinned or did good. All's I know she got a son who gone through serious tribulation and great courage to face down them three big trucks and put her in the ground proper. And that says something, yes sir. So she should go to heaven all right.*

Everything I need to know about Ruthie is in her use of language. I can hear how she says these words. I recognize her. I put on my jeans, a T-shirt, and my favorite cowboy boots and I'm ready to audition.

Except for my hair. My hair doesn't make me look like a carny worker. Definitely doesn't make me look like a carny worker with tattoos. Makes me look like a woman who gets it styled twice a week with a round brush and an ionic dryer.

I've got a wig I wore in *The Convent* when I played a

crazed biker blowing away nuns with Molotov cocktails. It's long and wild and gray and scraggly. As close to carny as I'm going to get. I can't put it on myself so I stop at a beauty salon for help. The stylist thinks it will look more natural if I use my own bangs. She positions the wig so far back on my head I look like I've got a growth on my skull. A hairy growth. By the time I notice it, it's too late. I'm already in the casting office.

The office is small and cramped. Two casting assistants sit at their desks, three feet away from the actors, and talk on the phone to agents about their clients' deals.

"Hi, this is casting calling about *Carnivàle*. We need a quote on David. Oh really? Well, I'm afraid that's not going to happen."

"Hello, *Carnivàle*. Who? Oh yes, no, no, he did a very nice job. We're just not going in that direction."

"The role of Lila? Are you kidding? Haven't you read the script?"

There are five of us crammed into a six-foot space. Four chairs. Actors are arriving faster than they're leaving. I recognize one actor who starred in a series in the late seventies but I'll be damned if I can remember his name. He looks more nervous than I am.

And I'm nervous. I want this job. There's a woman sitting next to me with the same sides. She looks a lot more like the character than I do. Well, except for the wizened part. This woman is taking a chance sitting in a chair with arms. She's definitely not wizened. Still, her hair is long and straight, parted in the middle, lots of gray. I'd hire her.

There's a sign-up sheet so I can tell who I follow. As the casting director walks each actor out and says good-bye, he crosses off that name. My audition time is 4:00. At 4:45, I'm still waiting. I spend the time going out into the bathroom, doing a relaxation exercise. This involves standing very still, getting in touch with my nerves, and then laughing hysterically or crying until I calm down. It's a technique I learned in Warren Robertson's acting class thirty years ago and it works for me. Except for the crying, which makes my mascara run. I try to cry without a lot of tears.

Finally I'm up. I follow the casting director down a short hallway into a room that's even smaller than the waiting room. There's a chair for me to sit in and off to my left, a camera about three feet away. Four men sit side by side on a banquette against the back wall, two others are against the right wall, and the director is jammed in behind the camera with the casting director scrunched down next to the lens.

Smiles and introductions all around. Howard is there, which is nice for me but adds to my nervousness. Don't want to let him down or embarrass myself in front of someone I know. But they're a warm group of people and that helps. The director doesn't smile. Maybe there's the feeling that I got foisted on him as a favor and I'm nothing like what he's looking for. I don't know. I can't let it bother me.

I do the scene. I'm no longer nervous. I do exactly what I set out to do. The director doesn't smile but he wants me to do it again and he gives me some direction. I do the second take.

There's more urgency in his voice this time and he has me do it with yet a different direction. The changes are subtle but they're there. I'm happy. Someone asks me if I'm afraid of snakes. I don't love them but I'm not afraid of them. I've worked with rats and tarantulas. As long as it's not cockroaches, I'll take the job.

Smiles again all around. The casting director walks me out.

"You were fantastic! That was fantastic!"

"Well, thank you. I was a little nervous 'cause I've never worn a wig to an audition."

"That's a wig? I never even knew it. You were just fantastic."

Later that night Howard talks to Billy's writing partner, Jane. "Tell Billy Adrienne was fantastic today."

*Great,* I thought. *Well, let's see what happens.*

Nothing. Nothing happens. No one calls with an offer. No one says anything to my agents. So . . . I was fantastic but they hired someone else. Oh well, at least I didn't embarrass myself. I did what I set out to do and someone else was simply more right.

Two weeks later I'm in New Jersey overseeing the remodeling of our kitchen. Billy calls as I'm going to bed.

"I just talked to Howard. He said they love you and you're definitely still in the running for that part."

"You're kidding. I thought that was long gone."

"Nope. I wasn't supposed to tell you but I couldn't keep it to myself."

"Wow. Well, that's good news. But I'm not gonna think about it until I hear something through the right channels."

I'm just falling asleep when the phone rings again. It's Billy.

"I can't keep this to myself. I'm so excited I've got to tell you. But you can't tell anyone else, not your manager, not your agent. What Howard actually said was they're trying to work it so you don't have to go to network. They just want to offer you the role."

"Going to network" is showbiz parlance for a final audition in front of the network executives. There are usually three or four actors who go to network for the same role, all of them having negotiated their contract prior to the audition. That way, when someone gets hired, he can't ask for more money. Sometimes four people will go to network and none will get hired. Then the casting directors have to start all over again. I've only had to do it once. Back in the seventies, Norman Lear had so much power, all he had to do was say he wanted me and I was hired. But several years ago I auditioned against Raquel Welch and Loni Anderson for a half-hour sitcom. The executives were on the floor laughing and I walked out of the room certain it was my job. They hired Connie Stevens, who wasn't even at the audition, then fired her and hired Dyan Cannon. Going to network is unbelievably nerve-wracking.

I'm as touched by Billy's excitement for me as I am excited for myself. I spend the rest of the night awake, wishing he hadn't told me. Worrying that I might have to go to network and I'll blow it. Worrying that someone will change his or her mind. Worrying that the agency will get the offer and blow the deal. I have to talk myself down. Just put it away until an actual offer comes in, Adrienne. There's nothing you can do about it.

I pretty much succeed in doing that. Don't mention it to anyone. Make my mind move away to something else whenever I find myself daydreaming about it. Then I have an epiphany. I firmly believe that I am manifesting whatever is happening to me, so obviously the best thing to do is to visualize it as a done deal. Stop trying to avoid disappointment by not getting excited, and instead make it happen with whatever psychic ability I possess. I start imagining the phone call, seeing the contract, feeling the money descend on me. I'm going to make this happen.

The Friday before Christmas my manager calls. He's heard from the casting director that they will be making me an offer right after the holidays. Now I *really* start to believe it might happen. Now I mention it to one or two close friends. I don't say what it is, exactly, only that I might have an offer for a pilot.

Actually, I don't know what it is. When the offer finally does come in, the first week of January, I still haven't read a script. I've read one interesting scene. A bunch of carny workers take in a young boy. I have no idea what the rest of the story is.

I pick up the script on my way to UCLA to drop off Cody's college application portfolio. I read while I'm driving. I read at the traffic lights. I read while I wait for the professor to show up and I finish while I'm sitting on the lawn surrounded by college students. From the first page, I'm blown away. Yes, it's about carny workers but carny workers in the dustbowl during the depression. No wonder I recognize Ruthie—this is the poverty my mother lived through. And it's not really about carny workers, it's about satanic evangelists and freaks with supernatural powers. It's *The X Files* meets Marjoe Gortner out of David Lynch. It's a *Star Wars*-like epic, good versus evil. And it's great!

My excitement increases when I go in for my costume fitting. Ruth Myers is the designer. Primarily a designer for feature films, with a background in classical theater, Ruth is a tiny, dark-haired woman from Great Britain who knew she wanted to design costumes from the time she was four. Within minutes I know I can trust her; I know she understands exactly what will work on me and what won't. And she understands the character. I rave about her to anyone who will listen. The hair and makeup artists come in to consult. We all agree that I won't wear any makeup save mascara. This is my dream as an actress. I hate makeup. When we did *Fiddler* on Broadway, Jerome Robbins wouldn't allow it. I never cheated. As soon as I see a scene where the actress has just awakened (*Collateral Damage*) or just stepped out of the shower (*The Russia House*) and is in full eye makeup, I know I should ask for my money back because the movie is going to be bad. Where's the director? Doesn't anybody notice these things?

I meet some of the cast when we gather to do a prerecord of the song we'll be singing at the gravesite. Dan Knauf, the writer-producer, is there. He was in the room during my audition but I was so nervous then that I don't recognize him now and immediately put my foot in my mouth by asking what he does on the show. He's warm and sweet and I hope he understands.

Debra Christofferson, who plays Lila, the bearded lady, comes in. She reminds me that we met when she did *A Midsummer Night's Dream* with my former boyfriend Alex, and before that, when we attended a metaphysical workshop run by another former boyfriend, Dennis Adams, the healer who deals in miracles. Hey, if he's praying for this project, it can only be great.

Michael J. Anderson joins us. He plays Samson, the dwarf who runs the carnival. And then Sarah and Karyne Steben, identical twins who will be playing Siamese twins. The girls are from Montréal and have been doing a trapeze act with the Cirque du Soleil for the last ten years. They regale us with backstage stories of what goes on underwater in the Las Vegas production of *O*.

The rest of us meet for the first time at the table read on the Friday before we start filming. We're working in studios in Santa Clarita, thirty miles from my house. On a Friday afternoon, you have to allow an hour and a half to get there. The exec from HBO doesn't know this and she arrives an hour late so there's plenty of time for introductions. Scott Winant, Howard's producing partner, tells me he's always loved my work but he never would have thought of me for this part. I give a quiet thanks to Howard. Finally we start. This is not like a table read for a sitcom where if you don't deliver something close to a performance you lose your jokes the next day. This is a situation in which you have twenty actors, all with very different styles of reading. Nick Stahl and Clea Duvall, the two young leads, barely speak above a whisper. Michael Anderson tends to stutter. K Callan fills her performance with tears. It's a bit disconcerting. I leave the reading wondering whether anyone will be replaced and not quite so certain about the final product.

The set is fantastic. Up in the hills behind Magic Mountain Amusement Park. There's nothing up there but a field of cilantro and us. Incredible sideshow sets have been designed. An old working Ferris wheel is in place. Vintage Model Ts and pickup trucks ring the outside of the carnival. Ruth's costumes for the townsfolk and the roustabouts immediately transport us to the Depression. HBO has spent twelve million dollars on the pilot, more money than they've ever spent on a comparable project.

The only downside is whether or not the series will be too expensive to continue to produce.

All my scenes are shot outside. We start work at 4:30 in the afternoon and by the time my close-ups come along, it's 1:30 in the morning. I'm so cold I can't stop shaking. I've got mini heating pads in my boots, in my pockets, and in my bra.

Between every take I race into one of the circus tents and toast my face on a portable heater. The set costumer layers me with a robe and a full-length down coat and then whips them off when Rodrigo yells action.

Rodrigo Garcia is the director. Rodrigo started out as a director of photography. Recently, he's been directing *Six Feet Under* for HBO. Last year he wrote and directed his first feature under the auspices of the Sundance Festival. It's called *Things You Can Tell by Looking at Her.* It's really good. He gets wonderful performances out of his cast, and he's photographed them beautifully. I can tell by the words he's written that he cares for women; he's sensitive to them. He knows what he wants, he's funny and sweet and helpful and smart. Not a traffic cop. An actor's director. I trust him.

My third day of shooting is the funeral scene, the one I auditioned with. The one in which I play the concertina. I've spent forty-five minutes with an accordion player learning the basics but the night before we're supposed to shoot I go online to research it and realize he hasn't even taught me to hold it correctly. I freak out and call Snuffy Walden, our music supervisor, who volunteers to drive to the set at 5:00 A.M. and help me. We're shooting this scene in Lancaster, two hours east of my house, and I've driven out the night before to stay in an area hotel. I don't have the heart to ask Snuffy to get up that early. Instead I spend the evening standing in front of a mirrored closet, making up bogus fingering for random chords while I practice looking like I know what I'm doing. They've taken the insides out of the concertina so I have to fake the resistance it would give me if I were really opening and closing it, but at least I can't make the wrong sounds.

Time comes to do the scene. We get the singing and playing out of the way and then I do my speech. Rodrigo asks me to do it a bit differently, which makes me question my choices.

Three days later, when Rodrigo has seen the dailies, I ask him how the scene was.

"It's great. You were right and I was wrong."

"What do you mean?"

"I always do that," he says. "The actor has spent all this time preparing, getting it right, the way it should be, and then I come along and make a suggestion and when I see it in dailies, I like what they did without me better."

"Well," I say, "I wanted to give you what you wanted. You're watching, you know what's right."

"No, no, it's not a question of right or wrong. You gave me red and then I wanted to see blue and green. Different, that's all."

Filming ends and we go our separate ways. The producers have until May 15 to pick up the options on our contracts. It's the middle of February. Rumors are flying and everyone is very optimistic. Ruth Myers tells me they've already asked her if she's available to do the series. Someone else says they overheard an executive asking the prop department how much notice they would need to get the sets ready. The last thing the line producer, Anthony Santa Croce, says to me is, "I'll see you in June."

In March I'm offered a musical for the month of June. I call Howard's office to ask if he knows, in the event we are picked up, how soon we would start production. Everyone is still very positive but the final version will not be delivered to HBO until April 19, so there's no way to know until after that.

In early April I go in to do some looping on the film. This means there's some problem with the sound on some of my lines and they need to redo them, or they need to add extra dialogue. Dan Knauf is waiting alone in the recording studio. He says they've released Nick Stahl to do *Terminator 3,* so if we do get a pickup, filming won't start until at least September. Sounds like good news to me because if Nick's career is taking off, all the more reason for HBO to want a show in which he is the star.

As it turns out, only one of my lines needs to be replaced. Howard thinks the delivery was a little too "Rizzo"—my character in *Grease.* There's a twenty-minute discussion about adding a line in another scene, but no one can think of what I should say. I finally suggest two words and everyone loves it and that's the end of my dubbing session. I see just enough of two scenes to know that I love the look of the film. The lighting is perfect, the sets are great, and the characters are fascinating.

I realize I am living my life believing I am going to be doing a series starting in September. Every minute I spend with the kids I think, well, spend as much time as you can with them now because when you start work you won't be able to. It's like I'm enjoying a summer vacation. I'm setting myself up for disappointment but, you know what, I might as well be enjoying this time to the fullest, believing I've got a great series coming up, rather than walking around feeling anxious because I'm not working. I've got a choice of how to react and I choose anticipation. Makes me happy.

The network has to pick up our option by May 15. I'm in New Jersey that day, putting dishes away in the new pantry. It's the first anniversary of my mother's death. I'm unpacking her wine glasses and sterling and china. Every time the phone rings, I tense. I'm walking around with my face up to the sky, talking to my mother.

"Come on, Ma. I need your help here. Make this happen. If you've got any power up there, make this happen. Please."

At 3:30 the phone rings.

"Adrienne? I have Hal Stalmaster for you." Hal is one of my agents. After the longest thirty seconds in the history of the world, he gets on the line.

"Hi Adrienne. How are you? It's Hal."

Who the hell cares how I am? I'm a nervous wreck. Stop with the small talk and tell me if I have a job or not. "I'm fine, Hal. What's going on?"

"Well . . . HBO just called and they're picking up your option. You're supposed to start filming in September."

I hang up the phone and break into tears. Billy is ecstatic. And I'm pretty sure my mother is, too. My only sadness is that I can't call her up and tell her in person. But I think she knows. I think she had a hand in it right from the beginning.

# Sex Scenes and Snakes

*Excerpt from ninth-grade term paper entitled "To Be or Not to Be: Acting as a Vocation," written January 5, 1960.*

*"I am in good physical and mental health and am also a born optimist. I have no idea how to prove my courage or perseverance but I would like to think that if I have the will to go ahead now, I will be able to go ahead when the breaks are hardest."*

E. G. Marshall worked with Madagascar hissing cockroaches in his segment of *Creepshow.* I wouldn't even visit the set.

I've worked with tarantulas in *Fantasy Island,* bees in *The Fighting Nightingales* (an unsold pilot I did in 1978, immediately after *Maude* went off the air), and rats in the rat movie, but roaches? I'll starve first.

When I auditioned for *Carnivàle,* the producers asked how I felt about snakes. Well . . . I love them in boots. In fact, when my toes finally broke through my python Tony Llamas,

I had another pair specially made. They were the star attraction on the first-grade playground at recess.

Ruthie was billed as the snake dancer in *Carnivàle* but it wasn't until episode six that I heard rumors I was going to have a scene where I actually danced. I was raised on Eastern music. I grew up doing Armenian dances at weddings and baptisms and graduation parties and reunions. My cousins and I had to fight our uncles for space on the dance floor. I watched my mother practice her belly dance lessons in our living room. So I wasn't too worried about looking foolish, but I wanted to take some lessons so I could come in prepared.

I called the local exotic dance studio, the same place Cody had gone to Gymboree when he was three, and explained that I was going to be dancing with a snake and I wanted to learn some basic belly dance steps.

"Oh, you don't want belly dancing," said the teacher, whose name was Anisa. "Dancing with snakes is a whole other thing. You need to work with Mesmera, she's the one who can help you."

Only in L.A. could I find a woman named Mesmera who dances with snakes for a living.

I Googled Mesmera and, lo and behold, there she was: offering dance lessons, a newsletter, and exotic travel seminars. She was a sweetheart on the phone and I made an appointment to go to her home to work with her and her snake.

Snakes, plural. She keeps eight or nine in a bedroom.

These aren't garter snakes; these aren't your garden-variety gopher snakes. These are indigo snakes and corn snakes and boas and a gorgeous twenty-five-foot albino python who's so big she can no longer lift him herself.

Snakes aren't interested in learning choreography. You can move them around if you're gently firm with them but they pretty much do what they're going to do and you ad-lib the rest. Mesmera taught me how to handle them and I was as ready as I could be to do the scene.

I loved it. I really had a great time. I worked with an Australian milk snake named Fred and a diamondback boa named Taxi. Taxi was about seven feet long and weighed fifteen pounds. His size gave him top billing.

I started the dance with Fred wrapped around my arm. He slithered up my neck and looked me in the face while we flicked tongues at each other. Then I handed him off to Nick Stahl who was waiting in the wings and I got down on my knees, lifted Taxi out of a basket on the floor, and followed his lead. The idea was to make it as erotic as possible.

After four hours of moving Taxi to different parts of my body and filming from various angles, we decided to try one take where he started in my hair and then slid down my body to wherever he was going to go.

He went all right. I had just lifted him up in front of me to place him on my head when I felt something wet hit my foot. I jumped back in time to avoid most of the digested rat he'd decided to pass. He got my thigh and my ankles but I saved the rest of the costume. I couldn't stop laughing. Snakes only go to the bathroom once a month. Maybe it was his gift to me.

Toward the end of the filming that day, I noticed my back was starting to bother me. I'd been doing a lot of repetitive movements, in which I started on the floor and then stood up with Taxi wrapped around my body. I figured I'd pulled a muscle.

By the next day, I couldn't get out of bed. I was in terrible pain. Billy was starring off-Broadway in his play *Silent Laughter* and the kids were with me. I put ice on my back and took a couple of Tylenols and waited for it to get better.

And waited. And waited. I had my big lovemaking scene with Nick Stahl coming up and I wanted to be ready to film it. I'd agreed to my back being photographed nude from the waist up, but I didn't know what the costume department was going to have me wearing and I decided I needed to buy the most flattering lingerie I could find.

The problem was I couldn't lift my legs to try on underwear and I couldn't bend over to pull them up. I was in too much pain.

Vanity won out. I limped from Macy's to Victoria's Secret to the Gap, trying on forty-five bikinis, thongs, briefs, and boxers. It took me three hours because the pain was so bad I couldn't move and I had to keep blowing my nose from crying. The image of Nick and the crew staring at my ass in unflattering lingerie kept me shopping.

When the time came to do the scene, all I could think about was how was I going to lie down on the bed without screaming. I couldn't turn over, I couldn't sit up, I couldn't hold Nick in my arms. Forget about passion, forget about lingerie, forget about working with a sweetheart, gorgeous, fantastic, twenty-seven-year-old actor. My first-ever love scene (unless you count *Swamp Thing*), and all I could do was grit my teeth and take painkillers.

*Carnivàle* was the perfect job for me. I loved everything about it: the words, the people, the schedule, the location, even the food from the caterers' truck. Ruthie was such a many-layered personality—a woman my age who was sensual and powerful and vulnerable and caring. I loved every minute on the set, even the painful ones.

A year later, during the second season, we brought Taxi back for an encore appearance. This time he was supposed to strangle me during a dance. We scheduled a rehearsal so I could practice uncoiling him from my neck without hurting him.

I was happy to see him. I'd grown fond of him during our first five hours together in spite of the torn disc he'd left me with. I think he remembered me, too. He'd saved up another predigested rat and shit all over me again.

# The Stylist

**IN 1978, CBS** HAD BEEN ON THE AIR FOR FIFTY YEARS. If they had a party to celebrate, I don't remember. They did take a cast photo. A hundred of us dressed in black evening wear and Lassie in the nude. *Maude* was in its last season on the air so Bea and I were there along with Walter Cronkite, Lucille Ball, Alfred Hitchcock, Dick Van Dyke, Dale Evans and Roy Rogers, and every living luminary who had ever graced the stages at CBS Television.

Now it's 2003 and CBS is turning seventy-five. The network is planning a celebration in New York and they send a note asking whether my husband and I will be able to attend. Billy goes nuts. "Yes, yes! Everyone I ever watched growing up is going to be there! Send that thing back immediately and tell them yes."

The follow-up invitation arrives in the mail. An original Peter Max painting adorns the cover. We will be flown to New York in a private jet along with Betty White, Dennis Weaver,

Chad Everett (looking even sexier than he did on *Medical Center*), Loni Anderson, Linda Gray, Telma Hopkins, June Lockhart, Larry Hagman, Joan Van Ark, and Don Johnson. The event is being held at the Hammerstein Ballroom, beginning with cocktails at 5:00, dinner at 6:00, and then a live telecast at 8:00. Attire is black-tie and there will be a red carpet.

Uh-oh.

This means press. This means photographers. This means showing up in the "What Was She Thinking" section of some national tabloid if you're wearing the "wrong" dress, the "wrong" shoes, the "wrong" jewelry or, God forbid, your purse doesn't go with your outfit.

In the years I was away from series television, celebrity fashion became an industry all its own. What you're seen wearing is as noteworthy as the work you're doing to merit you being seen in the first place. The gowns and jewelry and hairstyles are more memorable than the performances and the awards. Forget the fans, it's the photographers and fashion police who need pleasing.

I've never used a "stylist" in my life. I don't even know how they work. What do they charge? Where do they get the gowns? What if nothing fits?

I swear to God, every time I see a magazine layout of the "best-dressed" actresses at some event, I think, *Did this woman look in the mirror? Why would anyone put that dress on that body?* And sometimes I think, *Why would anyone put that dress on any body EVER?*

Anyway, I'm going to attend the CBS party, it's going to be televised, and I need to decide what to wear. I have several "black-tie" gowns I can fall back on if I can't find something new, so this seems like the perfect time to try working with a stylist.

If I can find one.

I call Clea Duvall. Clea plays Sophie on *Carnivàle,* and she always looks great. She tells me her publicist sets up an appointment for her at Armani and she goes in and picks something out. Not for me. What if nothing fits me? What if there's nothing there I like? I'll have to fake an appendicitis attack to avoid embarrassing myself when I want to leave.

I call my publicist. He handles Don Rickles and Dick Clark. They don't use stylists. He's more than willing to help me but he doesn't know any more than I do. He says he'll ask around.

I talk to my Pilates partner. She comes from a show business family and knows everyone. She knows stylists, she says, but they're all going to rip me off. She says she'll ask around.

I ask my voice teacher who has a client list filled with high-profile actresses. He says he'll ask around.

I ask the moms from the boys' first grade. One of them knows a junior-high mom who styles commercials for a living. I've got my first name.

I ask our makeup artist on *Carnivàle.* She has a friend who also styles commercials. My second name.

I call HBO. Another name. This is a woman who styles some of the actresses for *Six Feet Under* and *Sex in the City.* Exactly what I need.

Until I talk to her. A twenty-minute phone call in which she says, "You know what I mean?" so many times I start counting them. I give up at fifty-two. By the end of the phone call I have no idea what she means. All I know is that when she works for HBO, she charges them twice what she charges a private client. And the one client she brags about always looks to me like she should be leaning into an open car window on Hollywood and Vine. I can't get a straight answer out of her about her fees. When she says, "I'd rather work with someone with talent for ten thousand dollars than someone without for thirty-five thousand," I'm so totally confused I thank her and hang up.

Back to square one.

My voice teacher has a name for me. A fellow whose clients include two highly successful actresses who always look beautiful. We make a date to meet at a bakery down the street from my house.

I like him immediately. He's warm, professional, knowledgeable, and open. We hit it off. I know from his résumé that he's gifted and I would be in good hands with him. He answers my questions. He charges a flat fee per event. For that fee he does everything from dressing me to overseeing my hairstyle and makeup and showing me how to pose for the best photos. He talks about how a certain dress might require a specific hairstyle and different makeup. How everyone is vying for the paparazzis's attention and which jewels pull the camera's eye to the face. How all the stylists fight to get the dresses they want from the designers and how he has a seam-stress who can take a size 10 and make it fit my size 4 body and then return it to its original condition before handing it back to the designer. And that's okay with the designer.

The one thing he says, just before we part, is, "We all get our jewels from the same place." That sticks in my mind. I don't wear much jewelry. A wedding ring, a ring on the middle finger of my right hand, and a watch. I don't have pierced ears because I never wear earrings. I don't like necklaces and rarely wear bracelets. Poor Billy, when we met all he wanted to do was buy me diamonds. I don't like diamonds. The jewelry I do like is definitely not mainstream. And the idea of borrowing an expensive piece makes me unpleasantly nervous.

I'd hire this fellow in a heartbeat except I can't justify spending the amount of money he charges. It's probably not a lot compared to a lot of others but *Carnivàle* is on hiatus, we don't know if we'll be picked up for another season, and Billy is putting all his money into producing his play *Silent Laughter* off-Broadway. Plus we're starting construction on the house again. I don't want to spend money frivolously.

That night, after our meeting, I have a nightmare: I'm at a cocktail party for CBS, mingling with other stars. The organizer of the event comes up to me and I realize I'm the main presenter and I have to be ready to go on stage in five minutes. I don't have on any makeup and I'm not wearing a fancy gown. I've brought one with me but I don't know if it's a better choice than what I'm wearing. Billy says I should "change into the blue" and then he disappears. Now I realize I don't have an opening joke! I go racing through the crowd, searching for Billy to give me something funny to say. I finally find him outside with another sitcom writer; they're having a cigarette break although in real life Billy doesn't smoke.

"I need a joke, Billy! I'm on in five minutes and I don't have an opening joke!"

He thinks for a minute and then says, "Conspicuous consumption." There's a beat and then the other comedy writer breaks up laughing. Okay, I think, if I deliver it correctly, they'll get it. And they'll know I'm talking about all this pressure to buy the right dress and the right accessories. They'll howl. I go running back toward the dressing room to change clothes and put on my makeup.

I wake up with my heart pounding and my stomach in knots. I've just had a performance-anxiety dream and I'm not even performing, I'm just trying to get dressed.

On to the next meeting.

It's with the girl my makeup artist recommended. She's very nice but she's not a salesperson. Nor is she a stylist who works with designers. She is a designer, or rather she was a designer when she lived in Europe, but since she's been here, she's been working as a stylist for commercials. What that means is she shops for all kinds of clothes at various stores that let her take things out "on memo" and bring them back if they're not used. The items the actors use are then paid for by the production company. Well, I can do my own shopping at the same stores so there's no sense paying her to do it.

The mom from the kids' school is also a stylist for commercials. We have a great time together and she volunteers to contact designers for me but I don't have the time it will take to make those introductions. She charges $500 a day to shop for her clients and she even agrees to charge me by the hour if we want to go shopping together. I think I might like to do this at some later date but right now, it doesn't solve my problem.

Finally, my publicist has the name of someone who worked with one of his other clients on a commercial. He says that everything this fellow showed up with was just right, and since he's fairly new to L.A., he's willing to charge me only $1,200. Unlike the other three appointments, I make a date to meet him at my home.

By the time we meet, I've convinced myself that he's the person I should work with. I haven't even met him yet but I'm running out of time and he comes highly recommended and I can afford him.

He brings his book for me to see some of his other work. There's a layout of another actress he's dressed. I don't like anything she's wearing, it all seems a little trashy, but I know the actress and that's the type of part she usually gets hired for so I chalk it up to her image and taste.

I'm running out of time. I hire him. I show him a few of the things I already have that I think might work. He doesn't ask me any questions really, doesn't ask what I like, what I don't like, what I think works well on me, etc. We just make a date for two days hence and he says he'll have plenty of stuff for me to choose from.

I race home on the day we're supposed to meet because he's coming at 4:30. He's an hour late and I've got to leave at 6:00. As soon as he starts laying out the dresses he's chosen, I know I'm in trouble. Half of them are strapless. I can't wear a strapless. I'd have to tape my tits to my nose to keep them in place.

I hate everything he's brought. The colors are dull, the fabrics are overwhelming, the prints just aren't me. I don't want to hurt his feelings but my stomach is doing flip-flops. I start trying some of them on in the hopes that they'll look better on me than on the hanger.

Wrong. Nothing fits. Nothing works. There's one he really likes—it's black lace over a nude slip but it's got Lycra or something in it because it clings to my body like a jumpsuit. The price tag is still on it. Eighty bucks. These are obviously not designer dresses.

He's not concerned. He has plenty of other sources, he says, and he'll find something I like. We make a date to meet later in the week. He'll also bring some wraps in case I decide to wear the black velvet Richard Tyler gown I wear in my nightclub act.

Now I'm getting nervous. I drive to Beverly Hills and start combing the racks at Neiman Marcus, a store I've been in only once. There's a long gown I think will work. I get it home and try it on for Billy and Jane who are writing in his office. Neither of them likes it as much as the pale pink gown I've already got in my closet and, besides, as soon as I study it carefully, I don't like the way it fits. Back to Neiman Marcus to return it.

I e-mail my sister-in-law in New York. Can I wear pale pink in New York in November? I ask. She's not so sure.

In desperation, I call the first stylist. He had been gracious and understanding when I told him I couldn't afford him, and he'd offered to help me with anything he could, so I ask for his advice. Pink in New York in November? He says it will be fine if I have a really great wrap and offers to have a fur waiting for me at my hotel. I tell him I don't want to impose. Besides, I'm afraid to wear fur. Bea Arthur and Betty White will be there. They might not throw paint at me but they won't be happy.

I race back to Neiman Marcus and look for a wrap. The cheapest one I can find that seems right for the dress is $2,700. For that amount, I could have hired the original stylist.

The fellow I'm working with shows up with more dresses, and several of them are styles I'd choose for myself, but none of them fits. The ones I like are samples and we can't alter them. The event is now a week away and I still don't have anything to wear. He's brought a fake fur jacket to go with my black velvet dress. It looks like a dried-out skunk someone stuck in an electrical outlet.

Finally, I pull out my pink gown and show him and he says it's just fine, even though he'd nixed it on his first visit. I've got shoes to go with it but I need a wrap and a purse I can carry my glasses in. He says he'll go shopping again.

I wake up in the middle of the night wondering if he's charging me $1,200 for the event or $1,200 every day he goes out shopping. If so, I'm up to about $6,000. I can't get back to sleep.

The day before I leave for New York, he brings me a lovely pashmina wrap and two purses. Neither of the purses is large enough to hold my glasses. He's worked very hard for several days and, graciously, charges me $1,500 for the whole process. I could have, for that money, bought my own purse and pashmina and had a thousand dollars left over to spend on stupid fan magazines telling me what I should be wearing.

That's what I'm going to do next time.

# Eighteen Days in Queens

*Excerpt from ninth-grade term paper entitled "To Be or Not to Be: Acting as a Vocation," written January 5, 1960.*

*"There are really not many good, sound reasons for my entering acting as a vocation. The employment is very unstable, many actors go for months, even years, without a good part. And if it weren't for their outside jobs, they'd probably starve to death.*

*Personality and talent requirements are high but academic ability is quite low. The hours vary and the opportunity for advancement is quite shaky but there are no sex or age requirements.*

*Still, I feel a person should pursue a job because he enjoys it, not for the money or rank. And I know there is nothing I would rather do than act."*

*Carnivàle* is on hiatus after our second season. While we're waiting once again to learn whether we'll be picked up, I accept a part in another low-budget film. Why? It's the starring role and the character is all over the map emotionally. Yes, it's a horror film but at my age the opportunities to carry a film are few and far between. When's the last time you saw a woman in her fifties blowing away the bad guys?

I don't know why I like this kind of thing. Heroine with a gun. Saving people. Maybe it's my Armenian heritage. I grew up on stories of strong women who survived the Turkish massacre: My cousin's mother-in-law wandered naked in the desert for weeks, surviving by drinking her own urine until she could no longer nurse her two-year-old son and had to abandon him in the hopes the Turks would take him as their own. Then she was captured by the Kurds and forced to work in the opium dens until she escaped and made her way to Beirut and, eventually, America. She remarried, discovered that her first husband was still alive and had also reached the States, never saw him because she was afraid she'd be prosecuted for bigamy, and was then widowed when she was four months pregnant with twins. She lived to be eighty-four, pinching my cheeks and laughing at *Maude*.

Anyway, at the same time, I'm heavily into rehearsals for *The Property Known as Garland,* a two-character play Billy has written in which I star as Judy Garland backstage in a theater in Copenhagen during her last performance. It's almost a fifty-page monologue and every moment I'm not with the kids, I'm memorizing lines and watching videos of Judy's performances to capture her movements and idiosyncrasies. I've only got two weeks to learn the show. I know the movie script has problems, but I wait until my contract is finalized and rehearsals for *Garland* are over before I even read it for the second time.

It's a good role with some not-so-good dialogue. I talk to the director, who is also the co-writer, and he sounds very open and willing to hear suggestions. He's had success as a music video director, but this is his first feature. I'm not sure he's shaving yet. I can tell he's directed music videos because when I mention a particularly confusing point in the script, he assures me the audience will get it when they see the movie the second or third time.

It's an eighteen-day shoot in New York and New Jersey. In February. I'd love to stay at our house at the Jersey shore but the majority of the shoot is at Fort Totten, a military base near the Throgs Neck Bridge now used by the New York Fire Department as training facilities. My hotel is directly across the highway from the American Airlines terminal at LaGuardia. So much for walking in the New Jersey woods or shopping in Manhattan.

We start filming on a Saturday. An hour-and-a-half drive from my hotel to the first location. I doubt there's a person on the crew who's over thirty years old and each one is sweeter than the last, especially the writer. He arrives with carrots and tomatoes his mother has sent for me, and a promise to bring me lunch the following day from the local bakery. Word has gone out I'm a vegetarian (in fact, I just don't eat red meat) and for the rest of the shoot I'm inundated with greens.

It soon becomes apparent that the movie is severely under-budgeted. Four days into the shoot they stop printing the back side of the call sheet because it requires too much ink. By Thursday, I'm the only actor getting the day's scenes printed on "minis"—three or four pages of dialogue printed on half-size paper to carry to the set for rehearsal. They can't afford the extra paper.

The night we start filming outdoors, the temperature in Queens drops to zero. That's *without* the wind-chill factor. We're supposed to work until 4:30 A.M. It's so cold one of the actresses can't close her hands over the gun she's holding in the scene. I can't deliver my dialogue without shaking. My nose is a deep shade of burgundy. My makeup base has frozen in its container; we have to liquefy it in front of the heat vents in my trailer. We can't have running water in the trailer because the pipes will freeze. I pour antifreeze down the toilet to flush and use antibacterial wipes to wash my hands. I keep the heater in the trailer set to 91 degrees but the room feels like it's in the mid-60s. The crew tries to stay warm in a portable tent with two electric heaters that look like red aluminum foil and work just about as well. I invite anyone who stops at my door to come in and get momentarily warm.

The second Saturday is the night we're supposed to film in an abandoned cemetery on Staten Island, an hour from the hotel I'm in. All day Friday the production crew is checking the weather reports. There's a blizzard coming in. Finally, at three in the morning, they decide to change the shooting schedule. We'll do interiors instead, at a closer location, starting at sunset and going past sunrise.

The snow starts Saturday around noon. Twenty-six inches are expected along with fifty-mile-per-hour winds. The highway patrol is asking people to stay off the roads. To be on the safe side, we leave an hour earlier than usual. By the time we get to the location, six inches of snow are on the ground and one of our production vans is stuck in a ditch with several crew members in it. We can't shoot. This will be our day off, what's left of it. I'm back at the hotel just in time to eat dinner and go to bed to start another eight days in a row. It's so cold outside, the window in my room has cracked.

The crew remains stuck in the van for seven hours. By the time someone gets out to pick them up, one of the fellows has to be treated for frostbite. They leave the van in the ditch. In karmic retribution for leaving the crew members frozen in the snow, perhaps, the van disappears. Maybe impounded, maybe stolen. No one knows. The budget escalates.

I took this job because I liked the character. A single mother who comes home to find her daughter locked in the cellar, threatening suicide. When her daughter kills herself, the mother reconnects with her druggie son to find out why. They uncover a government experiment involving the "Unholy Trinity": mind control, time travel, and invisibility. The mother turns out to be a hero and a villain at the same time. A nice challenge for me.

It's not until we're in production that I recognize the real challenge—keeping the film believable. I'm having trouble finding the reality in a scene where my grown son sings "I'm a Little Teapot" as he walks into the cellar to die. And I join him in the chorus.

The director is a sweetheart and the director of photography is very talented. Between the two of them I'm certain the movie will look great. But I'm not sure the director has ever worked with actors before and not all of us seem to be making the same movie; the performance styles range from comatose to Grand Guignol. Add to that a complete lack of logic in some of the scenes and it's a toss-up for me whether to laugh or cry. My instinct as an actor, especially one who started in theater, is to take direction and make things work as written. If I do that on this project, we'll have problems. I've been around too long and I know too much and one of the things I'm sure of is that this script needs help. Fortunately the writer and director are willing to make changes. I lobby to eliminate the teapot scene, as well as the scene in which I ask my son what the bad guys want from me and in reply, he pulls up the zippered full-length coat I'm wearing, pulls up the sweater and thermal T-shirt I'm wearing underneath it, discovers the words STAY AWAY carved on my stomach, and then answers, "I think I know." How could he possibly know? I ask. I've got on more clothes than a bag lady in a blizzard. And who put it there? And when? And why didn't I notice? It's *my* stomach they were hacking away at.

The cemetery scene gets postponed to a Friday night. It's a change of locale; we're going to Staten Island, about an hour away from our original location. The night before, we're filming exteriors again. This time we're right next to the water on Long Island Sound and it's minus-6 degrees with the windchill. I don't know how the crew is surviving. At least I can get back to my heated trailer between some of the shots. The real challenge becomes continuing to give a shit about the performance when hypothermia is setting in. Act? I can barely make my frozen lips move. By four o'clock in the morning I can't feel my ears and my feet are on fire. Now I understand the oxymoron "burning cold." But I've got it easy; the crew doesn't finish until 7:00 A.M. and they've got to be back at work in eight hours. And half of them are working for free.

My pickup for Friday is scheduled for 4:00 P.M. We hit rush-hour traffic and we're two hours late getting to the set but it doesn't matter because we've still beaten the director, the crew, and my motor home. I finally get in my trailer at 8:30. I've been on the clock for four and a half hours and I'm not even in makeup yet. There's no electricity. They've moved the trailer without cleaning it and a bottle of antifreeze has spilled all over the floor. We're slipping and sliding like Laurel and Hardy. One of the crew moves the second RV closer to mine so we can plug into it for power. He smashes into my trailer's front bumper with the back of the other one. We get our first shot at 11:30 P.M., just in time to break for "lunch." By that time, the fumes from the trailer parked in front of me are so strong we're in danger of carbon monoxide poisoning. I've got a headache and I'm starting to fall asleep. We unplug the RV and move it. I spend the rest of the night with no electricity.

No electricity means no microwave and that means no dinner for me. The crew is getting one meal a day catered and there's not always enough to go around. Usually it's salad and one meat dish. If there is anything left, it's served for the second meal when we work overtime. Reheated Chinese food at 6:00 A.M. My friend and makeup artist, Stacey Panepinto, spends her own money on groceries for my RV. She gets yelled at if she leaves the set to buy us lunch. I don't eat meat so I'm living on Cup O Noodles, Honey Bunches of Oats cereal, and cherry tomatoes. And I'm the star.

We shoot my death scene on Saturday night. My "son" and I are in a cellar, my "daughter" outside the cellar looking down at us. She and I fight; she shoots me through the cellar door. Somehow the scene has been scheduled for a night the actress playing my daughter is not available. We film all our angles in the cellar without her. Instead of delivering my lines to an actress, I am delivering them to a klieg light set up outside the cellar door while the script supervisor yells the missing actress's lines from across the room.

The advantage to this, however, is that I can rewrite the scene without complaints from a talented but inexperienced actress who doesn't want to lose any lines because she's worried about how much time she has on screen. She doesn't realize it won't matter how much time she has on screen if the movie isn't good enough to be seen.

The following night, this same actress works outside until 5:30 in the morning. When she finishes, the line producer tells her she'll have to take a bus to catch the Long Island Rail Road into Manhattan and then a subway back to her home in Queens, ten minutes down the road from our location. The Second A.D. takes it upon himself to drive her home. They fire him.

Tuesday morning is a glorious day, sunny and cold. We drive an hour away to a suburban location in New Jersey. It's the screenwriter's parents' home and we're shooting in their garage. We're doing a three-character scene, most of it in a car parked in the garage with the door closed and the engine running. The fumes in my trailer were nothing compared to this.

I'm waiting to rehearse when Stacey asks what time the other actress in the scene is arriving. The transportation captain's face turns white. No one has given the actress her call time and no one has picked her up. We're ready to shoot in New Jersey and she's an hour and a half away in Brooklyn. So much for firing the Second A.D.

By the time we wrap, six accidents have occurred involving production vehicles. The last one takes place when a crew van backs into the car belonging to the girlfriend of one of the fellows in the art department. The line producer refuses to provide the production's insurance information to the girl, claiming she shouldn't have been visiting, and kicks her off the set. For the first time since we started work, I get pissed off. The girl's boyfriend promises me he'll file a police report.

It's the eighteenth day of the shoot and our last night on the film. The final setup is a medium close-up of my chest and head as I get shot with a single-barrel rifle. We've shot this setup earlier in the week but the special effects didn't work. Ideally we'd be using a squib, a device filled with fake blood that's attached to my body and explodes outward on command. The production can't afford the insurance necessary when squibs are used so they've asked the special effects department to come up with an alternative. What they've rigged is tubing attached to a spraying device, filled with fake blood. I hold it in front of my body at an angle unseen by the camera, the director yells bang, the effects department presses the sprayer, "blood" sprays out, and I fall backward out of frame into the arms of two big, strong crew members. That's what's supposed to happen. When we tried it earlier in the week, the blood sort of piddled out in light droplets, dribbled down the plastic garbage bag they'd wrapped around my legs, and stained my suede boots and the entire back of my fairly expensive jeans, which we need for the rest of the shoot. On top of that, you could see the sprayer in the shot.

So we're trying again. We've been working thirteen hours already and I'm into overtime. More expense for production. Maybe it would have been cheaper to use a squib. This time we have more blood in the sprayer, fewer holes in the tubing, and I am wearing "plastic pants" the wardrobe department has concocted by wrapping a pair of costume pants from another actress completely in garbage bags and taping them in place. From the waist down I look like an astronaut from a third-world country.

I hold the sprayer in place, the director yells bang, the effects department presses the sprayer, and a fine red mist fills the air in front of me. Definitely not the blood spatter caused by a rifle shot.

We try again. This time we forgo the sprayer. The Second A.D. has volunteered to hold fake blood in his mouth and spit it out from the side of my body as I am shot. At the last minute, someone suggests V-8 juice instead.

Another bust. The V-8 juice lands in a plop about four inches from my body. Either it's too thin or the A.D. doesn't have good jaw muscles. "What if we add crushed potato chips to it?" he asks. "That should thicken it up."

Suggestions are coming fast and furiously. It's the last take of a three-week shoot and everyone wants to wrap this film. We've got enough V-8 to fill a plastic water bottle. Someone from the art department will crouch next to me and squeeze the bottle on cue to shoot the juice past my body. Then he'll jump out of the way so the other two crew members can catch me as I fall backward.

This almost works. We see his head in the frame and there's not enough juice but it's worth trying again. Unfortunately we're running out of V-8. We dilute it with Yoo-hoo and we've got enough to spray two bottles at a time.

On the fifth try, the director asks to use the sprayer and the V-8/Yoo-hoo simultaneously. We're out of V-8. We substitute orange juice, add the Yoo-hoo, and color it with some of the fake blood. Now we've got four people scrunched behind my back trying to stay out of frame: my two catchers, the special effects artist with the sprayer, and the art department crew member with two plastic bottles of fake-blood-chocolate-milk-orange-juice to squeeze. Throughout all of this, one of the other crew members shoots gales of black smoke into our faces to create atmosphere. He and the camera crew are covered in juice, Yoo-hoo, smoke, and blood. Stacey can't take it anymore and leaves the set but that doesn't matter because you can't see my makeup anyway, there's too much junk in the air. I'm eating cold pizza and freezing and my plastic pants have started to melt from the heater I retreat to in between setups.

It takes two hours but we finally get the shot. The director shoots another angle of blood being splattered on a wall, just in case he can't use anything we've just done.

And so it ends. I've spent the last couple of days asking myself whether I would have taken the job knowing then what I know now. I think I've done some good work. I learned a lot. I learned how to go to work every day and continue to care about what I'm doing no matter how I think it might turn out. That's an important lesson and you can't do it in something that seems like gold from the beginning. I made some good friends, people I'd enjoy working with again. That's always valuable. And I realized, once again, that I have a choice about how to respond to life. I had the choice of whether to laugh or cry or get pissed off. I laughed. And wrote about it.

This is what I do, you know. I act. It's my job. It's what I do for a living. How I put bread on the table. In forty-two years, it's never felt like work, and after forty-two years, I'm still surprised that I get to do it. Sometimes it's easier to do the work than other times, and sometimes the work is better than other times, but it's always a joy and the fact that I can do it and get paid for it continues to amaze me. So, yes, definitely, I'd take this job all over again knowing what I know now.

And who knows, maybe it will work. The story is intriguing, the director has a real visual talent, the director of photography did a beautiful job. I was wrong about *Swamp Thing,* remember?

# And Finally . . .

THIRTY-FOUR YEARS HAVE PASSED SINCE WHOEVER THE girl I was then left *Grease* and New York and the Broadway stage. The woman I've become is going back. In the spring of 2006, I will be appearing off-Broadway as Judy Garland in *The Property Known As Garland.*

I have mixed feelings about returning. I am no longer the twenty-year-old with no responsibilities except to herself; nor am I the sixty-year-old with grown children who can manage on their own. My kids are in third grade and I hate leaving them, even for a few weeks. We've worked out the schedule so I can commute home to L.A. one day a week, and as soon as summer vacation starts we'll all be together at our farmhouse in New Jersey. But until then, I'm going to miss hearing Walker practice drums every day and William practice piano and I won't see all the baseball games. I won't be able to help Walker download rap songs on his iTunes or scratch William's back before he falls asleep. That's the hard part about taking this job.

The best part is saying the words. Billy has written a great script.

When he first started working on it and I heard some of the audio research material he was using—autobiographical tapes that Judy Garland had recorded in some of her unhappiest moments—I told him I wasn't interested in playing the role. There was too much pain there, too much neurosis. I've spent my life trying to grow and get healthy and live joyfully and what I was hearing on the tapes was a woman in so much pain, I didn't want to re-create it.

That's not what ended up in the script. Billy has written about Judy Garland, the indomitable spirit. The Judy Garland who loved to tell outrageous stories about herself and loved to make people laugh. The Judy Garland who loved her children and loved her work. The Judy Garland who took everything her career threw at her (from Louis B. Mayer forcing her to take diet pills at age twelve to her mother forcing her to have an abortion six years later) and never gave up. Bringing her truths to life on stage will be the biggest professional challenge I've faced since leaving home to start my career forty-two years ago. A hell of a lot harder than acting with rats in Russia.

*Excerpt from ninth-grade term paper entitled "To Be or Not to Be: Acting as a Vocation," written January 5, 1960.*

*"Corny as this may sound, I've wanted to act ever since as far back as I can remember. I've had to act to get attention and I've never thought of myself as anything else. For that matter, neither has anyone else.*

*I also realize that there is very little chance of my ever making the big time. But for my own personal reasons I wish to continue down 'the path to stardom' for, if nothing else, just the experience."*

I wrote that term paper forty-six years ago. I remember that girl, the one who wrote it. A lot of her doesn't exist anymore, but I do remember her. I remember her willingness to be anything anyone wanted her to be if only they'd like her, her inability to express her real feelings if she thought they wouldn't be accepted, her lack of belief in her talent, her lack of self-worth. Those are the parts that don't exist today. But I remember other things about her, too, that haven't disappeared: her optimism, her willingness to keep going, her fascination with emotional growth. I can see her walking out of her apartment in the Village, dressed in high brown boots and a wool dress with a wide leather belt. She's wearing a hat to keep her just-straightened hair from frizzing in the winter moisture and she's got her contact lenses in. She's carrying a black, eleven-by-fourteen-inch imitation leather portfolio with her photos and résumés and three-by-five index cards inside. She walks like she's determined to get where she's going and nothing is going to stop her.

Nothing did.

# Thank You

IN 1973 I WROTE IN MY JOURNAL: "PERHAPS SOMEDAY I can look back and do something with these memoirs. I want to create with words."

Talk about being slow to manifest.

I couldn't have written this book without my husband, Billy Van Zandt. He was the one who first told me, years ago, that I should be writing—that I could do it. He sent me off to our red farmhouse at the Jersey shore for days at a time so I could finish. And every night he read what I'd written and e-mailed me his guidance. I paid attention, too. Well, except for any bathroom references—I left those in against his advice.

I wouldn't have written this book without my friend and teacher Claudette Sutherland. She helped me find "my voice," told me when it was time to show my words to other people, and introduced me to her agents, Jane Dystel and Miriam Goderich. She read every word and told me when I needed to add more or move some around. Her encouragement and her belief in me kept me on my path.

And my dear friend (and downstairs neighbor back in the

1965 days of Richard) Wyatt Harlan who laughed when she read the "Rat Movie" chapter and insisted I had to continue. Her own writing is brilliant, and if she thought I could do it, maybe I could.

And Claudette's class: Andrea, Brett, Dani, Tamara, John, Justin, Frank, Brooks. I listened hopefully every Wednesday night as I read aloud my latest chapter, first for your laughter and then your critiques. They were my guidelines.

Without Jane Dystel and Miriam Goderich these words would never have found their way to Don Weise at Carroll & Graf, and I wouldn't have had such a great time getting them on paper. Without Don, I wouldn't have dug deeper and fleshed out the missing pieces; he helped me polish what I started. It's much better because of him.

A big thank-you to everyone at Avalon Publishing Group, as well. And to Suzanne Wickham-Baeird for letting people know what I've been doing.

My niece, Jaime Merz, shared her artistry with me, designing both my website and the cover of this book. It's so exciting for me to have an actual artist in the family and I love her work. My son Cody Carpenter is the other artist in our family, a brilliant composer and musician. I'm thankful to him simply for being the man he has become.

But it was Suzanne Pettit who started it all.

Suzanne and I met on the first day of Cody's preschool. Our sons became best friends and we became best friends. She was a part of every day of my life. She died on Memorial Day weekend, 1998, from a relentless breast cancer that didn't care about her two young boys and the hundreds of friends whose lives would suffer without her.

When she died, part of my life died, too. Life wasn't as fun without Suzanne. I tried everything I could think of to ease the loneliness. I spent more time with my kids, I hung out in Billy's office while he worked, I called friends in Texas and Tennessee. I read more books, visited more places. Nothing worked.

I even had coffee with a woman I had just met simply because she had survived breast cancer and she looked like Suzanne.

She was the one who told me about Claudette Sutherland's writing class.

I was fifty-five years old and I didn't know that people taught writing. Oh sure, I knew about screenwriting classes—everybody in Hollywood knows about that guy who teaches the weekend seminar on *Casablanca* to everyone else in Hollywood—but I figured that was for novelists and playwrights who wanted to learn to write movies. But to write a book from scratch? To take a class where I might be able to learn to do that? Maybe that would help fill the void left by Suzanne's absence. Maybe I'd even make a new friend.

I called Claudette and started class. The first thing she taught me was a writing technique called aide-mémoire. It's writing without making judgments, without using adjectives or adverbs. Writing from a totally objective point of view. As soon as she explained it, I understood that's how I'd always written.

My first aide-mémoire was about Suzanne:

*Suzanne's things covered every space in her bedroom: crystals and bird feathers and a long, wooden incense burner with leftover gray ashes. Her Walkman with a cassette of Gary Zukav's* Seat of the Soul *and a strand of prayer beads rested on the night table. She had photographs everywhere, some in standing frames, some in hanging frames, some taped to the furniture at eye level to the bed. Books rose in pillars from the floor, blocking my path.*

*Lesa sat by the foot of the bed next to a rolling metal stand with a stainless-steel machine on top. Lesa's cheeks were streaked with lines cutting through her blush. Her eyes were smudged black. She was staring at me.*

*Linda sat on the other side of the machine. She was dressed in beige Indian cotton and wore no makeup at all. She was staring at Suzanne.*

*Suzanne lay on the bed. Her eyes were closed. Her skin was cold. I covered her with the quilt. I sat down beside her and rubbed her right arm with long, slow strokes from her shoulder to her wrist. I told her I loved her but her eyes didn't open. And her skin stayed cold.*

*After a while, four strong men came into the room to carry Suzanne. Lesa and Linda and I left. Suzanne was already gone.*

This book was born a year after I started the class. A year later I had a publishing contract and an offer to collaborate on a novel as well. Claudette Sutherland has become one of my closest friends. All because of Suzanne.

These are the people I want to thank. And William and Walker Van Zandt, who never once complained when I had to sit at my computer instead of playing a three-hour game of Monopoly.

And anyone I ever met in my life who helped me grow.

And, oh yes, the guys who invented the iMac, the iBook, and the Internet.